"I was a big supporter, and i[...] Racist Action movement. T[...] opposition to racism and fa[...] and in the mosh pit continues ~~to be~~ inspiring to this day."
—Tom Morello, Rage Against the Machine and Audioslave

"*Antifa* became a household word with Trump attempting and failing to designate it a domestic terrorist group, but antifa's roots date back to the late 1980s, when little attention was being paid to violent fascist groups that were flourishing under Reaganism, and Anti-Racist Action (ARA) was singular and effective in its brilliant offensive. This book tells the story of ARA in breathtaking prose accompanied by stunning photographs and images."
—Roxanne Dunbar-Ortiz, author of *Loaded: A Disarming History of the Second Amendment*

"The foundation of Anti-Racist Action ushered in a new era of anti-authoritarian struggle in this country, by mounting a militant organized response to the growing influence of the American far right. ARA confronted fascism head-on with boots, fists, and whatever else they had handy and did their best to keep their comrades and communities safe. Decades before the mainstream media began wringing its hands over the question of whether it was 'okay' to punch a nazi, the ARA already had the answer: yes—hard. As the far right continues to increase its hold over the political system, and its adherents terrorize vulnerable communities with impunity, today's activists would do well to take a few pages out of ARA's playbook, and thanks to this new visual history it's all right there in front of them. *We Go Where They Go: The Story of Anti-Racist Action* offers a new generation of anti-racist, anti-fascist activists an essential dose of revolutionary history, while providing a bloodstained blueprint for the next chapter in the long, noble, and utterly necessary fight against fascism. The struggle is never over, and it's on all of us to wake up, read up, and stay ready. No pasaran!"
—Kim Kelly, author of *Fight Like Hell: The Untold History of American Labor*

"'History,' as *We Go Where They Go: The Story of Anti-Racist Action* observes, 'is a weapon.' Yet in this timely, much-needed book, set against the backdrop of today's resurgent fascism, it is far more than that. History is a teachable, or learnable, moment. History is remembrance, or never forgetting, and honoring our dead. Most important, history is possibility. Because, as the authors and many ARA participants so ably demonstrate on these pages, with such clear-eyed insights, those who collectively self-organize and take direct action can make history—a people's history of courage and solidarity. Thus, this engaging history is a compass, guiding us away from unnecessary perils and pitfalls and toward potentialities for not only community self-defense but also community care."
—Cindy Milstein, editor of *There Is Nothing So Whole as a Broken Heart: Mending the World as Jewish Anarchists*

"*We Go Where They Go: The Story of Anti-Racist Action* takes readers to the front lines of the little-known struggle against white supremacy and fascism that raged across North America at the turn of the twenty-first century. Based on insider accounts, this concise, riveting, and truly groundbreaking history of Anti-Racist Action is essential reading for the movements of today and tomorrow."
—Mark Bray, author of *Antifa: The Anti-Fascist Handbook*

"*We Go Where They Go: The Story of Anti-Racist Action* is the story of those who bravely went steel toe to steel toe against the nazis in the 1990s. It is a meditation on organizing when your life and community depend on it and the finest two-fisted street scholarship. Today's foes of fascism will find a treasure trove of perspectives, history, insights, and strategies here. It would be a mistake to call the nineties the 'lost decade' for radical action in the United States, and this book corrects the record."
—James Tracy, coauthor, with Amy Sonnie, of *Hillbilly Nationalists, Urban Race Rebels, and Black Power: Interracial Solidarity in 1960–70s New Left Organizing*

"There is a history of anti-fascist organizing and defense that has been a quiet one, but it is one we should all be proud of. This book will take the reader on a journey through that history, which I myself have been a part of, and they will be amazed—as we often are—by what they never knew and wish they had. I am very happy that finally the story of Anti-Racist Action is being told."
—Daryle Lamont Jenkins, founder and executive director of One People's Project

"*We Go Where They Go: The Story of Anti-Racist Action* is a rich, granular history of Anti-Racist Action, from its origins in the Midwest skinhead and punk scenes in the 1980s to its growth into a grassroots international network with nearly 180 chapters by the end of the 1990s. ARA not only effectively challenged nazis and the Klan on the streets, its activists struggled to connect their street-level actions with efforts to challenge more pervasive institutional racism. It took on sexism, abortion rights, and homophobia as key issues and allied with other groups fighting for social justice. Today, as democratic norms continue to erode in the declining imperialist centers, the threat of fascism resurfaces. This book reflects on fundamental questions of organization and strategy that anti-racist activists must consider in the twenty-first century."
—Tim McCaskell, author of *Race to Equity: Disrupting Educational Inequality* and *Queer Progress: From Homophobia to Homonationalism*

"This book is a must read for anyone wanting to know the unknown histories of activists who set out to destroy fascism in their communities. These activists did not seek fame or recognition but put themselves continually at risk. While the stories of comradery and conflict show the fissures of any movement, what I find important and necessary is to uplift these heroic voices in our activist history and in our radical imaginations."
—Sharmeen Khan, organizer with No One Is Illegal Toronto and editor of *Upping the Anti: A Journal of Theory and Action*

WE GO WHERE THEY GO
THE STORY OF ANTI-RACIST ACTION

Shannon Clay, Lady, Kristin Schwartz,
and Michael Staudenmaier

We Go Where They Go: The Story of Anti-Racist Action
Shannon Clay, Lady, Kristin Schwartz, and Michael Staudenmaier © 2023
This edition © PM Press

ISBN: 978-1-62963-977-2 (hardcover)
ISBN: 978-1-62963-972-7 (paperback)
ISBN: 978-1-62963-987-1 (ebook)

Library of Congress Control Number: 2022931958

Cover design by John Yates/www.stealworks.com
Interior design by briandesign

10 9 8 7 6 5 4 3 2 1

PM Press
PO Box 23912
Oakland, CA 94623
www.pmpress.org
Printed in the USA

"We go where they go. Whenever fascists are organizing or active in public, we're there. We don't believe in ignoring them or staying away from them. Never let the nazis have the streets!"
—Anti-Racist Action Network, First Point of Unity, Adopted 1995

CONTENTS

FOREWORD

ART & TEXT BY GORD HILL

DURING THE LATE 1980S, FASCIST & FAR RIGHT MOVEMENTS IN NORTH AMERICA SAW A **RESURGENCE** WITH MANY NEW GROUPS EMERGING, BOLSTERED BY A GROWING NEO-NAZI **SKINHEAD** MOVEMENT.

NEO-NAZI SKINS ATTENDED THE SAME CONCERTS AS ANTI-RACIST SKINS & PUNKS. IN SOME AREAS, ORGANIZED EFFORTS WERE MADE TO FORCE NEO-NAZI SKINHEADS OUT OF THE PUNK & SKA SCENES.

SKINHEADS AGAINST RACIAL PREJUDICE (**SHARP**) FORMED IN NEW YORK CITY IN 1987. LATER THAT YEAR, THE FIRST **ANTI-RACIST ACTION** (ARA) CHAPTER WAS FORMED IN MINNEAPOLIS BY AN ANTI-RACIST SKINHEAD GROUP KNOWN AS THE BALDIES.

ARA CHAPTERS QUICKLY **SPREAD** IN BOTH THE US & CANADA. MORE **DIVERSE** GROUPS BECAME INVOLVED WITH ARA, INCLUDING ANARCHISTS, COMMUNISTS, TRADE UNIONISTS, HIGH SCHOOL STUDENTS, ETC.

DESPITE THIS, THE STREET **MILITANCY** OF ARA, ALONG WITH ITS **DIY** APPROACH TO ANTI-FASCIST ORGANIZING, REMAINED UNCHANGED FROM ITS PUNK & SKINHEAD ORIGINS.

THIS **EXPANSION**, HOWEVER, GAVE THE MOVEMENT CAPACITY TO ORGANIZE ANTI-FASCIST RESISTANCE ON A **BROADER** LEVEL. THIS ALSO PROVIDED FOR A WIDE VARIETY OF **TACTICS** & A **DIVERSITY** IN THEIR FORMS OF **COMMUNICATION**.

THIS INCLUDED LEAFLETS, POSTERS, STICKERS, AND REGULAR NEWSLETTERS.

"WANTED" POSTERS WERE PRODUCED, WITH PHOTOS & INFORMATION *IDENTIFYING* FASCIST ORGANIZERS.

PATCHES & T-SHIRTS WERE *SCREEN PRINTED* AND SERVED TO BOTH COMMUNICATE (THROUGH GRAPHICS & TEXT) AND TO RAISE FUNDS FOR ORGANIZING WORK.

GRAFFITI WAS ANOTHER PART OF ARA'S COMMUNICATIONS STRATEGY.

NOT ONLY DID IT CONVEY ANTI-RACIST & ANTI-FASCIST *SLOGANS*, IT ALSO SERVED TO COMMUNICATE THAT THE AREA IN WHICH THE GRAFFITI WAS PLACED WAS ANTI-FASCIST *TERRITORY.*

CONCERTS WERE ORGANIZED, INCLUDING *ROCK AGAINST RACISM* SHOWS, WHICH PROVIDED AN OPPORTUNITY FOR ARA MEMBERS TO *SOCIALIZE,* DISTRIBUTE *INFO,* & *RECRUIT* MEMBERS. MONEY RAISED HELPED *FUND* ORGANIZING WORK.

ARA WAS ALSO INFLUENCED BY MOVEMENTS IN *WESTERN EUROPE.*

IN THE UK, THE MOST ACTIVE GROUP AT THE TIME WAS *ANTI-FASCIST ACTION* (AFA). AFA USED A DUAL STRATEGY OF *IDEOLOGICAL* & *PHYSICAL CONFRONTATION.*

IN W. GERMANY, ANTIFA EXISTED SINCE THE EARLY 1980S & ENGAGED IN MILITANT DIRECT ACTIONS, OFTEN USING THE *BLACK BLOC* TACTIC.

BY THE EARLY '90S, THE GERMAN ANTIFA WAS A *LARGE* NETWORK OF *AUTONOMOUS* GROUPS WITH MANY YEARS OF EXPERIENCE.

IN NORTH AMERICA, ARA WAS ONE OF THE FIRST GROUPS TO *CONSISTENTLY* USE BLACK BLOC TACTICS. AS IN GERMANY, THIS HELPED PROTECT THE *IDENTITIES* OF MILITANT ANTI-FASCISTS FROM BOTH *FASCISTS* & *POLICE.*

THROUGH ALL THESE METHODS, ARA *COUNTERED* THE FASCIST RESURGENCE & HELPED *DEFEAT* NUMEROUS FAR RIGHT GROUPS BY THE MID-90S.

ARA ALSO LAID MUCH OF THE GROUNDWORK FOR TODAY'S *ANTIFA* MOVEMENT IN NORTH AMERICA.

ACKNOWLEDGMENTS

The four coauthors heartily acknowledge the individuals and organizations that offered their support and assistance in the crafting of this book. We are especially grateful to all the comrades and friends who agreed to be interviewed. While some were quoted more or less than others in the final product, each was essential to our own understanding and writing. Thank you as well to those who provided us with copies of documents and images, including Steve and several other veterans of ARA, Sarah Reando from Webster University in St. Louis, and Aly Maderson Quinlog from the Visual Art Library in New London, Connecticut.

Several people went the extra mile (or kilometre) by providing direct and in-depth feedback on our writing drafts. For essential fact-checking work, pointing out blind spots we would otherwise have missed, and challenging and sharpening our political and historical points, we thank our "friend readers," including Katrina K, Kieran Frazier, Matt, Michael Novick, Sheila, Steve, Sunday Harrison, Todd F, and Xtn. Their experience with anti-fascism spans many states and provinces.

Kristin and Shannon both carried out research for this book in academic contexts, and we would like to thank our advisors. They did not play a direct part in and cannot be held responsible for the contents of this book, but we thank them for their guidance in our education and our approaches to writing and history.

We offer our thanks and appreciation to Stef Gude, our editor. Her skill, attention to detail, political sensitivity, and lightning efficiency were essential to getting this project to the finish line. We are also grateful to the staff at PM Press, including Ramsey, Joey, Jonathan, and Michael, and to Gabriel Kuhn who provided feedback on an early draft of this manuscript.

This book was a labor of love, and each of us spent many hours working on this project over multiple years. While we may one day see some nominal income from book sales, financial gain was never a motivator. We have been fortunate to have loved ones who saw the value in this project and cut us some slack when it impacted our paying jobs, our current political work, and our responsibilities at home. As just one example, our families will never recover the Sundays we four spent on Zoom almost every week in 2020, 2021, and some months into 2022. We are grateful to all our loved ones for their support.

CHAPTER 1

INTRODUCTION

The nazis had a wedding hall, but ARA had a baseball team.

Near the end of May, it finally starts to feel like summer in the Twin Cities of Minneapolis and St. Paul, Minnesota. It begins to feel like anything is possible, and optimism runs deep regardless of your politics. St. Paul's local neo-nazi band, Bound for Glory, fresh off a show in Idaho in honor of Adolf Hitler's birthday, decided to plan a high-security concert in St. Paul for Saturday, May 20, 1995—and the local branch of Anti-Racist Action (ARA) decided to stop them. Years before, ARA had used physical confrontation to make it impossible for nazi bands to perform publicly in the Twin Cities, and they weren't about to let it start all over again. Through what long-time member Kieran later called "pre-internet age detective work," ARA determined that would-be nazi show attendees had been told to pick up tickets and a map to the secret venue at a public park on St. Paul's Eastside.

On the day of the show, ARA-affiliated activists reserved a permit for a picnic and softball game in the park, but this was no typical ball game. The ninety or so anti-fascists who showed up shared one or two softballs, a handful of mitts, and an assortment of about seventy-five aluminum and wooden bats. Those not playing ball rode bicycles around the perimeter of the park and used walkie-talkies to alert everyone when a suspicious car approached. Beyond the bats, one other weapon was on hand: an older comrade, a Vietnam veteran supportive of ARA, was positioned away from the group with a single concealed firearm. The agreed upon plan was that the anti-fascists would accept a brawl and take a beating if it was unavoidable, but that if any fascist pulled a gun this comrade was authorized to act as necessary.

ANTI RACIST ACTION

A youth organization in the twin cities fighting racism through education and direct action.

Were looking for new members who are interested in taking a stand against racism.

Our future plans include:
Anti-racist demonstrations and benefit concerts

For more information and suggestions write:

Anti Racist Action
12   27th Ave. S.E.
Minneapolis MN. 55414

The first ever Anti-Racist Action flyer, c. 1987, Minneapolis. Courtesy of the artist, Brandon Sanford.

In the end, everything went right for ARA and wrong for the nazis. There was no violence at all; whoever had been expected to hand out tickets and maps never showed. A handful of cars with nazi fans drove into the park, and each time, as Kieran put it, "a large crew of community baseball players headed over to greet them." Without exception, the nazis drove right back out again empty-handed.

ARA sleuths had also identified the concert venue, an empty wedding hall on St. Paul's Westside. For a couple of days prior to the show, activists went door to door in the neighborhood to alert people about the hate to be unleashed that Saturday night. As a result, when the picnic and ball game had successfully concluded, and dozens of militants drove to the venue to confront the band, they found hundreds of confused and angry neighbors already filling the street in a spontaneous protest. The neighbors wanted the show shut down at least as much as ARA did. The police, and eventually even the mayor of St. Paul, arrived on the scene to defuse the community's anger and "to avoid a riot," according to Kieran. "They finally announced that the show was being called off for public safety reasons." Police drove the band members and the few fans who had managed to show up away from the venue. The protest turned to celebration as the sun set on a warm early summer evening.

We Go Where They Go

What was ARA, and what does it have to do with today's radical social struggles? First founded in 1987, Anti-Racist Action was a militant, direct-action-oriented, radical left political movement active in the United States and Canada. It was based in punk counterculture, and as it grew it drew in a broader array of young people, as well as older left-wing organizers from different radical traditions.

Anti-Racist Action lived up to its most famous motto, "we go where they go," by taking direct action in the streets against Klansmen, neo-nazis, anti-abortion extremists, and other far-right organizing, as well as against racist and brutal police. The previous story highlights several indispensable elements that defined ARA's work and identity: a commitment to linking mass mobilizations against fascist targets with direct and sometimes violent confrontation by a militant core of anti-fascist activists; the skillful collection and wise use of counterintelligence; and the notion that the cultural terrain constituted a political arena.

These features recurred throughout the era of ARA, resulting in a number of victories against the far right in North America, some larger and some smaller than preventing a nazi concert, many of which have been forgotten or are simply unknown to today's activists. ARA was a major precursor to and helped define "antifa," contemporary US and Canadian anti-fascism, a term increasingly used by some ARA activists during the 1990s and early years of the new millennium. We are telling ARA's story now to document the hard work done by so many, and so that today's anti-fascists can glean useful lessons and inspiration from this experience.

ARA contended with perennial challenges faced by left-wing organizers. It functioned as a decentralized network and attempted to navigate competing demands for local democratic decision-making and for broader ideological coherence and accountability. As a political grouping based in youth cultures, it drew from the energy and vitality of its membership but was sometimes limited by short-term thinking and impatience. ARA groups that managed to defeat their local fascists or push them into hiding sometimes struggled to find new targets or campaigns or petered out entirely. As an initiative involving a lot of white people, ARA sought to make practical contributions to anti-racist struggle. For better and for worse, the priority was not personal transformation of individual members overcoming their own racism or building successful relationships with people of color but collective action against manifestations of white supremacy. ARA never reached coherent positions on any of these challenges. Persistent lack of consensus sometimes limited ARA's political development, but it also created a dynamic environment where people could and did work together despite otherwise irreconcilable disagreements.

In political terms, ARA reflected the leftist, anti-authoritarian side of the punk culture in which it was based. As it grew in the 1990s, ARA deliberately sought to be a united front of views: obviously incorporating ideologically committed anarchists, it also included Trotskyists, other Marxists, and people whose politics were most heavily informed by feminism, radical nationalisms, and other far-left ideologies. Having said that, plenty of ARA's participants were neither strongly aligned with nor claimed any specific political tradition; many might have been anarchist almost "by default," reflecting a do-it-yourself approach and an allegiance to punk rock.

Cover of ARA Toronto's news bulletin *On the Prowl* no. 16 (2000), with original artwork illustrating different aspects of anti-racism.

April 22, 1995, Toronto. Credit: David Maltby, RIP. Courtesy of Toronto ARA Archive.

ARA was also a popular movement. To be sure, it was never "mainstream" like liberal anti-racist institutions, such as the Southern Poverty Law Center (SPLC), nor did it ever approach the massive size of popular movements like the 1960s student movement or the Black Lives Matter movement of the present day. But during the era covered in this book, Anti-Racist Action mobilized hundreds of chapters and thousands of activists, reaching a peak, according to Columbus ARA member Gerry Bello, of 179 chapters in 1999. Throughout the movement's lifetime, members and chapters were security-conscious but generally public-facing. Indeed, ARA's strategic orientation could be characterized as an attempt to develop a kind of mass or popular militancy in the streets. ARA was, then, significantly more aboveground than the anonymous, closed-off styles of anti-fascist organizing that are now relatively common in North American antifa circles.

Notwithstanding its public profile, ARA distinguished itself from social movements of its time by embracing a wide diversity of tactics, including property damage and physical violence. Liberal approaches to the problem of rising fascism opposed direct confrontation and typically emphasized simultaneous "unity rallies" held on the other side of town to avoid "giving publicity" to fascists. Healthy and sometimes contentious debates about strategy and tactics inside ARA always proceeded from a baseline repudiation of this liberal approach. Physical confrontation was a reality and a tactic in ARA's campaigns against fascists, and many examples appear in this book. Often, as with the Bound for Glory shutdown, the threat of violence prevented violence, but ARA militants backed up these threats frequently enough that they were not perceived as empty. As with questions of democracy, accountability, and racial dynamics, ARA never came to consensus on the role of violence in its work and produced propaganda that oscillated between gleefully violent and nonviolent, but almost all ARA members contrasted their tactical use of force as an aspect of community self-defense with their nazi opponents' open embrace of violence for its own sake.

Who Were "They," Anyway?

Members of ARA never agreed on and only rarely debated precise theoretical definitions of fascism or racism, but for our purposes here it is crucial to have a clear understanding of ARA's terrain. This prehistory begins in Greensboro, North Carolina, on November 3, 1979, when members of the United Racist Front (URF) confronted and opened gunfire on an anti-Klan march organized by a local communist group, killing five anti-fascists.[1] The URF, notably, included both KKK and neo-nazi groups, though subsequent investigations revealed the involvement of multiple local and federal police infiltrators. None of the killers were ever convicted, and the stage was set for the intermingling of Klan and nazi ideas and individuals over the coming decades.

The defining feature of the post-Greensboro period was what Michael Novick labeled "the nazification of the KKK," after the two types of far-right groupings had eyed each other suspiciously for decades.[2] Nazification was perhaps best personified by Tom Metzger, one of the most innovative and influential far-right organizers of the 1980s. A Klan activist turned neo-nazi, Metzger epitomized several Reagan-era trends on the far right: he straddled the line between so-called "suit and tie" nazis and an emergent milieu of street-fighting fascists, served as a media-savvy mouthpiece for white supremacist politics via his cable access show and mainstream media appearances, and, perhaps most importantly, bridged the far right's generation gap by founding White Aryan Resistance (WAR), a US movement of fascist skinheads, in an explicit attempt to merge fresh blood with aging far-right leadership.[3]

A design from *Turning the Tide* (February 1990), a journal produced by Los Angeles ARA-affiliate People Against Racist Terror.

Iconic 1994 graphic by Toronto's "agitprop crew." It reflected the strategic assumption of many ARA organizers of the 1990s that, notwithstanding the racist foundations of North American society, fascist organizations of the day were not (yet) firmly rooted and could be kept on the margins through determined pressure. Today, the extreme right has taken root in the Republican Party in the United States. At the same time, the strength and commitment of anti-racist forces continues to grow. How should anti-fascist strategy evolve in response to these changes?

Influenced by British anti-racist skins, ARA preferred to call them "boneheads."

Beyond Metzger and WAR, other elements of the far right were emboldened by the rightward turn in US politics during the 1980s, but many of them rejected Reagan and the Republican Party and instead pushed further into revolutionary politics and paramilitary territory.[4] Such ideas had already circulated on the fascist fringes courtesy of the 1978 novel *The Turner Diaries*, written by William Pierce, head of the National Alliance, which was consistently one of the larger fascist groups but also among the least likely to engage in street-level activism. *The Turner Diaries* had a huge impact on the revolutionary wing of the white-power movement thanks to its potent mix of ideological race hatred and practical guidance for underground activity.

The Order, for example, a white supremacist terrorist network founded and led by Robert Jay Matthews and active in 1983–1984, took its name straight from *The Turner Diaries* and carried out actions directly inspired by the book. The Order targeted Jews and people of color with violence, most prominently assassinating Denver radio host Alan Berg in 1984, and carrying out a string of high-profile robberies, mostly of armored trucks, funneling the proceeds into the white-power movement. David Lane, an Order member, coined the so-called "fourteen words" slogan ("we must secure the existence of our people and a future for white children") and the numeric code 14/88, which references "Heil Hitler" (H being the eighth letter of the alphabet). While the Order itself was short-lived, both the 14/88 symbology and the small-cell paramilitary approach to neo-nazi organizing have lived on in far-right circles into the present era.

By the 1990s, as ARA was coming into its own, the legacy of the Klan/nazi marriage spawned multiple variants of white nationalist politics that began to resemble the many-headed hydra of the current twenty-first-century far right. We'll learn more about these groups as we encounter them throughout the book: small and frequently competing Klan organizations; a nascent "white-power music" industry; sustained suit-and-tie outfits like the National Alliance; up-and-coming sects like the World Church of the Creator; and "lone wolf" or small-cell structures responsible for bombing everything from abortion clinics to the federal building in Oklahoma City in 1995 (probably the most famous example of fascists implementing the how-to aspect of *The Turner Diaries*). One major feature of North American fascism in the 1990s, as opposed to the 1980s, was the development of militia and patriot movements, particularly in rural areas, and their growing crossover with the Christian right, although, compared to fighting Klan or nazi groupings in their own backyards, these rural movements were less of a focus for ARA.

In Canada, where ARA also took root, fewer fascist players existed, with huge variations across the vast country with a relatively thinly spread population. However, the Canadian fascists of the 1990s were linked to their American brethren ideologically and practically, while also maintaining ties with surging European fascist movements and trends that got a big shot in the arm in 1989, with the fall of the Berlin Wall, reunification of Germany, and the collapse of the socialist bloc.

The ideological and strategic differences among all these far-right tendencies were substantial and often irreconcilable—homegrown nativism versus European-oriented neo-nazism, white supremacy versus white "separatism," open revolution versus coded reformism. However, they all had at least one thing in common: they were all opposed by Anti-Racist Action.

What's Inside This Book?

Offering both a chronological and thematic review of Anti-Racist Action's history, we will examine how ARA began, how it grew into a national network and movement, dive into its culture and politics, and, finally, examine how and why it declined, with a final chapter devoted to its legacy and lessons.

Chapter 2 will explore ARA's founding period, beginning when members of the Baldies, a crew of anti-racist skinheads in Minneapolis, organized with other youth to isolate and beat back a crew of white-power skinheads encroaching on their social scene. Setting the tone for ARA's future, the Baldies used a diversity of tactics, explicitly joining education and outreach with direct-action physical violence against their neo-nazi rivals. Baldies members created the name Anti-Racist Action in 1987 to broaden their organizing outside of their skinhead scene and promoted their organizing model to other punks and skinheads throughout the Midwest and beyond, including in Chicago, Cincinnati, Milwaukee, Winnipeg, Edmonton, and other cities, in part through an anti-racist skinhead network called the Syndicate. This stage of ARA's history was perhaps most intense in Portland, Oregon, where local nazis

ARA members hold a banner at a May Day parade, Minneapolis, c. 1989. Courtesy of Kevan F. Willington.

Created in 1999 for the protest against the far-right Human Life International conference held in Toronto, this image reflects ARA's growing commitment to challenging the Christian right and defending both reproductive freedom and LGBTQ+ communities.

affiliated with White Aryan Resistance (WAR) murdered Mulugeta Seraw, a local Ethiopian man, who was a student, in 1988. Portland ARA rallied a broad swath of chapters to beat back the fascists and hosted the first two national ARA conferences in 1990 and 1991.

By 1990, ARA chapters in the midwestern US were opposing frequent rallies by a surging Ku Klux Klan and soon became a nucleus for a new wave of anti-racist organizing, covered in chapter 3. While ARA maintained its base in punk and youth counterculture, it grew from organizing within social scenes and hangouts into a more public political arena of rallies and marches and expanded into broader populations of students, leftists, queer youth, and others. Several anti-racist groups participating in anti-Klan actions convened a conference in 1994 to launch the Midwest Anti-Fascist Network (MAFNET), renamed the ARA Network in 1995. The 1994 conference was hosted by ARA's Columbus, Ohio, chapter, a linchpin during this period, hosting the next four annual conferences and publishing the ARA newsletter with the largest distribution, a peak of seventy-five thousand copies per run by 1999.[5] (ARA never had a single official national newsletter.) Chapter 3 also describes how different political organizations related to the growing network as it developed an organizational structure that balanced experimentation with coordination. A major anarchist network, the Love and Rage Revolutionary Anarchist Federation, had the strongest influence on this process.

Some of ARA's biggest and most successful chapters, located in Canada, are examined in chapter 4. The first ARA chapter in Canada, a mixture of young punks and seasoned, primarily anarchist, activists, came together in Toronto in 1992 to oppose the Heritage Front, Canada's most successful fascist organization since the 1940s. With tactics that included doxxing, public protests, and street fighting, Toronto ARA helped bring down the Heritage Front by 1994, but Canadian ARA activity continued—most strongly in Ontario, as well as in Québec, on the prairies, and on the East and West Coasts. We will see how Canadian ARA chapters networked to counter Paul Fromm, a fascist who sought to exploit public spaces as a platform, and how ARA collaboration across the US-Canada border built ARA campaigns against the growing distribution of white-power music. We will also examine an ARA chapter in Kitchener-Waterloo, Ontario, which defended street-involved youth from police harassment and fascist targeting.

Having established an early timeline, in the subsequent three chapters, we will analyze three enduring aspects of ARA's organizing: first, the different, even contradictory, ways that individual ARA activists and chapters understood and tried to practice anti-racism beyond the direct anti-fascism that ARA was best known for; second, ARA's work for reproductive freedom; and third, the youth counterculture(s) in which ARA arose and frequently operated. Each theme is essential to understanding the politics and culture of the loosely defined network, challenging as it can be to pin down. In each case, the perpetually unresolved tension between local self-determination and network-wide accountability influenced both ARA's successes and its problems. While multiracial skinhead crews in the Midwest started ARA, as skinheads became a smaller portion of its membership, ARA became whiter. Was it, then, a "white anti-racist group" or a multiracial movement? Was it best off focusing on its area of expertise—direct anti-fascism—or expanding to fight structural and systemic racism? In chapter 5, we explore ARA members' thoughts on and approaches to these questions.

Probably the most significant development in ARA's internal politics occurred in 1998, when the ARA Network explicitly broadened its focus to include campaigns for reproductive freedom. While a pro-choice platform may seem an obvious choice today for a leftist activist movement, it was by no means guaranteed in a highly decentralized network. ARA's network-level embrace of reproductive freedom was the culmination of years of on-the-ground organizing against the anti-choice Christian right. It amplified the voices of women and queer militants within ARA, while enriching ARA's analysis of the North American far right. We examine this topic in chapter 6, covering both pro-choice work and ARA's internal struggle around adopting a pro-choice platform.

Chapter 7 takes a deeper dive into ARA's cultural base and organizing, examining music, visual arts, publications, and relationships with the media. As much as it was anti-authoritarian, punk culture nevertheless reflected the trends of wider white-dominated society and wasn't immune to racism or other reactionary politics. Some of ARA's most important organizing took the form of its anti-racist, anti-sexist, and queer-positive participants claiming space and combating all forms of oppression within their scenes—i.e., fighting (and largely winning) the "culture war" for punk rock. ARA's base in youth culture also very concretely influenced its organizing; ARA chapters almost never sought funding from foundations or government programs, for example, and preferred to finance themselves locally through donations, merchandise sales, and fundraising events, such as concerts. In this chapter, we will also see how the ARA Network grew significantly when it accompanied several national music tours in 1997 and 1998. With acts like the seminal hardcore band Avail, the major-label ska band the Mighty Mighty Bosstones, the annual Warped Tour, and the US's first national hip-hop tour, Smokin' Grooves, ARA organizers were able to promote the creation of new chapters all over the US and Canada.

Chapter 8 will offer a broad view of what newer chapters got up to, covering a wider geography than the midwestern strongholds of ARA, while ARA's national network was shaken from the inside and out. On May 9, 1998, an anti-Klan rally in Ann Arbor, Michigan, escalated into an anti-racist riot, with ARA members and other militant locals fighting together against the Klan. Two months later, several anti-fascists were arrested at a rally in Kalamazoo, Michigan, based on photos taken in Ann Arbor; such coordinated police surveillance of ARA activities was new, and ARA organizers felt they faced more serious legal consequences than they previously had. At nearly the same time, on July 4, 1998, two of Las Vegas ARA's most prominent members were murdered in the desert outside the city, victims of a trap set by the neo-nazis they'd been opposing. Although violence had been a part of ARA since its beginning, the Las Vegas murders were a tragic shock. Finally, at that year's annual October conference, when many members hoped to reorient themselves to the challenges of Michigan and Las Vegas, the network learned of accusations of gendered violence within the influential Columbus chapter, sparking efforts to confront misogyny and sexual assault within chapters and the larger scene. ARA kept growing but reached its peak about a year later, in the latter half of 1999. Measured in simple numbers, the network then began a fairly rapid decline—but it was still far from over.

In 1999, an Illinois-based member of the fascist World Church of the Creator (WCOTC) went on a multistate shooting spree, a horror the WCOTC leveraged for increased publicity and rapid growth. Later that same year, the "Battle of Seattle," days of street blockades and property damage against a World Trade Organization summit, rocketed anti-globalization to new prominence for young activists, shifting away some of the energy that had fed ARA. Chapter 9 explores a series of transformations within and outside Anti-Racist Action at the dawn of the millennium. Between 1999 and 2003, ARA hounded the World Church, doxxing its members and disrupting public events. Eventually, the WCOTC allied itself with the larger National Alliance (NA), which was revving up from quieter organization building to a new, aggressive street presence. Meanwhile, the terrorist attacks of 9/11 reoriented essentially all North American politics, dramatically changing organizing conditions for the state, the fascists, and the ARA Network. ARA continued its work against both the WCOTC and the NA, through confrontations in Pennsylvania, Maryland, and Maine in 2002 and 2003 that helped undermine the viability of both groups. However, Anti-Racist Action had also shrunk in size and had begun to change its strategic orientation, as the rapid transformations of the internet pushed the network toward smaller, more anonymous, and more online counterintelligence and counterorganizing, not covered here. The ARA Network persisted, reconstituting itself as the TORCH Network in 2013, but our narrative largely ends in 2003.

Last, Chapter 10 will reflect the reason we believe this book is necessary: ARA has enduring lessons for our understanding of fascism and how to end it. We offer our thoughts on the legacies of ARA and its efforts, all the way up until today.

A Note on Authorship, Names, and Security Culture

This book attempts to do justice to the work of thousands of people over the course of almost twenty years. Three of the coauthors are ARA veterans, Lady in Columbus, Kristin in Toronto, and Mike in Chicago, while Shannon was too young to participate during the period this book covers. Although we are deeply proud and supportive of the work we and so many others undertook over many years, we have attempted to avoid cheerleading. Our goal has been to produce an accurate narrative history of ARA, the good and the bad, the successes, the missteps, and the failures. We have chosen to write in the third person until the final chapter, and while we each drafted different sections, we have all read, added to, and edited each chapter in a truly collaborative process that reflects one of the better elements of ARA itself—a rejection of hierarchy and a commitment to collective work. We have also attempted (with mixed success, we acknowledge) to "smooth" our overall authorial voice, but, be forewarned, you will see elements that reflect each of us throughout.

In researching this book, we interviewed over fifty former ARA members, as well as people who worked outside but alongside the group. These comrades talked with us about their experiences, shared items from their personal archives, and helped us better tell the tales that need to be told, while keeping some things completely off the record. To better understand the impact of ARA's work on our opponents, we spoke with former fascists Frank Meeink, in Philadelphia, and Elizabeth Moore, in Toronto. We also spoke with Devin Burghart and Matthew Lyons, two researchers of the far right in the United States, and Bill Dunphy, a reporter who covered the far right in Canada, in the 1990s, along with a former Toronto City councilor and three witnesses to events in the Toronto area.

We also want to explicitly acknowledge that we simply know less about some places than others. Our research is heavily based on interviews with ARA veterans, many of them contacted through the same informal networks that existed back in the day.[6] Our three ARA veteran coauthors knew a lot of people who knew a lot of people, but the truth is our networks just might be more likely to catch people who were in the Midwest than the one activist driving an ARA chapter in their small hometown somewhere in Utah. We regret that we don't know what the ARA chapters got up to in Kalispell, Montana (population 15,388, in 2000), in Jasper, Alabama (13,399), or in McCall, Idaho (2,178). The absence of Southern ARA groups from this book (with the partial exception of Louisville) is particularly unfortunate.

One topic we will explore throughout the book is ARA's majority white membership. We do this as four white anti-racists, and we take responsibility for the limitations of our perspectives.

We refer to our sources using a mix of full names, first names, and pseudonyms, out of respect for the very real and entirely legitimate concerns people have about being targeted for retaliation or violence in our present moment and likely future. This too is a legacy of ARA, which was committed to balancing its efforts to organize mass opposition to the far right with the need for a security culture to protect people from harm at the hands of violent fascists. We are immensely grateful to everyone who helped us bring this book into existence.

A Final Thought Before We Begin

History is a weapon, and the aim of this book is to arm a new generation of anti-fascists. We very much hope you enjoy the ride as we take you through the high points, and some low ones, in the history of ARA. And we hope that you learn some things along the way that are valuable in our current period of struggle against white nationalism and the far right.

NOTES

1   On Greensboro and the URF, see Kathleen Belew, *Bring the War Home* (Cambridge, MA: Harvard University Press, 2018), 60–63.

2   Michael Novick, *White Lies, White Power* (Monroe, ME: Common Courage Press, 1995), 51.

3   For more on Tom Metzger's life and legacy from a militant anti-fascist perspective, see Kdog, "American Strasser," Three Way Fight, December 9, 2020, accessed April 1, 2022, http://threewayfight.blogspot.com/2020/12/american-strasser.html.

4   See Belew, *Bring the War Home*; Novick, *White Lies, White Power*.

5   *Anti-Racist Action Network Bulletin* no. 11 (c. August 1998).

6   References for all interviews can be found on pages 284–85.

CHAPTER 2

SKINHEAD SCENES AND THE FIGHT FOR TERRITORY

ARA was born as the solution to a very concrete problem: a multiracial, anti-racist crew of Minneapolis skinheads needed to keep a crew of white-power skinheads off their turf. Their battle—rooted in skinhead and punk culture, emblematic of a broader clash between opposing strains of skinheads—paralleled turf wars happening in cities across the Midwest and throughout North America and led to the creation of a short-lived intercity network called the Syndicate.

Arising in 1960s Great Britain, skinhead culture, like the neighborhoods it hailed from, was initially multiracial. British working-class whites and West Indians, mostly Jamaicans influenced by the "rude boy" culture of Kingston, Jamaica, came together around ska and dub, two Jamaican music genres that overlap with reggae. British skins then embraced punk culture to such an extent that an entire subgenre of punk, Oi!, is essentially synonymous with skins. In general, though, skinhead culture has few consistent, well-defined markers besides working-class roots and a distinctive fashion: bomber jackets, Doc Martens, shaved heads. During the global economic crisis of the late 1970s and early 1980s, skinhead culture split when wide swathes of white Britain blamed increasing unemployment and other troubles on immigrants of color from the Caribbean and South Asia. In tandem with a rise in British neo-fascism generally, a new breed of white-power skinhead arose[1]—what anti-racist skins like to call "boneheads."

Minneapolis

In 1986, the Baldies were the first skinheads on the scene in the Twin Cities.[2] Initially, they were a group of seven friends who knew one another through the local punk scene and had a common interest in skinhead culture. Their main activities were partying, attending punk shows, and skateboarding. Baldies member Joe said the crew was "like a replacement family for me."[3] Founding member Mic Crenshaw (pronounced like "microphone") described the group in simple terms: "We were good friends, we were multiracial, and we were militantly anti-nazi." As for their initial attraction to skinhead culture, Mic explained: "We liked the look, we liked the working-class roots ... [and] we wanted to be little tough guys."[4] All seven founding members were, in fact, guys, embodying a righteous masculinity typical of anti-racist skinheads.

Foreshadowing a commitment to youth leadership and engagement that would later define Anti-Racist Action, the Baldies were young; like Mic, they were all around sixteen when they named their crew. Mic explained some members "were, like, twenty-one. We used to get them to buy us beer." Still, "older" Baldies were in their early twenties. They were also proud and explicit about being a multiracial crew. Along with Mic, an African American, the other founders were Gator, who is Ojibwe, and "a couple working-class white kids," and the crew went on to explicitly recruit among youth of color. "I think people of color in the organization had more clout," Mic said, because members understood that they faced racism "as part of our historic existence in this country.... That awareness in our crew gave people of color a degree of reverence."

Trouble was brewing, though. Mic explains, "We started to see white kids who were showing up at shows, showing up in the neighborhoods we hung out in, dressed like skinheads, but when we would ask them where their beliefs were, they would say they were white power."[5] About six months after the Baldies formed, a twenty-year-old skinhead named Paul Hollis formed the White Knights "in a blue-collar neighborhood of East St. Paul" with an explicit white-power ideology.[6]

By the late 1980s, seasoned white-power organizers like Tom Metzger of the California-based White Aryan Resistance had begun explicitly targeting skinhead and punk culture to recruit young people into aging radical-right political circles.[7] Later, in 1988, Oprah Winfrey hosted a televised panel of four white-power skinheads who used her show's national platform to essentially promote unfiltered white supremacy;[8] other media across the United States jumped on the bandwagon and played up sensationalist images of white-power skinheads on the rise. Frank Meeink, a former nazi skinhead turned anti-racist activist, described a segment on Geraldo Rivera's show, which escalated to an on-air fistfight, as "the fuckin' marketing of the fuckin' year." Media coverage of racist skinheads in the 1980s "was huge. It is what made us stronger in them years, above the anti-racist groups. It really was what pushed us over the top." Thanks to that, the popular perception of the bald fascist stormtrooper—skinheads as inherently radically racist and right-wing—was born, but anti-racist skinheads continued to exist.[9]

The Baldies embraced a "militantly anti-nazi" identity after the arrival of the White Knights. According to Mic, "That became the point at which a group of friends that was more of a social clique, now we had a purpose, and our purpose was to fight those guys." But while this political stance became an explicit part of the Baldies' program, other beliefs varied. Like broader skinhead culture, the Baldies were proudly working class. "That's where my roots are. That's where I come from," said Joe. Some Baldies, like Joe and Gator, "combined traditional midwestern populist distrust of the System with vaguely democratic-socialist ideas about how to fix it."[10] Others were "anti-racist U.S. patriots," according to Kieran;[11] Kieran himself was a committed anarchist. Notwithstanding their internal differences, the Baldies were undeniably the anti-racist crew. They shared "some basic class politics to understand that by splitting black people and white people up it makes regular people weaker as a class."[12] A sharp distinction thus existed between the anti-racist Baldies and the racist White Knights—Minneapolis became a battleground between the rival strains of skinhead culture.

The Baldies and White Knights ran into each other at punk shows or just around town, especially on the streets of Uptown, the Baldies' preferred neighborhood. According to Baldie and ARA member Lorraine, Uptown was where all of Minneapolis's cool kids and youth scenes converged: "On a given night, like, especially in the summer, there could be about a hundred kids out there from every group." Minneapolis weeklies wrote scene reports on it; Prince wrote a song about it; nazis weren't wanted in it.

The Baldies pushed fascist skins out of shows and neighborhoods to deny them a safe space to organize and recruit. In a 1989 interview with the punk zine *Maximum Rocknroll*, Kieran described this activism simply: "We made it clear to the Nazi skinheads that they will not organize at shows, they will not organize at hangouts, we will not be friends with these people." He continued, "From our experience the tactic that has

NAZI SKINHEADS BEWARE!

This area has been declared a nazi-free zone by Anti-Racist Action. Racist violence will not be tolerated!

Contact A.R.A.at:

Minneapolis, late 1980s.
Courtesy of Brandon Sanford.

worked in Minneapolis includes physical confrontation, which is fighting them and kicking the shit out of them."[13] The Baldies would first give a warning: lose the racism, or next time you'll be treated to "righteous violence."[14] "We would see them and we'd fuck 'em up, and sometimes they would see us and we'd be outnumbered and they would jump us," observed Mic.[15] They mainly stuck to street fighting, but this could escalate, as when Mic "decided to throw a brick through the window" of White Knights founder Paul Hollis's apartment.

While the racists were a serious threat in Minneapolis, the Baldies were the dominant force, mostly through sheer numbers. As Kieran said in the *Maximum Rocknroll* piece:

> Some people get this fear that [racist] skinheads are these supermen that can't be beat, but the fact is that any two people should be able to beat any one person if it comes down to that. One of the reasons why the Baldies won so much isn't because we're on some macho trip or that we're all huge people but because we've been able to get the numbers to support us.[16]

Kieran didn't see violence as its own end, "because it's important to talk to people in the scene about racism and not letting it be acceptable. If you are going out there and [you] fight and the scene isn't going to be behind you, then it's not very effective."[17] However, violence as a tactic largely defined the Baldies' anti-racism, and certainly the way outsiders conceived of the group. Just like ARA later on, the Baldies were set apart from traditional activists by their willingness to engage in violent confrontation with white supremacists. Members like Mic remained unapologetic:

> Adults at the time who caught wind of what we were up to were always trying to get us to chill out. They were the ones who were, like, "You gotta use nonviolence, people aren't gonna respect you if you use violence, you guys are gonna get killed"—and we were always, like, fuck that, man.... Get the job done. These guys are violent, so how are we gonna confront them with nonviolence?

Still, the tactic certainly had its drawbacks. Kieran argued that their tendency to win helped the Baldies and their anti-racist struggle to grow, as "no one's going to join a gang that's losing all the time."[18] On the other hand, the Baldies' penchant for "righteous violence" could lead to a less righteous variety. They might be confronted by "big drunk jocks who come out of Figlio's and have heard how tough skinheads are,"[19] or nonaligned skins who "wanted to make a name for themselves."[20]

As the rival sides fought, the more politically active members of the Baldies moved to expand their organizing. After fascists jumped a black teenager and "started a mini race war at a St. Paul high school," according to Kieran, the Baldies decided "it shouldn't just be a battle between bald head kids."[21] Sometime in 1987, they named their organizing activity in an explicit attempt to broaden its base beyond skinhead and punk subcultures. A few members knew and admired a British group called Anti-Fascist Action but, according to Mic, were concerned that the word *fascism* "was often more limited to the organized left and academic circles, and common people on the streets didn't necessarily know what you meant when you said fascism ... but everybody knew what racism was."[22] Thinking it would better fit their activism and the wider American political context, the Baldies decided to revise the British group's name. Anti-Racist Action was born.

"The idea for ARA was not just to be a group of anti-racist skins but to involve all types of young people," according to Kieran.[23] Mic explained:

> We started to reach out to some of the gangs, the Black, Latino gangs, people in the Native American community and their street organizations. We built with other punks and anarchists, specifically Revolutionary Anarchist Bowling League. We used the anarchist bookstore ... as a center for our meetings and cultural events.[24]

They particularly pulled from other Uptown youth scene groups. If they knew the White Knights were coming to anything specific, Lorraine explained, "We would call everyone. Call SLK Posse, call the Latin Kings, call, you know, the skater kids." SLK was particularly close to the Baldies, described by a Baldie named Brandon as "trusted folks from our community that hung out with us, went to parties with us, fought nazis with us," but who weren't skinheads: a group of hip-hop kids, skaters, etc.

Minneapolis ARA was made up of an initial core group of Baldies, who teamed up with a diverse cross section of Minneapolis's youth culture to fight something that directly impacted all of them: nazis trying to encroach on their scenes. Their budding anti-racist movement was good at what it did. But Minneapolis wasn't the only North American city, or punk scene, plagued by fascist skinheads. As Mic recalled, zines like *Maximum Rocknroll* had "'scene reports' ... from the West Coast, you know, the Southwest, the East Coast, and you started to see, like, oh, these people are fuckin' having nazi problems everywhere right now."[25] In Midwest cities in particular, anti-racist skinhead crews were fighting the same fight as the Baldies in Minneapolis, defending their scenes from nazi interlopers. Before long, these different groups would come together, forging an intercity network of anti-fascist skinheads, a major precursor to the ARA Network that later spanned a continent. This early network was known as the Syndicate.

Cincinnati

Before meeting the Baldies, Cincinnati's scene evolved independently but in similar ways, described by Cincinnati skinhead Eric as "what we call in Marxism a combined and uneven development." Cincinnati's anti-racist activists began simply, around the same time as the Baldies, by keeping nazis out of their scene.

Eric had gravitated to the punk scene when he was fourteen, around 1985. Like most of his friends, he had dropped out of high school. In his eyes, the punk scene of the 1980s was a catch-all for every "freak": punks, skinheads, goths, runaways, queer kids, and basically everyone who didn't fit in to Reagan's America. For these outcasts, especially in a time before the internet, physical space—where they could feel safe and be themselves—mattered. Like the Baldies had Uptown, Cincinnati punks had Short Vine Street. Venues, hangouts, and parties were shared by everyone. Early on, this even included nazis.

Eric remembers "being at parties and hearing Skrewdriver," the English band that essentially invented and hugely promoted the idea of the nazi skinhead (before their lead singer was killed in a car crash by an anti-fascist tree). In 1985 Cincinnati, white-power skinheads weren't very politically organized, but they were "part of the scene." Thankfully, that didn't last long.

Eric remembers the specific party where conflict broke out. It was attended, as usual, by a varied crowd. Drinking on the porch of the Skin House, one of the nazis called one of the goths, a young Black kid, a racist epithet, and a fight broke out. After that, the conflict was permanent. Cincinnati's anti-racists fought to keep nazis out of the venues, houses, shows, and (when they were old enough) bars where they hung out around Short Vine Street. However, the fight against nazis didn't stay confined to the social scene for long.

In 1987, anti-racist skinheads counter-demonstrated a rally by nazi skins. According to Eric, "there was probably ten of them, and probably two hundred of us, and maybe two cops.... They were behind the American flag, and they were sieg heiling, and I knew all of them by name." For the nazis, the rally wasn't much of a statement—one thoughtfully told a reporter "we're protesting the protest against us."[26] But Eric remembers the rally: "probably, one, because I was on LSD"; two, because the anti-racists "intimidated" and "humiliated" the nazis, eventually chasing them into alleyways.

It was a victory, at the time—but afterward the violence increased. The nazis had cloaked their rally in an innocuous name (United Skinheads), but they were already calling themselves White Aryan Skinheads (WASH). Their anti-racist rivals crewed up in turn: the Noble Savages, the Queen City Boot Boys, Punks Opposed to Racism and Nazis (PORN). Eric, his brother, and their more militantly anti-nazi friends took on the name SHARP, Skinheads Against Racial Prejudice, a common moniker to this day. The name was first coined in New York City, and a few dozen skinhead crews and very many individuals were calling themselves SHARP within several years, but Eric reckons Cincinnati was among the first.

All of these Cincinnati crews continued the physical, turf war–like conflict against the nazis to keep them out of the scene. Eric explains:

> Where the clubs were is where the fighting was. They would hang out at the bars; we would hang out at the bars. And whoever was gonna win, it was like a war of attrition with them. Someone would call on the pay phone and be, like, hey, two WASH skins are up at Sudsy Malone's.... It rang at our house, and we'd go to a couple other houses and say, "Hey, man, Mike Farrell's up at Sudsy Malone's." We'd get six guys together and go kick his ass. And they'd do the same thing, right?

Eric compared Cincinnati's conflict to gang violence, just as Mic described the Baldies' struggle. But while the Baldies always dominated in Minneapolis,[27] Eric describes the Cincinnati scene as significantly more violent, escalating over time after the 1987 rally.

SHARP jumped nazis and were jumped. Both sides collected trophies, carrying razors to cut the laces of beaten rivals and take their boots. They taped RAID cans to bricks and threw them through house windows. Curb stomping was "real, and I've seen it," says Eric. SHARP members burned a leading nazis' motorcycle and watched bullets riddle the car in front of them as they fled. Gunplay, overall? "Not a lot, a little." For Eric, the conflict was "existential." If he wanted to visit a coffee shop,

> and nazis were in there, were they gonna kill me? Were they gonna stab me on the way out? If I wanted to go to a show ... would I be safe? ... Would nazis crash that show and be there sieg heiling in the front row, and then see me and beat the crap out of me because of that fight that happened last week? So it was an immediate need for survival, for most of us, to just be able to walk down the street. And once it got going, it was either [fight or] you leave the movement, which was—this was our life. This was our world. Where were we gonna go, back to the suburbs where, you know, they stop the car when you have green hair? ... When you have six or seven people, ten people, fifteen, twenty, thirty people that have that same feeling, you all get together and defend each other.

Like the Baldies, Cincinnati's anti-racist skinheads weren't necessarily leftists. Even SHARP had a solid current of Pro-Ams, skinhead
parlance for "Pro-American." Eric doesn't think "they were so, like,
politically pro-American"; "it was just part of the uniform." For his own
part, Eric started off interested in "the idea of, like, unity, family, all this
honor stuff." Cincinnati had some women skinheads; however, "it was a
lot of macho stuff. It was a *ton* of macho stuff, and I was drawn to this."
For Eric, fighting nazis "was a matter of survival before it was political."

Some other Cincinnati SHARP skins, though, were leftists from
very early on. Grover was an anarchist who sported patches of the West
German militant Red Army Faction; Matt identified as a communist by
about age fifteen. Led by such early leftists and driven by the anti-fascist
work they would continue in the Syndicate, a lot of Cincinnati SHARPs
moved left over time. One push to the left for Eric was "points of conten-
tion" within the skinhead scene: "Like, anti-gay rhetoric among the
Pro-Ams," he scoffs. "Some people move to the right when they hear
that. I moved to the left.... Like, skinheads hated homeless people for
some fuckin' reason. These Pro-Am kinda guys. And I thought that was
really awful, you know."

Still, some anti-racists didn't always fit into "the left." For example,
the International Socialist Organization (ISO) was around Cincinnati,
including at the 1987 rally, but Eric says they "wanted a purely legalistic
route, but we were in a war, and we did war-like things." The ISO "didn't
want to have anything to do with that," he says, while SHARP "didn't very
much care for them, 'cause they were just college kids." (Matt, meanwhile,
had some nice things to say about the ISO—he and Eric both stress the
diversity of viewpoints in the scene.)

SHARP did forge connections with more established activists,
whose outlook—although not necessarily ideology—lined up with theirs.
According to Matt, SHARP's relationship with any activist group essentially came down to whether the latter took the skinheads seriously and
treated SHARP's fundamental attitudes, including a willingness to use
physical confrontation, as legitimate. One such group was the John Brown
Anti-Klan Committee (JBAKC, usually pronounced "j-back"), a militant
anti-fascist group formed in the 1970s by activists who had had many
years of experience in the Student Non-Violent Coordinating Committee
and the Congress of Racial Equality.[28] Before long, Cincinnati SHARP's
"lefty skins" were studying and sharing JBAKC's writing. In fact, a JBAKC

chapter was still active in Chicago, supporting anti-racist skinheads who would soon be in the Syndicate alongside Cincinnati and Minneapolis skins.

Chicago

A group of nazi skins called Chicago Area Skinheads (CASH) formed in 1983. At that time, founder Clark Martell was ancient by skinhead standards—twenty-three—and a (relatively) experienced activist from the Aryan Youth Movement.[29] According to a 1989 *Chicago Reader* article, "It's interesting to note that, unlike most nazi skins, Martell apparently came to skinheadism through white power, rather than vice versa."[30] Selling bootlegged Skrewdriver tapes from a post office box, calling his mail order outfit Romantic Violence, Martell was probably the first white-power skinhead organizer in the US.[31]

Like in Minneapolis, Chicago's nazis were always outnumbered. According to Michelle, a skinhead from the Windy City, "being a skinhead in Chicago in the 1980s meant being anti-racist." For one thing, Michelle has heard others estimate a quarter of the scene was people of color; she reckons "it was probably closer to half." For some kids like Malki C. Brown, Martell and CASH couldn't even be called skinheads, just "racists that shaved their heads." CASH existed as a consistent nuisance and, at times, a very real danger, but most of Chicago's skins had better things to do.

"We hung out," says Michelle. Like Cincinnati and Minneapolis, the scene had a physical center: Belmont. She continues, "You didn't have to have an invite; you just knew to go down and that's where your friends would be." From there, the night was yours: go to a punk show, meet at Fleet's for a burger, or go to Medusa's, an all-ages juice bar—basically a nightclub with no liquor license—that "brought together all of Chicago's long-segregated nightlife tribes in a single throbbing melting pot: Goths, skinheads, punks, black house-music fans, white Boystown denizens, closeted suburban honor-roll kids."[32] CASH might come to shows or, according to Malki, "they'd drive by Belmont ... and we'd chase 'em down the street; they'd get stuck in traffic and we'd try to pull 'em out of their cars." By this point, the nazis knew they weren't welcome.

As was the case in Minneapolis and Cincinnati, Chicago's anti-racist skinheads had been fighting "a war,"[33] physically confronting nazis at punk shows and venues since at least 1985. As Malki put it, "It was just a part of the culture to make sure they knew not to come around and send a message that their position ... and their ideas were not acceptable." JBAKC activists were supporting the anti-racist skins by 1985, viewing the nazi skinheads as the violent edge of a deeper, overall "backlash" against the gains of the Civil Rights Movement and black liberation struggle.[34]

Malki joined this scene in 1987, coming from his high school's suburbs. Malki looked up to the older skinheads fighting CASH, like Dwight, Sonny, and Corky. Like Michelle, he rolled with, but never officially "joined," the Skinheads of Chicago (SHOC), the more "politically minded, explicitly anti-racist group" of the time.[35] If SHOC had a leader, it was probably Sonny, who was enigmatic—a black man with swastika tattoos[36]—but "magnetic and tough, and he liked to fight," as Malki put it. SHOC's founding "thought leader," though, was Corky, who, Malki says, took "a more intellectual approach to things." When the Baldies came through Chicago in 1988, following their friends' hardcore band Blind Approach on tour, they met some SHOC members and, shortly after, Corky told Malki about this ARA idea. What if they started something like that in Chicago?

Chicago ARA was born around 1988 and, attempting to make the local scene's anti-racism more explicit and organized, took on a wider mandate than beating up nazis. They visited high schools to "talk about how racism is used to divide people who should be united,"[37] encouraged record stores to stop carrying white-power music, compiled an anti-racist zine, *Colorblind*, and held Rock Against Racism shows, mostly organized by Malki. (They also still beat up nazis.) The new strategies asserted anti-racism as an aspect of skinhead and punk culture and raised money, for example, for the local Puerto Rican Community Center's HIV/AIDS clinic,[38] likely influenced by JBAKC's long-term support for the Puerto Rican national liberation struggle. For Malki, ARA seemed a natural continuation of work they were "already doing," now taking on a more overtly political tone. In an interview with Mic Crenshaw, Corky explained:

> There are people who brought ideology to the clique and who brought muscle to the clique and who really brought useful points of view. So thought and muscle. But it wasn't until summer of 1988 when y'all [the Baldies/Minneapolis ARA] came down that we got

This May 1989 Chicago Rock Against Racism show, presented by "COLORBLIND and ARA/Syndicate," raised money for a local Puerto Rican HIV/AIDS clinic called VIDA/SIDA. Courtesy of @boxcutterbrigade, Instagram.

the vocabulary that was missing.... While we believed it had some philosophical underpinnings, when it comes down to it, we were just fighting and drinking. But then when y'all gave us the language of anti-racist action, direct action, and confrontation and principled anti-fascism; it's, like—ahh—here we go. That's what we were missing.[39]

The political turn suited both Malki, influenced by his ex–Black Panther parents and the Civil Rights Movement, and Corky, who Malki described as "somewhere between a socialist concept to a [Black] nationalist concept." But, Malki said, "most people weren't trying to hear that." Their SHOC crew was the political side of Chicago's scene, but according to the *Chicago Reader*, "the common term of derision is 'communist,'" and at least one centrist skinhead called them "just as bad" as the nazis.[40]

One legend of Chicago's skinhead history is telling. When an out-of-town nazi skin rolled through, looking for a place to stay, he was directed to a couple of locals. They beat him to a pulp and left him hogtied at a Holocaust memorial.[41] What doesn't often pop out in retellings is that the same skins, before beating him up, had been partying with him.

This was not the culture in SHOC or their sister group, Chicago ARA; a single SHOC member joined that night's party just before the beatdown.[42] However, it reflects the overall political milieu. According to Michelle, some of Chicago's Black skinheads didn't "care if you [were] white-power;" the night of the hogtying, "they gave that guy every opportunity to not fuck up and say something racist."

The Syndicate

Members of the Baldies, SHARP, SHOC, and the nascent ARA groups were coming out of skinhead scenes with imprecise anti-fascist politics and gravitating increasingly to leftist political activism against fascism. They soon took a big step toward a more political conception of anti-fascism, while maintaining their roots in skinhead and punk cultures, when they formed an intercity network of anti-racist skinheads they called the Syndicate.

Post office boxes, letters, and printed media like zines stitched connections between scenes. According to Eric, in this pre-internet age, zines were "our social media, and that's how we found out everything: all the new music … what was going on in groups." The Baldies read about the "nazi problems" of other scenes in the zine *Maximum Rocknroll* (MRR) and realized they weren't alone. In 1989, early in ARA's growth, according to Kieran, "Getting ARA mentioned in the *MRR* scene reports created a big response … [W]e had letters pouring in."[43] Cincinnati SHARP, likewise, took out an ad in MRR sharing just their name and post office box and soon received mail from anti-racist skinheads in other cities.

Aside from using written media, punks and skinheads met each other through travel. As Eric from Cincinnati SHARP described it, "Gorilla Biscuits came to Toledo. We went up to Toledo, right? … I drove to New York City overnight to go see Bad Brains…. We were always in the car going to a show. Always…. And then you go to a show. You need a place to stay. You ask some local crew. You got floor space." Punk, with its do-it-yourself ethic, was built on informal but extensive networking. Anti-racist skinheads in multiple midwestern cities formalized those connections when they formed the Syndicate and began hosting conferences to come together for parties and the occasional brawl, but especially for political speakers, discussion, and events.

At the first conference, on January 14, 1989,[44] anti-racist skins joined the Black Law Student Union of the University of Minnesota on a march

AP photo

Some of the more than 100 skinheads from eight Midwest cities raised their fists in solidarity outside a library in the Uptown section of Minneapolis Saturday night. The group discussed ways to counter the racism of other skinhead groups.

Syndicate skinheads, Minneapolis, 1989.

to clean up racist graffiti on campus. Beside the Minneapolis, Cincinnati, and Chicago crews, there was Milwaukee's Brew City Skins. They were a "pillar" of the network, says Kieran, and "the Syndicate might not have happened if Brew City had not come up to Minneapolis on a whim and met the Baldies."[45] Another crew notably came from across the Canadian border: Winnipeg SHARP, which member Thomas describes as "in constant conflict" with local fascists like the Northern Hammerskins; they also had the support of some existing left-wing groups, some "old school union guys," and, most importantly, other punks and queer kids in their scene.

Other groups and individuals came to the Syndicate's founding conference from Boise, Indianapolis, St. Paul, Des Moines, Lawrence,[46] Omaha, Michigan, and New York.[47] Some of these groups were their own crews or just called themselves ARA; in some places, like Minneapolis and Chicago, skinhead crews and ARA existed side-by-side, overlapped, or, depending on the city and who you asked, the distinction might have been little more than in name.

Mic remembers the powerful emotion of this first conference:

> It was exciting. It felt like we were part of a political movement that was created by us, for us, in our time, and it was an electric moment. I remember standing up and looking around, and I actually shed a tear, because it was the first time that I was doing something empowering that had nothing to do with what adults thought I should be doing.... You knew that you had family. Like, these people believed in the same things you did. That was a powerful feeling and a powerful understanding to have.

The Syndicate soon hosted additional conferences in at least Chicago, Cincinnati, and Milwaukee. During the Milwaukee gathering, on June 17, 1989, Syndicate skinheads argued with a record store owner about stocking of white-power records, which the owner eventually, though reluctantly, handed over for destruction. (Michelle remembers a simpler strategy to deal with white-power records: surreptitiously "crack the records in half," so that a nazi customer "would get the record home and it'd be in pieces.") According to Malki:

> The conferences were big, and a big thing for us. We tried to host them as often as possible. People came in on a Friday; we would hang out and meet and greet, and then on Saturday would be a day of panel discussions, where you had different speakers. So, [at] the one in Chicago ... [the SPLC] spoke about neo-nazi activity across the country. [The] John Brown [Anti-Klan Committee] spoke ... about police activity and the types of things going on in the Chicago community, things that we should look out for. I think some of the Baldies spoke ... about further organizing ARA chapters [and growing] the movement.

By 1990, the Syndicate was a well-established force of anti-racist skinheads from all over the Midwest and nearby Canada. midwestern skinhead scenes had independently and simultaneously started fighting nazis, responding in similar ways to similar conditions. ARA also began to take root beyond the Syndicate, as people elsewhere started fighting their own local fascists.

ARA Beyond the Syndicate: Edmonton and Winnipeg

By 1990, Walter Tull remembers, boneheads in Edmonton had grown from one or two outcasts to a consistent violent danger, particularly after getting involved with more established white supremacists affiliated with the Aryan Nations. After boneheads invaded the home of a local journalist, Keith Rutherford, beating him with a baseball bat so severely that he was blinded, Walter, and a few others, including a Winnipeg SHARP who had recently moved back to Edmonton, demonstrated at the trial, formalizing the Edmonton Anti-Fascist League (AFL) shortly thereafter. For the next year or two, AFL "ran this protracted street fight with the nazis," Walter remembers:

> It started with us just meeting to put Nazi-Free Zone and No Hate Here posters through the downtown area one night a week. We'd meet at the punk bar; we'd get our wheat paste and split up in twos and go and do that. And it really kicked off, because one night I was out with my friend doing this, and I guess the nazis weren't that stupid, and they figured out what night we were doing it. So we ran into five of them and [Aryan Nations activist] Terry Long's henchman, and they beat the shit out of us. I got knocked unconscious. My friend got the wheat paste bucket poured over her head. I went to emergency.
>
> It's funny, they got the shit kicked out of them a few hours later when they ran into a group of British soldiers who were in town for military exercises and didn't take kindly to the skinheads. They got wheeled in—I'm still in the hospital, yeah, the same ER!—I saw two of the guys being wheeled in wheelchairs and one of them is unconscious. Karma! It was pretty good.
>
> Word got out that we'd been assaulted, and the next time we went out postering we had fifty people. [The nazis] all lived in this one house. We went to their house and confronted them. They came out with shotguns. It was pretty tense. And there's no cell phones, right? We had it planned; we had scouts that were within eyesight of the crowd, and if we gave a signal, they'd signal to the other person, to signal to the other person, who was at a payphone, to call 911. So, when the shotguns came out, [we] made the signal and we left. The cops showed up, and the nazis got busted for illegally altering their shotguns to hold more rounds than is legal.

Around the same time, in Winnipeg, the Syndicate-affiliated SHARP evolved into a new name, United Against Racism (UAR), to better welcome non-skinheads who wanted to be involved; as a result, both Edmonton AFL and Winnipeg's UAR still had connections with skinhead culture but weren't all skinheads. Street fighting was still included in their arsenals, but they were also taking on broader tactics. Both Walter and Thomas remember the significance of what we might now call doxxing, surveilling and publicly outing fascists who weaponized anonymity. Thomas says:

> Nazi skinheads jump out of a van, nobody knows who they are. They all have shaved heads; they're all white guys with boots.... But once you start keeping information about them, they're a lot more easily recognized, and it was a deterrent to them to attack us...
>
> We did have a lot of rallies and confronted them on the street, but as soon as they are not anonymous anymore, it really takes a lot of the power away from them, because once the community knows who they are, and they punch someone in the face, the police will charge them, or there will be some sort of retribution. Like, they'll be afraid that their cars will get wrecked or whatever, and that will hurt them a lot more than anything else we can do.

Los Angeles

Michael Novick was not a skinhead, and People Against Racist Terror (PART), the organization he founded, wasn't initially an ARA chapter—though, still active today, it's ARA's longest running chapter. Novick was a veteran of the New Left, the broad range of 1960s and 1970s leftism that included the anti-war student movement, and of JBAKC. PART is best known for publishing *Turning the Tide* (TTT), "a journal of anti-racist activism, research and education," beginning in 1988. Although PART was not based in youth counterculture, TTT stitched together ties and dialogue between militant anti-racists, especially punks and skinheads, in addition to promoting a fairly influential anti-imperialist/anti-colonial perspective. The fifth issue of TTT, for example, included a Chicago ARA letter asking TTT to list its members' contact info: "We should start offering ways of contacting other groups to form a network. Fight racism!"[48] The conversations in TTT joined ARA chapters in the Syndicate to budding groups on the West Coast, many of which were relatively short-lived, but which an ARA pamphlet later described as a "first wave," including Colorado ("Front Range ARA"), the Bay Area, San Diego, and Portland.

San Diego

George Matiasz, also not a skinhead, started San Diego ARA (SDARA) in 1990. For some time, while temporarily going to grad school in San Diego, he was "pretty much on the campus and in the community doing various kinds of political organizing ... anti-militarism and anti-draft groups," he says, and then "general anarchist organizing." When he started seeing *Turning the Tide* around town, he organized a first meeting. SDARA had skinhead members, but George saw the budding movement as fundamentally a force of the punk scene. Like PART in LA, SDARA didn't engage in a turf war conflict like the Syndicate crews were fighting—in retrospect, Matiasz admits they were possibly just too outnumbered by nazis—but, as he told the *Los Angeles Times* in a 1990 profile, their goal was "to educate people that racism isn't cool and to take control" to push nazis out of San Diego's punk scene. They were "plastering pockets of San Diego with 'Smash Racism' posters and scattering flyers at music shops" and inviting people to twice-monthly meetings held "wherever room [could] be found."[49]

Portland

Of all the West Coast "first wave" chapters, Portland ARA had the most similarities with and connections to the Midwest Syndicate. Closely related to, but not synonymous with, a local crew of SHARPs, Portland ARA had its name first "brought over" by visiting Baldies, and Portland activists had read about ARA in *Maximum Rocknroll* and *Skinhead Times*, a New York zine.[50] Portland also closely paralleled the Syndicate cities' combination of turf war conflict with other anti-racist activism. In fact, Portland's chapter embodies the entire history of ARA in many ways.[51]

On November 13, 1988, members of Eastside White Pride, a local nazi skinhead gang, murdered Mulugeta Seraw,[52] an Ethiopian refugee and a student at Portland State University, a father, and an avid soccer fan (and player), described by his uncle as "hard-working, caring, kind, and respectful ... acknowledged as a leader and a peacemaker."[53] Seraw's murder immediately sent ripples through Portland, especially in the Ethiopian community. For Portland's punk scene, it sent the clearest possible message that the threat of the racist skinheads who harassed and attacked them needed a response.

Tom, an ARA organizer and anti-racist skinhead, explained, "We all just kinda said we had enough and started forming groups and going after them." The same week as Seraw's murder, an ARA organizer named Jason remembers, "there was a show at the Pine Street. A bunch of the punks showed up, the spikey-haired crowd … and within a week, we had gotten a meeting together," under the name of both Anti-Racist Action and Skinheads Against Racial Prejudice, "and decided that we were gonna fight back."[54]

ARA and SHARP—like elsewhere, two groups, but clearly overlapping—agreed on a plan of action: at a subsequent show, they organized "a very serious presence," as Jason described:

> Everybody showed up with bats and stood out front.… A few groups of [nazis] walked up, and they'd see people going toward them, and they'd take off. There was probably a couple scuffles in the blocks around it, mostly people, like, pulling up in their cars and trying to jump out to attack. They would get beaten back down, and they'd jump back in their cars and tear off.[55]

The anti-racist punks repeated the strategy for two more shows—and for shows, at least, that was enough. Jason explains, they "expected this to go on for months," and instead:

> As soon as it was a fair fight, they were gone! They disappeared. There were three hundred of them in the Portland area in 1990, but they were all hiding out in Beaverton, out in Milwaukie, out in Southeast. There were ten of us that were engaging them on a daily basis, and sometimes multiple different places on the same day. Five of us would get in a car, we'd drive to Beaverton, beat up a couple guys at the mall, and then we'd drive to Clackamas and beat up a couple people out there. They thought we were everywhere. They thought there were tons of us. It was just the same five guys! [laughs] Not just guys. There were several women too.[56]

Portland expanded on existing ARA tactics. Like Thomas and Walter from Winnipeg and Edmonton, Tom especially remembers "early forms of doxxing."

> We would go, like, sit on houses and confirm that's where they lived, follow them, and try to find out where they worked, you know.… We would try to get them fired from their jobs and kicked out of their houses.… [We were] flyering neighborhoods.… There was a

guy who worked at the Olive Garden, and we had pictures of him on flyers and an info sheet about him, and his customers were coming in, and we were, like, giving [flyers] to them, and he got fired that day. We got it to the point where it's, like, the cost of doing business is more than just getting beat up or getting in a fight, it's, like, you aren't gonna be able to rent a place or be employed here if you're a white supremacist.

For this intelligence and surveillance work, ARA and SHARP often worked alongside the Coalition for Human Dignity (CHD), initially "a coalition between the city of Portland and a variety of different community organizations" formed in response to Seraw's murder.[57] The CHD evolved from meeting in city council chambers into a street-credible grassroots organization specializing in intelligence research on white supremacists. Thanks to that intel, ARA was able to get even more creative. When some Portland nazis planned a weekend trip to the white supremacist Aryan Nations compound in rural Idaho, for example, Jason remembers, "we'd just grab a bunch of Jolly Ranchers and go from house to house to house putting them in the gas tanks so that they all had car trouble."[58]

But while Portland ARA employed a variety of more creative tactics, street fighting continued—and, in fact, their fight against nazis was particularly violent. There were extensive brawls and multiple stabbings. A small group of boneheads, remembers activist M. Treloar, "attempted to break down the door of the office of the Coalition for Human Dignity with pickaxes." Nazis so frequently threatened activists' and community members' homes—and the police, who some community members initially turned to, were so dismissive—that ARA, SHARP, and the CHD developed a practice of "house defense," packing and guarding a residence to protect it from consistent physical attacks.

The house defenses were a highly successful community self-defense project but also illustrated the escalation of nazi violence. M. Treloar explains:

> So the boneheads fought with fists and knives, and then, eventually, when they became more organized, they were told and they learned, "Oh, if we're going after these people, somebody's got to bring a gun." I would say that they armed up way before we did. It's also inevitable in neo-fascist organizing to go from: "We're going to give a speech

here" to "We're going to come after people with guns." Because
they're not gonna win in a public debate, unless, sooner or later, they
bring out the guns.... They [armed themselves] here in Portland
fairly rapidly, going from a bunch of teenagers with baseball bats
to a bunch of teenagers with AK-47s and .45s.... At that point, [the
CHD] assisted SHARP in getting some weapons for purposes of
defense. From then on, I think, the wiser of them got their own
weapons, and that was also true among some of the ARA people.[59]

From its beginning, Portland ARA and SHARP were closely tied to
the Syndicate's midwestern skinheads through punk networks. At the
first Portland ARA/SHARP meeting, someone, likely a visiting Baldie,
"presented information about the organizing that was happening in
Minneapolis and Chicago." In 1990, Portland hosted the ARA Network's
first national conference,[60] organized and promoted through the
Syndicate, zines like *Turning the Tide*, and other connections. Chapters
and individuals from multiple midwestern cities, from "up and down the
West Coast," and from Canada attended the conference.[61]

The Political Evolution of the Syndicate and ARA

By the 1990 Portland conference, the Syndicate was a loose but established force, mobilizing like-minded anti-racist skinheads specifically,
but also working closely with other youth and some veteran activists like
Chicago members of JBAKC. In addition to carrying out direct action
and controlling youth scenes in member cities, they developed a broader
range of anti-fascist tactics, including doxxing and house defense, and
deepened their political analysis.

The political center of Syndicate anti-racists moved left over time,
led by those skinheads who were leftists from early on. Brandon and
Kieran, both Baldies and Minneapolis ARA members, were also members
of an activist group called the Revolutionary Anarchist Bowling League
and were one tie between Minneapolis ARA and Back Room Anarchist
Books, a store that offered both meeting space and radical ideas and
literature. In Cincinnati, Matt met the Trotskyist Revolutionary Workers'
League and joined in 1989, and Eric and "most of the political skins in
Cincinnati" joined by 1990.[62] (They left after about a year, starting the
new Trotskyist League/US.)[63] Older activists like Michael Novick and
Chicago JBAKC also influenced the Syndicate, as Eric described:

Local ARA members in Minneapolis at a march against US military intervention in Nicaragua in the late 1980s. Courtesy of Brandon Sanford.

It took their knowledge and experience for us to bridge that gap from fighting for two blocks and being kind of street crews to becoming political. It took that political intervention by these older radicals who had done it before, just like it does today. [They] started teaching us about organizing, community outreach, all this stuff that we'd just never had thought about.

Also, it took a while to break us from thinking that the most militant thing was punching somebody. It took us a while to realize, no, the most militant thing is having ten thousand people on the street protesting them.

Finally, anti-racist skinheads affiliated with ARA evolved around oppressive trends that existed within skinhead culture, namely sexism, machismo, and homophobia. Michelle describes some of the sexism she saw in the scene:

I'm not gonna say the skinheads in Chicago were overly sexist. I'm not gonna *not* say they were. [laughs].... In Chicago, I think if you were too much of a feminist, you were called a feminazi. That was a big word. "Oh, you're a feminazi." You're, like, no, I'm not anything like a nazi, I just want equality.... [Some male skinheads would] go an hour and a half out of their way just to make sure I got home safe at night. You know, they're good guys. So I don't want to bash the skinhead guys and say they were a bunch of pigs; they weren't, but they weren't thinking about it. It wasn't something, you know, that anybody really held them to.

Lorraine had a similar experience in Minneapolis. "I felt like the guys really ... made an honest attempt to treat us fairly, to be fair. But ... when we [women] needed to be represented, I sometimes felt like that wasn't [seen as equally] important as when the boys needed to be seen." A *City Pages* profile of the Baldies, for example, failed to mention a single Baldie woman, even though, Lorraine reckons, "There were at least six or seven girls who shaved their heads," and maybe "ten more girls who didn't shave their heads."

Though lacking recognition, the women of the Baldies were outspoken and active in countering the sexism they saw. Michelle remembers that during one Syndicate gathering,

after the meeting, and a party had started happening, [one Chicago skinhead] beat his girlfriend up. And it was some of the women from Minneapolis who actually tried to stop him, you know ... while his friends—I wasn't there, but I'm assuming most of his friends just stood by and watched him beat his girlfriend up. And I'm sure it wasn't the first time. One girl got her, I think, her nose broken, from Minneapolis, trying to stop it... That's how those women were. They were so pro-woman and anti–domestic abuse, anti-rape, and very vocal about it. And they weren't—you know, you call 'em a feminazi. They didn't fucking care what you called them. They were very strong, and they were beautiful women.... I learned a lot from them.

Though Minneapolis wasn't perfect, Michelle believes the Baldies were leaders against oppressive tendencies within the Syndicate. When she moved from Chicago to Minneapolis in 1989, Michelle thought:

They were definitely woke. They were more aware of sexism and homophobia and how those two sort of play off each other.... [I remember] talking about some really horrible stuff we were doing, that was, like, throwing eggs at a gay club in the neighborhood. And we were, like, laughing. You know, I was probably, like, fifteen at the time—and I don't excuse it, you know, 'cause I should have known better. But here we are, telling the skinheads from Minneapolis, like, "Yeah, we did this!" And they were, like, "You did what? What the fuck is wrong with you guys?"

In the time between the Baldies' first fights against nazis in 1986 and its height around 1989–1990, the Syndicate became more politically formal, with more influence and analysis from explicit leftist politics. Nonetheless, the Syndicate was based in a culture that was not fundamentally activist. While political leftists were involved from early on, the Syndicate, particularly certain chapters, had a very strong presence of anti-racist Pro-Ams. Over time, the two sides were seeming less like they could share a movement. As Malki from Chicago explained, people increasingly gravitated toward political "poles"; Eric saw the same thing in Cincinnati, and then in the Syndicate. The Syndicate came to an end quickly, but it's worth noting that there was no acrimonious split.

According to Matt from Cincinnati, this division between pro-American and leftist skins fostered ARA's transition from a movement driven, in practice, by skinheads into the broader activist network it was intended to be. Pro-Ams generally remained in anti-racist but less political skinhead crews, like Cincinnati's SHARP. In Portland, by 1992, the anti-racists in a shared ARA/SHARP milieu "became more SHARP, very much more street-oriented," says Jason, "like, 'We're just going to fight them in the street and keep it there.'"[64] Although Portland anti-racists hosted the first national conference of ARA groups, they weren't closely involved when a new ARA network formalized in the Midwest in 1994.

Those who were farther left continued with ARA. Minneapolis ARA went dormant after their victory over the White Knights, but re-formed in 1991 in response to a new wave of local white-power organizing. They included more conventional activist tactics, like a June 1991 march through St. Paul's Eastside to counter Northern Hammerskins implicated in burning a cross on the lawn of an interracial couple, and organized with a broad coalition of students against a new "White Student Union" at the University of Minnesota later that year.[65] The *New York Times* reported on both the large coalition and a brawl between members of

the White Student Union and anti-racists involving tear gas and resulting in head injuries.[66] The new "University ARA" wrote in a pamphlet:
"We began with a strong analysis of how heterosexually dominated and
controlled the old ARA was. The new group also agreed that physical
confrontation can be used as a tactic against racist presence, but that we
needed to build an understanding of how men use violence to dominate
and control."[67] Minneapolis ARA and the Love and Rage Revolutionary
Anarchist Federation, which would continue to be influential in ARA,
also organized an "Anti-Racist Summer Project in 1992," joining organizers from inside and outside the Twin Cities in a months-long effort
to deepen anti-fascist organizing in both Eastside St. Paul and at the
University of Minnesota.

A cultural war for the soul of punk scenes and skinhead culture
was transforming into a vibrant political movement and a strong youth
culture. Teens and some twenty-somethings, supported by militant New
Left veterans, were coming together across the country and continent
through subcultural scenes, DIY zines, and touring bands. They were
building strong groups capable of fighting organized racists locally and
regionally—and it was just the beginning.

NOTES

1   Meleah Maynard, photos by Kara LaLomia, "The Lost Boys," *City Pages*, January
     31, 1990, accessed April 1, 2022, http://insurgence.proboards.com/thread/210; Bill
     Wyman, "Skinheads," *Chicago Reader*, March 23, 1989, accessed April 1, 2022, https://
     www.chicagoreader.com/chicago/skinheads/Content?oid=873583.
2   That is, the first skinheads of their time. An earlier crew was disbanded.
3   Maynard, "The Lost Boys."
4   Sole, "Solecast 44 w/ Mic Crenshaw on the Anti-Racist Action Network & Radical
     Politics," *Solecast* (podcast), June 15, 2017, accessed April 1, 2022, https://tinyurl.
     com/2psvxs34.
5   Ibid.
6   Matt Snyders, "Skinheads at Forty," *City Pages*, February 20, 2008, accessed April 1,
     2022, http://archive.altweeklies.com/aan/skinheads-at-forty/Story?oid=204827.
7   Kdog, "American Strasser," Three Way Fight, December 9, 2020, accessed April 1,
     2022, http://threewayfight.blogspot.com/2020/12/american-strasser.html;" Clive
     Thompson, "In Your Fascist Face: The Inside Story of the Rise and Fall of an Anti-
     Nazi Youth Movement," *Toronto Star*, November 6, 1994, ProQuest NewsStand; Linnet
     Myers, "War of the Skinheads," *Chicago Tribune*, May 11, 1989, accessed April 1, 2022,
     https://www.chicagotribune.com/news/ct-xpm-1989-05-11-8904110718-story.html;
     "How the Midwest Was Won: The Bloody Rise of Anti-Racist Action," 94.1 KPFA
     (podcast), February 16, 2018, accessed May 13, 2022, https://kpfa.org/area941/
     episode/midwest-won-bloody-rise-ara.

8   "How a Gang of Skinheads Forever Changed the Course," Oprah Winfrey Show, January 2, 2015, accessed April 1, 2022, https://youtu.be/5BRDSvO_eDA.

9   Martin Sprouse and Tim Yohannan, "Interview with Anti Racist Action (Minneapolis)," *Maximum Rocknroll*, November 1989, accessed April 1, 2022, https://libcom.org/article/interview-anti-racist-action-minneapolis-maximumrocknroll-1989.

10 Maynard, "The Lost Boys."

11 Sprouse and Yohannan, "Interview with Anti Racist Action (Minneapolis)."

12 Ibid.

13 Ibid.

14 Rory McGowan, "Claim No Easy Victories: A History and Analysis of Anti-Racist Action and Its Contributions to Building a Radical Anti-Racist Movement," *Northeastern Anarchist* no, 7 (Summer 2003), accessed April 1, 2022, https://theanarchistlibrary.org/library/rory-mcgowan-claim-no-easy-victories.

15 Sole, "Solecast 44 w/ Mic Crenshaw on the Anti-Racist Action Network & Radical Politics."

16 Sprouse and Yohannan, "Interview with Anti Racist Action (Minneapolis)."

17 Ibid.

18 Ibid.

19 Maynard, "The Lost Boys."

20 Snyders, "Skinheads at Forty."

21 Sprouse and Yohannan, "Interview with Anti Racist Action (Minneapolis)."

22 Snyders, "Skinheads at Forty."

23 Sprouse and Yohannan, "Interview with Anti Racist Action (Minneapolis)."

24 Sole, "Solecast 44 w/ Mic Crenshaw on the Anti-Racist Action Network & Radical Politics."

25 Ibid.

26 Peg Loftus, "Demonstrators, Neo-Nazis Face Off," *Cincinnati Enquirer*, October 25, 1987; courtesy of Matt.

27 Malki C. Brown interview.

28 Hilary Moore and James Tracy, *No Fascist USA! The John Brown Anti-Klan Committee and Lessons for Today's Movements* (San Francisco: City Lights Books, 2020), 53.

29 Wyman, "Skinheads;" Winfrey, "How a Gang of Skinheads Forever Changed the Course."

30 Wyman, "Skinheads."

31 Odette Youssef and Colin McNulty, "Romantic Violence," *Motive* (podcast), September 11, 2020, accessed April 1, 2022, 34:37, https://www.wbez.org/stories/2-romantic-violence/718b54f2-fe19-4dd6-96b7-7cc1706d04ad.

32 Mike Thomas, "Medusa's," *Chicago Magazine*, October 30, 2017, accessed April 1, 2022, https://www.chicagomag.com/Chicago-Magazine/November-2017/Medusas.

33 Youssef and McNulty, "Romantic Violence."

34 Ibid.

35 Wyman, "Skinheads."

36 Photo of Sonny, courtesy of Malki C. Brown, June 16, 2020.

37 Myers, "War of the Skinheads."

38 @boxcutterbrigade, "When we decided to do a fundraiser for Vida Sida, a grassroots HIV/AIDS clinic that focused on the Puerto Rican community in Wicker Park, we knew that it would challenge some of our associates."

39   Celina Flores, Erin Yanke, and Mic Crenshaw, "Episode Four: The Minneapolis Baldies and Anti Racist Action," December 4, 2020, *It Did Happen Here* (podcast), accessed April 4, 2022, https://itdidhappenherepodcast.com/episode4/index.html.

40   Wyman, "Skinheads."

41   Ibid.

42   Myers, "War of the Skinheads?"

43   Sprouse and Yohannan, "Interview with Anti Racist Action (Minneapolis)."

44   *Syndicate*, April 1989, 4; courtesy of Malki C. Brown.

45   Kieran, email message to authors, February 17, 2021.

46   Corky, "Syndicate Meeting," *Colorblind*, c. 1989, 9–10; courtesy of Malki C. Brown and Michael Novick.

47   "Anti-Racist Skins in Mid-West, East Coast Set Up 'Syndicate,'" *Turning the Tide* 2, no. 2 (February–March 1989): 1, accessed April 4, 2022, https://antiracist.org/vol-2-2-feb-mar-1989.

48   Kris and Corky, Letter, *Turning the Tide* 2, no. 4 (May–June 1989): 4, accessed April 4, 2022, https://antiracist.org/ttt-vol-2-4-may-june-1989.

49   Deanna Bellandi, "Skinheads, Punks Push Anti-Racism Message to Peers," *Los Angeles Times*, October 8, 1990, ProQuest Newsstand.

50   Tom interview.

51   For those readers interested in an in-depth profile of Portland anti-fascism, we recommend *It Did Happen Here,* a podcast and soon-to-be book from PM Press.

52   Elinor Langer, *A Hundred Little Hitlers: The Death of a Black Man, The Trial of a White Racist, and the Rise of the Neo-Nazi Movement in America* (New York: Metropolitan Books, 2003), 31–36.

53   Celina Flores, Erin Yanke, and Mic Crenshaw, "Episode Two: The Murder of Mulugeta Seraw," *It Did Happen Here* (podcast), November 20, 2020, accessed April 4, 2022, https://itdidhappenherepodcast.com/episode2/index.html.

54   Celina Flores, Erin Yanke, and Mic Crenshaw, "Episode Five: They Thought We Were Everywhere: Portland ARA," *It Did Happen Here* (podcast), December 11, 2020, accessed April 4, 2022, https://itdidhappenherepodcast.com/episode5/index.html.

55   Ibid.

56   Ibid.

57   Celina Flores, Erin Yanke, and Mic Crenshaw, "Episode Three: Building Community Defense," *It Did Happen Here* (podcast), November 27, 2020, accessed April 4, 2022, https://itdidhappenherepodcast.com/episode3/index.html; Celina Flores, Erin Yanke, and Mic Crenshaw, "Episode Seven: A Research Capacity: The Work of the CHD," *It Did Happen Here* (podcast), January 1, 2021, accessed April 4, 2022, https://itdidhappenherepodcast.com/episode7/index.html.

58   Flores, Yanke, and Crenshaw, "A Research Capacity."

59   Celina Flores, Erin Yanke, and Mic Crenshaw, "Episode 6: House Defense," December 18, 2020, in *It Did Happen Here*, podcast, 27:45, https://itdidhappenherepodcast.com/episode6/index.html.

60   The conference was timed to coincide with a lawsuit against three fascist organizers: the SPLC was representing Seraw's family in their case against one of Seraw's murderers, as well as father and son nazis Tom and John Metzger of White Aryan Resistance. As Tom Metzger had formed WAR in an explicit bid to bring a younger generation into the far right, they'd been spending time in Portland to help Eastside White Pride step up their organizing. ARA did make a showing at this trial, and let

the fascists know they were watching, but according to CHD organizer Jonathan Mozzochi, Portland activists had "a very contradictory relationship to the Metzger trial, especially ARA and SHARP, but also people in CHD … because it was not really central to any of our work and what we organized around. You know, that was sort of stage-managed American justice."

61   Tom interview; "Portland Resists Racist Terror!" *Turning the Tide* 3, no. 6 (October–December 1990): 3–4, accessed April 4, 2022, https://antiracist.org/ttt-vol-3-6-oct-dec-1990.

62   Eric Johnson interview.

63   Matt interview.

64   On January 1, 1993, an agreed-upon fight in a parking lot between SHARP and the nazis escalated into a SHARP member shooting and killing a nazi; see Celina Flores, Erin Yanke, and Mic Crenshaw, "Episode 9: The Story of Jon Bair," *It Did Happen Here,* podcast, accessed January 15, 2021, https://itdidhappenherepodcast.com/episode9/index.html.

65   U-A.R.A., "Anti-Racist Action, Pamphlet for Rock Against Racism," *in Anti-Racist Action: A Reader,* accessed April 4, 2022, https://issuu.com/randalljaykay/docs/arareader-rotated.

66   "CAMPUS LIFE: Minnesota; Conflict Escalates over Organization Devoted to Racism," *New York Times,* October 20, 1991, accessed April 4, 2022, https://tinyurl.com/2p9ha6th.

67   U-A.R.A., "Anti-Racist Action"; the pamphlet also explains that, after several successes in 1991 in different contexts, Minneapolis "ARA realized that it would be much more effective to split up into three separate subgroups: University ARA, South Minneapolis ARA, and St. Paul ARA."

ANTI-KLAN ORGANIZING

On April 7, 1990, the US Knights of the Ku Klux Klan marched in Oxford, Ohio, a college town of around twenty thousand. They were trying to capitalize on a local controversy: two high school students had been suspended for wearing Klan robes to school as a Halloween "prank." About forty Klanspeople showed up; about three hundred people counter-demonstrated, heckling and harassing the Klan along their march route.[1] The Klan was "interrupted," Associated Press reported, "when Klansmen began fighting with 'skinheads.'"[2] "And, uh, we crushed the Klan that day," remembers Cincinnati ARA's Matt. "I remember at one point," he says, "the march passed next to a railroad trestle with all the rocks from the railroad bed. And so, it just started raining rocks, and you could literally pick your target…. We crushed 'em." The Klan had planned to rally after the march, but the local sheriff revoked the permit, with the Klan's blessing.[3] While the Klan went home, the anti-racists proceeded to the local police station; four of their number had been arrested but, according to Matt, "We were able to get our people who were arrested unarrested," because they simply "besieged the jail." Mac, an ARA member in Columbus, Ohio, remembers:

> Hundreds and hundreds of people … [were] basically shouting, you know, "Let them go." And I went up, and, I mean, before I could get to the door, they grabbed me. I said, "Look, I'm a lawyer,"[4] and this one sergeant said, "Yeah, right" … and shoved me up against the wall. But I had my lawyer's card, and they let me in, and eventually we negotiated where all of the people arrested got to go without any charges if we just promised to leave town.

The 1990s fight against midwestern Klans is the story of how Anti-Racist Action developed into a formalized, though always decentralized, activist network. Between 1990 and 1994, anti-Klan work introduced activists previously associated with the Syndicate to other anti-racist activists from across the Midwest and beyond, some called ARA, and some who adopted the name later: anarchists, students, punks—even a couple adults. More than a name, or even shared politics, what united these groups was their attitude and tactical focus on militant confrontation and direct action. A MAFNET (Midwest Anti-Fascist Network) conference was held in 1994, renamed the Anti-Racist Action Network (ARANet) in 1995. As ARANet grew to include many hundreds of activists organizing on many fronts, anti-Klan work continued to be one of the network's driving forces.

This chapter will trace this history and explore several key themes. First, it will examine anti-fascism in the public sphere, as opposed to the Syndicate's more subcultural fight for the soul of skinhead culture and punk scenes. It will explore ARA's continued use of militant, even extralegal, tactics, as well as some nitty gritty details of anti-racist mobilization and building and running a network before the internet. Finally, it will consider the political tendencies that fed into ARA, and the network's growth beyond its original multiracial skinhead chapters into a broader, though whiter, population.

So Much Klan, So Little Time

"Klans. Plural." Gerry Bello, a longtime member of Columbus ARA, could remember several off the dome even twenty years later: the Knights of the KKK, the American Knights of the KKK, the Christian American Knights of the KKK, and more. Unlike the original KKK of the Reconstruction South in the 1920s, or even the anti–civil rights backlash of the 1950s and 1960s, the midwestern Klans of the 1990s were not part of an overarching organization but were generally individual groups that even "competed" for members.[5]

These midwestern Klans traveled widely. They invaded small towns and major cities, holding white supremacist rallies and speaking events in an attempt to recruit followers and disseminate white-power ideology. No two events were exactly the same, but their format was predictable. Kieran, of the Baldies and Minneapolis ARA, explains:

The Klan would basically get a permit to rally either at a state capitol or at a city hall front steps. And then they'd be protected by a big legion of police. And then there'd usually be a bunch of people from the community who'd come out against them with a range of politics and ideas: sometimes it would be sort of liberal Christians; sometimes it would be, like, militant black youth; sometimes it would be all of, you know, a combination of different types of people. And then there'd usually be some supporters or some people who were interested and intrigued by the Klan who'd come out too.

While local governments would generally sponsor "unity rallies" held at the other side of town, ARA and other demonstrators went to confront the Klan directly, shouting, chanting, or otherwise drowning out the Klan or throwing things, and even physically confronting the fascists. Kieran describes a popular community/youth militancy:

In several places ... they [anti-Klan rallies] turned into anti-racist riots. In many (most) places, there were scuffles or fights with Klan supporters; frequently there was fighting with the police (pushing through police lines), throwing projectiles, attempting to block arrests or unarrest people, going after the Klan—and their police protection—coming or going from the rally.

Steve, of Lansing ARA, describes:

The idea was just to disrupt them, to not allow them to speak, just no platform for any fascists, not to allow fascists to be in the crowd. You know, push it as far as we could, so the police would have to shut down the rally. That was kind of the idea. I think sometimes there was [street fighting/physical confrontation]. Sometimes it was just, like, it was so overwhelmingly anti-fascist that folks wouldn't show up—and often I don't think there was a lot of people who really wanted to show up!

It's worth understanding what the Klan had in common with nazi skinheads, or "boneheads," and what they did differently. Klans were often more activist-oriented, focused on public politics like holding rallies and demonstrations and speaking to media, while nazi boneheads coalesced around white-power music and crews that offered fraternity and belonging. The Jim Crow Klan had been generally anti-nazi, because nazis were the enemy of the state, but when much of the US white-power movement later declared themselves "at war" with the US government (because it wasn't explicitly racist anymore), different white-power organizers increasingly made common cause, united by anti-state, as well as racist, views. By ARA's time, at the end of the 1980s, some Klans sported paramilitary fatigues alongside their traditional white robes or directly merged with small nazi groups.[6]

KKK membership numbers are notoriously hard to gauge, given the movement's secretive nature, but throughout the 1990s various midwestern Klan groups were highly active. The Southern Poverty Law Center (SPLC) maintains that after a brief surge in the late 1970s Klan memberships overall entered a continuous decline through the 1980s and 1990s.[7] In retrospect, it is worth noting that the national decline in Klan membership reported by the SPLC coincided with ARA's hard work during the 1990s. Unfortunately, the SPLC and other liberal institutions' failure to this day to give credit to direct-action anti-Klan efforts described here is exemplary of the whitewashing of the history of the Klans' decline.

Have Klan, Will Travel

Matt remembers Oxford during "the birth of ARA" as a real network and movement in the Midwest. While anti-racists in different cities were heavily in touch through zines, newsletters, phone calls, and correspondence and may even have shared the name Anti-Racist Action, until they met in person at an anti-racist event, they might not have known each other as much as they knew *of* each other. At Oxford, for example, the Cincinnati crew first met Columbus ARA. It had formed around 1989 to, again, kick nazi skinheads out of their local punk scene and would prove to be one of the ARA Network's strongest chapters throughout the 1990s.

Through a continued boots on the ground succession of anti-Klan events, the informal network that would become ARA grew. By 1992, Matt recalls attending meetings in a small city called Lima, Ohio, because it was accessible to activists in Columbus, Cincinnati, and Detroit. Some Antioch College students were also active against the Klan, like Gerry, who reckons they didn't think of themselves as members of ARA yet but were close with Columbus ARA: "That's who was poking us and going 'Hey, you coming?' 'Yeah, we're coming.'" Around this time, anarchist organizer and Michigan State University student Steve, from Lansing, first got involved.

It is worth noting that all these individuals are white. ARA's base was expanding in many ways to include students, lawyers, autoworkers, and more, but the early highly multiracial skinhead crews were less prominent. As Kieran, of the Baldies and Minneapolis ARA, explained, ARA grew over the decade to include "more women involved, more queer people involved, more people of different generations, and probably, you know, in numbers there were probably more people of color, because it got bigger, but percentagewise it became more white overall." This demographic shift in ARA would prove to be a theme for the rest of ARA's history, especially in its anti-Klan work.

Multiracial skinhead crews declined in prominence in ARA, while other social and political networks became more important. Mac, for example, who was "really the only non-youthful, [non-]punk rocker type" at Columbus ARA's founding meeting, came out of the 1960s New Left student movement and had spent the 1970s organizing against fascists, especially the Klan, with a group called Those United to Fight Fascism (TUFF); Mac explains, I "started to go through my networks from TUFF and go to different cities" to promote ARA. The Trotskyist League/US was a small group and, as Marxists, were in ARA's political minority but played an important role in chapters in Cincinnati, Detroit, and Ann Arbor, where they had members.

Most significantly, the Love and Rage Revolutionary Anarchist Federation was the clearest and most consistent proponent of an anarchist position in ARA, the most prominent political ideology throughout ARA's history. Love and Rage members involved in ARA at the outset included Kieran from Minneapolis,[8] Steve from Lansing, and a longtime anti-fascist, anarchist and autoworker in Detroit named Mike. Love and Rage had begun in 1989 as an anarchist newspaper and developed into a network of groups with a clear set of shared political beliefs and a commitment to working together. Later, Love and Rage established an "Anti-Fascist Working Group"; as Kieran described it, basically a "caucus of anarchists who were in Love and Rage [and] ARA" to discuss and strategize around organizing in the network. The Minneapolis, Detroit, Lansing, Toronto, and later Flint and Harlem ARA chapters all, at one point, included members affiliated with Love and Rage.

Nonetheless, while these organized connections between ARA members were important, ARA is not best thought of as a coming together of different ideologies. Most groups that would become ARA,

Anti-fascists confronting the "Gay Bash 93" rally held by the white supremacist USA Nationalist Party, with crossover members from the KKK and Aryan Nations. The anti-fascist coalition included May Day Skins (New York City), ACT UP (Philadelphia), Grassroots Queers, the University's Lesbian Gay Bisexual Alliance, and ARA. New Hope, Pennsylvania, November 6, 1993. Courtesy of Dan Sabater.

according to Matt, weren't "coming out of" the organized left but "going toward it." Some ideological connections allowed "organizers to go from city to city to city, but it's in the process of those organizers going from city to city to city that ARA [was] built. And [it was also] built out of people who [came] from no tradition at all, right?" What really laid the groundwork to grow Anti-Racist Action into a formal network was their activity on the ground.

Toward the end of 1993, very large counter-demonstrations took place against the Klan in Columbus, Cleveland, and Indianapolis. A great success for anti-racists, the October 16 rally in Indianapolis was reported in the *Indianapolis Star*:

> A few dozen members of the Ku Klux Klan had their say on the steps of the Statehouse on Saturday, but their message of "white power" was drowned out by protests, police sirens and sporadic violence.
>
> A crowd estimated at more than 1,000, including hundreds of anti-Klan demonstrators, hundreds of police and scores of Klan

sympathizers, was drawn to the Downtown area by the 35 Klan participants. Most of the Klansmen were from out of state.[9]

Then, on March 5, 1994, a Klan rally in Painesville, Ohio, took place: another event key to the formation of a formal ARA network. Detroit activist Paul reported, regrettably, "three hundred cops ... prevented anti-fascists from dispersing the handful of actual robed Klansmen themselves." Nonetheless, demonstrators had "prevented the Klan from holding a successful rally." Mainstream media agreed; the Klan in Painesville "had a hard time delivering [their message] amid shouts of rage and indignation from peace protestors," and "their feeble attempt to get their message across had been silenced."[10] For Paul, the crowning proof of ARA's success was "a public admission of defeat by the Grand Dragon of the Unified Knights of the Ku Klux Klan, who called the event a "disgrace," and "the subsequent fragmentation of that no-longer-unified Klan group."

The lesson Paul drew was that "two thousand anti-fascists prevented the Klan from holding a successful rally ... largely because many different anti-fascist and anti-racist organizations mobilized jointly for the action." Paul and others took the huge Painesville success as a call to formalize their preexisting networks, as Paul's letter a month later shows:

> [A]ctivists from several organizations, as well as independent activists, have started working together to form a network of anti-fascists throughout the region, tentatively called the Midwest Anti-Fascist Network (MAFNET). Initiators of MAFNET include anarchists, socialists, and other leftists, antiracist groups, and other progressive organizations and individuals ... from Illinois, Michigan, Ohio, Missouri, Wisconsin, Iowa, and Minnesota.

The conversations continued in Bowling Green, Ohio, on August 27, 1994. Mac and Dana from Columbus ARA, Paul from Ann Arbor and the Trotskyist League/US, and Steve and Mike from Lansing and Detroit ARA and Love and Rage met and discussed plans for the founding conference of MAFNET. Soon after, Columbus ARA snail-mailed an invitation to "friends":

> It is time for us to build our movement in a more stable, serious organized way. We can increase our numbers, involve thousands of people, initiate new and imaginative programs to fight racism—the

possibilities are unlimited. Please plan to be a part of this historic weekend.

And a historic weekend it was: it's in a book now.

Network Conferences and Character

On October 15–16, 1994, a year before it renamed itself ARANet, the Midwest Anti-Fascist Network was born. Two hundred twenty-one participants from eleven US states and Canadian provinces,[11] "as far

ANTI-FASCIST CONFERENCE
MIDWEST ANTI-FASCIST NETWORK (MAFNET) FOUNDING CONFERENCE
COLUMBUS OHIO
OCTOBER SAT.15&SUN.16 1994

NORTH HIGH SCHOOL
- ★ WORKSHOPS
- ★ SPEAKERS
- ★ BOOTHS
- ★ NETWORKING
- ★ MUSIC/PERFORMANCES
- ★ CHILD CARE
- ★ FOOD
- ★ BASKETBALL/SOCCER/VOLLEYBALL

"In recent years the undercurrent of intolerance and social injustice in our society has grown in strength, which is made apparent with the rise of hate crimes and Klan rallies. It's time to begin building a society of tolerance with diversity and respect. Come join us at this conference."

FOR MORE INFORMATION CALL (614)294-5226 OR WRITE TO ANTI-RACIST ACTION (ARA) P.O.B. 02097 COLUMBUS OH 43202

away as Alabama, New York ... and Toronto," gathered for the founding conference at North High School, in Columbus, Ohio.[12] This was the first of a series of annual conferences hosted by ARA, bringing supporters together for a variety of workshops, decision-making plenaries, and parties.

The fifteen workshops at the network conference clearly show how ARA was rising out of countercultural scenes and militant politics. "What to Do When the Klan Comes to Town" and "Confronting the Nazi Music Underground" reflected the network's two main enemies. Do-it-yourself punk rock–style was evident in "Setting up a Pirate Radio Station" and "Defending Yourself." Socialist groups were present in "What Is Fascism? A Marxist Analysis" and "Labor and the Fight against Fascism." Members talked about "Black/Jewish Relations" and "Eco-Justice." Members of the Mayday Crew from New York City presented on the "History of Anti-Racist Skinheads" and the Lesbian Avengers offered a women-only workshop on "History, Tactics, and Fire Eating."

Signe Waller, survivor of the Greensboro massacre of 1979, also presented. Remembers Kristin:

> I found it riveting to hear about the visceral racism of the Klansmen, coupled with their hatred of labor unions and left-wing organizers, the collusion of local police and the FBI in the murders, and the determination of survivors to keep speaking out. That Waller attended the conference to meet with us younger organizers, to share that experience and what she had learned from it, was meaningful. It really felt that we were part of something historic.

Although the network did evolve in the following years and at subsequent conferences, the fundamentals of its culture and political analysis were established by the end of this 1994 conference. Most fundamental were the points of unity, with the wording hammered out in 1995 as follows:

1) **We go where they go.** Whenever fascists are organizing or active in public, we're there. We don't believe in ignoring them or staying away from them. Never let the nazis have the streets!

2) **Don't rely on the cops or the courts to do our work.** This doesn't mean we don't ever go to court. But we must rely on ourselves to protect ourselves and stop the fascists.

3) **Non-sectarian defense of other anti-fascists.** In ARA-NET, we have lots of groups and individuals. We don't agree about everything and we have a right to differ openly. But in this movement an attack on one is an attack on us all. We stand behind each other.

4) **ARA-NET intends to do the hard work necessary to build a broad, strong movement against racism, sexism, anti-Semitism, homophobia, discrimination against the disabled, the oldest, the youngest, and weakest of our people. We intend to win.**[13]

In discussions leading up to the 1994 conference, the points of unity drafting process, according to Matt, "was a pretty natural coming together.... Anti-fascism had a tradition, and its tradition is non-sectarian defense [and] where they go we go." The points of unity incorporated this tradition and put words onto the work that the network's activists were already doing. As Gerry says, "The first three points of unity are, you know: 'How do we do what we do?'" Political groups' points of unity are often largely theoretical, but for ARA they were defining, essentially the only official political position ARA ever had. "It wasn't like the throwaway points of unity that all organizations put together ... and then ignore," says Matt. ARA didn't "want ten points of unity. We [didn't] want twenty, you know. We want[ed] four or five.... We wanted it short and sweet ... where you could just remember it.... We wanted it to be real, right?"

The points of unity also reflected some aspects of how ARA members viewed the world of anti-fascist organizing beyond Anti-Racist Action itself. Most members viewed many larger and more mainstream organizations skeptically. The Anti-Defamation League (ADL) and the Southern Poverty Law Center (SPLC), for instance, clearly ran afoul of the second point of unity. Both the SPLC and the ADL developed working relationships with law enforcement and marketed themselves as "anti-extremist" research centers that tracked both far-right *and* far-left groups. The ADL went even further, collaborating with local police and the FBI to spy on an array of left-wing groups from the late 1980s onward, including Anti-Racist Action.[14] Needless to say, ARA wanted nothing to do with this open collaboration with "the cops [and] the courts."

Partly as a result, ARA groups relied on their own local research and regional networking efforts rather than the well-funded efforts of groups like the ADL, SPLC, or NWCAMH. As Devin Burghart recalls, it was precisely local and regional knowledge and experience that set ARA apart from mainstream groups like these: "In many ways the kind of work that ARA was doing was identifying hotspots and important issues before they became mainstream."[15]

At the same time, ARA tended to view some smaller but still "mainstream" groups like the Coalition for Human Dignity (CHD), in Portland, and later the Center for New Community (CNC), in Chicago, which did not work directly with the police, as fundamentally different from the ADL or SPLC. While largely rejecting their grant-funded nonprofit structure, many ARA members respected the work they did and in some cases worked successfully alongside them in the context of specific campaigns, reflecting a practical aspect of the third point of unity.

Agreeing to the points of unity was the only formal and explicit "requirement" to join the Anti-Racist Action Network. Otherwise, ARA was always very decentralized and horizontal. Few decisions were ever made on a network-wide level; those that were were sometimes made by majority vote for simple things, while in some cases participants agreed that a two-thirds majority was required (e.g., for a proposal to change the points of unity in 1997 or to expel a chapter in 1999).[16] This decentralized structure was a defining and crucial feature of the network, because it allowed individual chapters to respond to local conditions with a certain amount of experimentation and local initiative and prevented anyone from being "in charge of" activists in another area.

At and around the time of the 1994 conference, ARA did go through some growing pains. Anarchists, Marxists, and others had closely cooperated to organize the conference, but some "unprincipled" Marxist formations also participated.[17] Gerry viewed the establishment of the network's horizontal structure as a victory for anarchists—a slim majority or maybe just "the biggest minority" in the room—over would-be entryists—people trying to take over or gain a few more recruits, even at the cost of breaking up the larger group. As Gerry describes it, "We created the organization as a network so that there were no committees to stack with your people, right? You know, there were no order-giving bodies to take over; there was no guiding political line outside of how we do our anti-fascist work." Importantly, though, the ideas and debates around this decentralized structure were not a simple split between anarchists and Marxists. Matt, from the Trotskyist League/US, agreed that a decentralized structure was "the only way we [were] going to get these groups of people in the same room and organizing together." Cincinnati ARA alone, he says, "had anarchists, Trotskyists, pro-Ams.... If we were going to bring that Cincinnati crew into the national network, well, it would have to have the same kind of framework ... [that] allowed for all of that."

ARA never had a strong institutional framework or a united political ideology. Instead of formal leadership or institutions, chapters in different cities were bound together by a militant outlook and attitude, by horizontal networking and communication, and by annual conferences held in October. Delegate meetings, with just a few representatives from each chapter inclined to send them, also happened each spring, to discuss strategy and proposals, but big decisions were left to the full network conferences.

The 1994 conference established an internal network bulletin, a key example of the horizontal communication that proved fundamental to ARA, "simply ... a letter board containing correspondence between members of the Midwest Anti-Fascist Network [and then the Anti-Racist Action Network] ... a forum of news, ideas, conversations, criticisms, and arguments," according to the first internal bulletin.[18]

In the network's informal and horizontal structure, chapters being willing and able to put in the work of communication and coordination was key. Although Toronto, Minneapolis, and Chicago were "hub" chapters, Columbus ARA was a sort of "default network office" until about 1999. Set apart by their logistics and resources, Columbus had a dedicated office space, a constantly growing mailing list, the network's most widespread newsletter, *ARA News*, funded primarily by radical lawyers like Mac.

But the office "wasn't really an office," according to Mac. "I had an apartment, and my wife and I split up ... so we had four big rooms that were not being used, and we just started doing that stuff out of my apartment." Columbus grew their mailing list "every time we went to do a show ... every time we went out to a protest, some of our organizers would be out on the edge signing people up." The Columbus newsletter, *ARA News*, soon became a key outreach tool for the ARA Network, growing to seventy-five thousand printed copies and a mailing list of twenty-one thousand in 1998,[19] with thirty-one thousand mailed out in 1999.[20] The cost was substantial, estimated by Mac at "$15,000, all inclusive ... about every 4–5 months" in 1997.[21] (We review more of ARA's written materials in chapter 7.)

All in all, the organizers who formed the network in 1994 had a strong desire to build toward "proactive," not reactive, organizing against fascists. As Columbus ARA wrote in a conference report published by the *Columbus Free Press*, "We hope to do a lot more than just stop things from getting worse. We want to make things better, starting now."[22] Likewise, "while militant mobilizations to stop KKK/nazi rallies are necessary," the Trotskyist League/US also wanted to avoid "responding piecemeal," wanting, instead, to plan "an organized offensive against the growing number of fascist rallies, bars, bands, elections campaigns and other activities."[23]

"They Couldn't Keep Us Off Them": ARA on the Grind

According to Columbus's Gerry, ARA's "pace of operations for the 1990s was extreme." ARA members had protested a Klan rally in Indiana just two weeks before the MAFNET conference, and they were back protesting two Klan rallies in Michigan a week after. The Klans they protested were often familiar faces, or familiar hoods. In December 1990, a Klan group erected a holiday cross in a downtown Cincinnati plaza to protest a local Jewish group's menorah in the same plaza, a tradition the Klan maintained, and ARA members maintained their counter-protests. The Klan erected their cross "at 3:00 a.m. under cover of darkness and protected by a small army of police" and were nowhere to be seen when about 150 network supporters gathered later that day to drape a banner reading "This is a Klan Free Zone" over the cross. Before long, the police moved in suddenly, and "as a result ... the peaceful debate broke down, people scattered in all directions, and some people responded by knocking down the cross." (A dramatic photograph of the moment soon appeared in both the *New York Times* and in *USA Today*.) Six anti-racists were arrested, including Matt.

The pace only picked up. In early 1994, one Ohio Klan announced its intention to hold at least eighty-eight rallies, one for every county in the state, over a couple of years. *ARA News* reported, "It seemed like we were gearing up for another protest every other weekend," until Klan leader Vince Pinette was arrested for domestic abuse on July 9, 1994.[24] In January 1995, the Arkansas-based Knights of the Ku Klux Klan organized simultaneous protests of Martin Luther King, Jr. Day in several cities.

DEFEND THE

CINCINNATI SIX!

On December 17, 1994 the Ku Klux Klan put up the annual cross on Fountain Square in Cincinnati, Ohio. The Midwest Anti-Fascist Network (MAFNET) went door to door throughout Cincinnati and passed out 25,000 newsletters promoting racial unity. MAFNET also organized a counter-demonstration against the Klan. About 200 people came to show the city they were fed up with the free reign the Klan are given during the holiday season. 30 of Cincinnati's finest showed up in riot gear. When the cops decided that the protesters had enough free speech for the day they attacked the crowd. In the melee, some protesters took the opportunity to tear down the Klan's symbol of racist terror. The cops maced, beat, and cuffed six protesters. Three of the six were charged with resisting arrest and rioting. The three others were charged with felony assault of police officers, and face <u>years</u> in prison! These charges are false! Video taken by MAFNET supporters show brutal police actions. Some of these same cops have been recently suspended in another brutality case. Those that were arrested need our support. They deserve a pat on the back for standing up to hate-mongers, not jail time!

•**Drop all charges against these anti-fascist fighters!**

•**Show zero tolerance for racism!**

•**Join the Struggle! Join MAFNET!**

For more info write to: **Anti-Racist Action** pob. 02097• Columbus, Ohio 43202

A flyer in support of anti-Klan protesters arrested at a 1994 Cincinnati demo. As Matt recalls, "Lots of punk rock benefits, etc. [were held] to raise funds.... We all ended up having different charges and trials, and lawyers, some together, some separate. I ended up also with a civil suit brought against me by the Klan.... Mac and Kathy Adams were my main lawyers.... We ended up winning a couple of those cases on appeal, and even sued the cops for wrongful arrest and won some money, which was put toward the office in Columbus." Courtesy of Matt.

KLAN KROSS KOVERED

CINCINNATI
12/17/94

**THIS IS WHAT IT LOOKS
LIKE WHEN YOU GET
TRAMPLED BY HORSES...**

ARA News (February 1995)

In June, they rallied twice in a day in Circleville and London, Ohio. In 1996, the Klan had fifteen rallies over thirteen weeks.[25]

Klan rallies happened so often that, according to Gerry, "If the weather's good, you know what you're doing on Saturday; you just don't know where." Coauthor Lady reckons that she has "personally been to very few Klan rallies" compared to other ARA members, but, nevertheless, she remembers the intensity:

> Quitting my job the day before a rally was scheduled, and not scheduling the next job to start for a week gap in case I got pinched or hurt, calling off of work to attend rallies, keeping a change of clothes and toiletries in the trunk of multiple friends' vehicles, so I didn't have to pack, and could get to my job without smelling like pepper spray or wearing black [battle dress uniforms], steel toe boots, and a black hoodie to work, picking up more people in cities along the way to fill the car, and reading all of that state's/city's firearms and weapons laws before traveling to it.

As was the case among some early Syndicate skinheads, it was not uncommon for ARA members to arm themselves in self-defense against fascists who were a proven violent threat. At the time, though, only the police would ever open carry—not the Klan, not ARA. Thus, while some ARA members would bring firearms, ARA generally did not explicitly posture that they were armed or advertise it as a political position in the way we might see today, particularly in the United States.

By consistently going to the small towns and county seats where Klans held their events, ARA was growing. Some chapters were very much oriented toward or built around a college; some were heavily high schoolers. Says Gerry of one small town:

> Goshen, Indiana ... that was eight punk rock kids that all lived in the same trailer park.... That was also a thing that made ARA different from other left-wing groups; we were going to small-town America. That's where we worked, right? That was the reality of where the struggle goes, so.... We're [growing] there because there's something wrong going on there, and they want to do something about it. You know, they meet us and they want in. Small-town America is not, absolutely not, full of fucking bigots.

A list of upcoming ARA events. Note that five of six weekends in a row have Klan rallies, in four different states: Kentucky, Ohio, Indiana, and Oklahoma. *ARA News* (April 1996)

Highly mobile anti-Klan organizing brought ARA to diverse locations across the US, especially in the Midwest, and this meant ARA grew. This large number of chapters, in turn, strengthened ARA's continued fight against the Klan. According to Gerry:

> What enabled us to do this was having fourteen, fifteen chapters just in Ohio, another six in Indiana. Okay, we can get a car out of each one, or two cars out of each one. You know, put that together and make it work...
>
> It took us until 1996, 1997, to really build to be able to do that reliably, every, every, every single time, to outnumber them in that fashion. But to give you an idea of the operational mindset and the operational tempo and the strategic philosophy, like, we ground them down, and that's how.

ARA's "grinding" consistency and dedication is what set it apart and is how ARA had an effect on the Klan. According to Gerry, the Klan "want to get people riled up to join them and feel empowered. So our job at a Klan rally is to make it as not empowering as possible." When the Klan "reach failure after failure after failure after failure"—that is, when the Klan is consistently outnumbered, shouted down, and generally despised in every town they go to, "they have to go into a group self-examination about that in some way or another, and that's never good for group cohesion.... It's demoralizing to them, and eventually it breaks them," says Gerry.

As a result, Klan rallies steadily evolved, and ARA's tactics actually co-evolved with those of the police. Gerry explains:

> First it began with, they couldn't keep us off them.... There was a time when you didn't have pens.
>
> Then they moved it to, you had one designated demonstration area you had to get searched to go in, right? Fenced off, so you're surrounded by riot cops inside a metal box. You're not getting in there with anything. Like, nothing that you can start a fire with. They're taking your cigarettes. They're taking your lighter.... Early on with the one-pen situation ... a couple of Klan guys would come in there, typically big biker types, and jump some shit off. And these guys could take a punch, right?...
>
> Eventually they moved it to a two-pen situation, you know, go through a metal detector and declare one side or the other.... And then what they would do is they would coddle the pro-Klan demonstrators in every possible way and fuck with us in every possible way.
>
> So sometimes the plan, when we had sufficient strength and sufficient numbers, was [to] not go in the pen and block the entrance to their pen. You know ... "What's up, master race?" ... And that sort of evolved into different variations of essentially zone defense: we're gonna try and pick off stragglers; we're gonna try and catch up with their bus, along with handing out literature, getting people on the mailing list, talking—you know, general political organizing stuff.

The Cops, the Klan, and Whiteness

ARA organizers often perceived police bias in favor of the Klan, in keeping with the left's long held view that "cops and Klan go hand in hand." Before the 1979 Greensboro massacre, a United Racist Front informant warned the police of plans for violence, but the police did not intervene; more recently, a review of US protests in 2020 found police were 3.5

times more likely to use force against peaceful left-wing demonstrations than against peaceful right-wing demonstrations.[26] In the 1990s, ARA organizers saw the same trend.

Steve, from Lansing ARA, remembers an April 1994 Klan event in his town where hundreds of police mobilized to defend the Klan and were quick to disperse anti-racists with batons and gas. For Steve, that event "kind of taught us how the state goes to such a length to protect the fascists.... [Compare] the lengths the state would go to to actively destroy the Black Liberation Movement, and then the lengths they went to to protect the Klan at any cost." Gerry's partner at the time of the Lansing event was a journalist, and she walked in while the cops were briefing.

> Okay, so the cops—and they've got a gillion fucking cops for this shit—are all sitting in a circle ... before we even get there, talking about their feelings because, sensitive new age cop time. And this one guy goes ... "Hi, I'm Bob, and it's my birthday." [Others respond,] "Hi Bob, happy birthday!" "And for my birthday I just want to beat some commie ass." "We support you Bob!"...
>
> No, I don't have the recording of that, it was a long time ago, but, like, that shit happened. They're talking about what warm fuzzies my blood will give them, you know, and the context is we're counter-protesting—these people are protesting for racism, and nobody's talking about kicking their asses. We're saying this is bad, and everybody wants our blood real fucking bad.

Police bias in favor of fascists and against anti-racists increased the risks of coming out against the Klan, particularly for people of color. Furthermore, Klan rallies often took place in small towns and rural county seats, in areas that were often heavily white. These were important factors in the increasing whiteness of ARA, compared to the multiracial skinhead crews of its founding. Chicago ARA member Sheila remembers, "I often found myself wondering: What the hell am I doing in this or that burg—chasing [the] KKK? Knowing that my grandparents had warned me away from even leaving the highway, as they had escaped small-town racism in southern Illinois before my mother was born."

A Minneapolis ARA member named Rocky shared some similar sentiments: "I did feel a certain sense of, like, they might actually kill me. Not only am I Black, I'm, like, flamboyantly gay, with bleached blond hair. So I can pretty easily get beat the fuck up ... [just for] being in their face." Rocky continues: "But no matter what trepidation I had in my head, I didn't let it affect what I wanted to do.... I felt like I was standing up for something. I definitely know [having Minneapolis ARA] and all those people around me—I felt safe."[27]

Rocky was one of the only people of color in Minneapolis ARA in 1994–1996. Similarly, Sheila recalls often being the *only* person of color at some of ARA's more obscure small-town anti-Klan rallies.

For some, it made sense for ARA's anti-Klan work to be heavily white. Chicago ARA member Tito, who is Chicano, echoed Sheila and Rocky's sentiments of sticking out at anti-Klan rallies and connected that precise argument to why he believes ARA *should* be heavily white:

> What the fuck business do I—I'm sorry, I'm getting a little worked up—but what the fuck business do I have in fuckin' Pontiac, Illinois? I didn't even know that place existed, dude.... The reason I don't know it exists, in my state, is because I don't go there. It's not my community. Driving miles and miles away to fucking Peoria, Illinois, do you think that [fellow Chicago Chicano member] Manny and I had any fucking business there?
>
> Everyone has a right to demonstrate against fascism. I don't think it's right that people of color are out there breaking their fuckin' necks because these white [non-fascist] motherfuckers let these [fascist] motherfuckers run loose...
>
> And that was my argument, and that's my belief now.... [People of color] don't *have* to be there. They're not obligated to be there because they're people of color and ARA hates racists. Nah, ARA *should* be predominantly white; ARA should be going to these small communities and handling this.

One white member of Cincinnati ARA believed that "we were in competition with the Klanspeople, on the buses and in our schoolyards." Going back to ARA's early days, for example, those skinheads and punks who were white were often the precise target demographic of the fascists; per this line of thinking, every white person fighting the Klan was a white person not in the Klan and, according to that Cincinnati ARA member, "the idea of recruiting white people is exactly what we wanted to do."

Another white ARA member, Rath Skallion, joined the Columbus chapter in 1996 and regularly worked in the ARA office, responding to calls and email from people who had heard about ARA, mainly through *ARA News*. "We were doing the exact same thing that the fascists were, recruiting young [white] people," she says. "So it was gonna be a question of: Who was going to get to them first? I was amazed at some of the smaller places—that I had never heard of before—and they're reaching out to ARA. So I think it was really impactful, the level of recruitment that we tried to do." At the same time, many ARA members, including Rath, viewed this heavily white makeup as a weakness for an anti-racist movement. We will consider this further in chapter 5.

The Klan in Decline

By 1997, ARA was giving the Klan, in Gerry's words, "failure after failure after failure after failure." An April event in Pittsburgh, for example, was a "total shut out, slam dunk, didn't hear from that Klan group again, embarrassment." Although the Klan had been delayed in nearby Monroeville, "where they caused a disturbance at a local Burger King," their group of about fifty did eventually show up in Pittsburgh, joined by Pennsylvania's American Nazi Party. But "their message never made it across the street," "drowned out" by chants from upwards of ten thousand counter-demonstrators.[28] An example of an ideal anti-Klan rally, the counter-demonstration was attended by ARA chapters from outside Pittsburgh (there was no Pittsburgh chapter at the time), alongside locals from the "Grant Street Anti-Klan Coalition" and the "Campus Coalition for Peace and Justice," as well as other leftists, including a local communist party. There were no fights or arrests,[29] and the event was a success, according to Gerry, because the anti-Klan protesters had "such great numbers that we [didn't] even have to fight.... Such great numbers that the only picture you can see of your rally is [of the] counter-rally from the helicopter."

After Pittsburgh, ARA "didn't hear from that Klan again,"[30] but the anti-Klan struggle continued. On December 6, 1997, the Klan rallied in Beloit, Wisconsin. In 1998, there was Cicero, Illinois, which helped kick off a high period of Chicago ARA, and a string of Michigan events, including at Ann Arbor (discussed in more detail in chapter 8). In Hamilton, Ohio, Gerry remembers police mistaking a local family buying groceries for anti-Klan demonstrators and beating them. The mayor of Warren, Ohio, called the Columbus ARA office to warn them not to come to his town when the Klan did. One of the final Klan events of this wave was

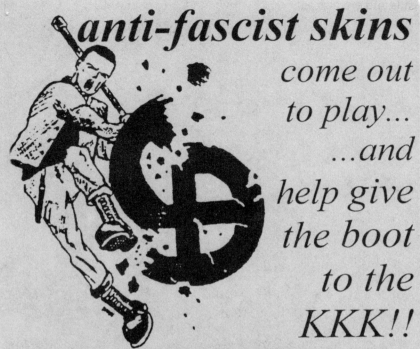

anti-fascist skins

come out to play...

...and help give the boot to the

KKK!!

on march 14th at 1pm at the town hall (50th St. & 25th St.) in Cicero, Il, the Klan will be having a rally, lets help kick these racist scum off our streets. for more information contact **Anti-Racist Action**: 773/252-6019

if going to protest the klan, 3 tips: 1) unfortunatly, most people dont understand skins, punks, and others like us, and can think were the nazis and racists, so,clearly identify yourself as an anti-racist, this will help others to not confuse you with the racist trash, 2) go with a crew for protection, safety, and strength, 3) be prepared to fight the klan and those protecting these bastards, the pigs, but be smart, the cops and klan are brutal forces and can/will use any excuse to do you in, so work with the other anti-racists around us, in unity there is power.

Showing up to oppose a Klan rally in a majority-Latine Chicago suburb of Cicero, in 1998, was a key element in the revitalization of Chicago ARA over the next several years. This flyer indicates the local group's continuing outreach to anti-fascist skinheads, years after the decline of the Syndicate.

In December 2000, Chicago ARA joined thousands of local anti-fascists in opposing a Klan rally in the historically Jewish suburb of Skokie, Illinois, where neo-nazis had infamously attempted to march in the late 1970s. Many snowballs were thrown at the Klan, some of which might have had stones or batteries inside them. Photo from Chicago's *ARA Research Bulletin* (May 2001)

in 2000 and was not a rally; a theater in Louisville, Kentucky, was showing a controversial play, *Corpus Christi*, exploring the life of a gay Jesus. The Klan had shut the play down during its first weekend, so a few ARA chapters traveled to support Louisville ARA in protecting the theater against the Klan.

ARA had consistently opposed the Klan throughout the 1990s, while Klan membership continued to decline. As late as 1999, Columbus ARA "literally had a Saturday Klan and a Sunday Klan," but the truth is the Klan was so hounded by ARA that their attempts to organize were hamstrung. According to Matt:

> You could just see that we were winning.... We limited what the Klan could do. They had marches, and we fucked up their marches.

Skokie, Illinois, December 2000. Original
art by Josh MacPhee.

And then they had to be stationary, and then they had to be in
the pen, and the police and Klan were constantly reacting to what
ARA was doing.... We could see in real time that we were having
an effect attracting the attention of the motherfuckers. We fought
the Klan to a standstill; I wouldn't say we beat them, but we made
it very, very difficult for them to do their work, and we changed
the parameters of how they could even organize.

The Klans were being beaten by ARA, ground down through endless
opposition, and fractured by internal conflicts and power struggles. Anti-
Racist Action had grown through this opposition. In terms of mobilization
and sheer frequency of activity, ARA was probably at its height during their
1990s campaigns against the Klans, with anti-Klan organizing helping ARA
to grow as a network that could take on a variety of progressive causes.

While anti-Klan organizing was growing ARA in the Midwest, ARA
also was growing in Canada, resisting boneheads on the streets and
Holocaust-denying propagandists in the newssheets.

NOTES

1   John Dougherty, "Hate vs. Hate in Oxford," *Dayton Daily News*, April 8, 1990.

2   "Klansmen, Skinheads Fight at Oxford Rally," *Palladium-Item* (Richmond, IN), April 8, 1990; courtesy of Matt.

3   Dougherty, "Hate vs. Hate in Oxford."

4   A significant part of Mac's lawyering was suing police over misconduct.

5   Beverly Peterson, dir., *Invisible Revolution: A Youth Subculture of Hate* (New York: Filmakers Library, 2001), accessed April 4, 2022, https://vimeo.com/131350523.

6   Kathleen Belew, *Bring the War Home* (Cambridge, MA: Harvard University Press, 2018); Michael Novick, *White Lies, White Power* (Monroe, ME: Common Courage Press, 1995), 51.

7   Klanwatch Project of the Southern Poverty Law Center, *Ku Klux Klan: A History of Racism and Violence*, 6th ed. (Montgomery, AL: SPLC, 2011).

8   When Kieran was charged with assaulting a nazi bonehead, Daniel Simmer, while working security at an anti-racist event in 1993, Love and Rage publicized his case and the efforts of the Anti-Fascist Defense Committee that campaigned for Kieran. He was acquitted in 1996.

9   Andrea Neal and Mark J. Rochester, "Klan's Message of Hate Drowned Out by Violence," *Indianapolis Star,* October 17, 1993, newspapers.com.

10 Armetta Landrum, "Klan's Rally in Painesville Unsuccessful: Performance Unlikely in Cleveland," *Call & Post* (Cleveland, OH), March 10, 1994, ProQuest Newsstand.

11 M.C. Reddy, "Anti-Fascists Meet in Ohio," Spunk (online anarchist library), accessed April 4, 2022, http://spunk.org/library/pubs/lr/sp001715/afaohio.html.

12 "New Anti-Racist Network Formed," *ARA News* (Columbus, OH), November 25, 1994.

13 *ARA Network Bulletin* #3, October 1996. Emphasis in the original, although exact wording and presentation varied. The ARA Network formally amended the fourth point in 1998, to add explicit support for reproductive freedom (see chapter 5). The phrase "weakest of our people" was dropped in most published versions around the same time, with no formal decision.

14 Abdeen Jabara, "The Anti-Defamation League: Civil Rights and Wrongs," *Covert Action Quarterly* no. 45 (Summer 1993): 28–37; In 1999, lawyer Lawrence Hildes discovered that the Seattle office of the Pacific Northwest ADL had shared information about ARA and other anti-fascist organizing against the Aryan Nations in Idaho with the Northwest Coalition Against Malicious Harassment (NWCAMH), which went on to share it with police. The NWCAMH had first contacted Hildes's client, an ARA woman, in "support" after her home was firebombed, presumably by Aryan Nations supporters; Tom Burghardt, "Who Watches the 'Watchdogs'? Files from the 'Public-Private Partnership in Political Repression,'" reproduced in *Anti-Racist Action Bulletin* (October 2001): 14–15.

15 Devin Burghart interview.

16 *Anti-Racist Action Bulletin* no. 9 (c. February 1998); *Anti-Racist Action Network Bulletin* 2, no. 3 (May 1999): 17.

17 Gerry interview.

18 Columbus ARA produced three bulletins (December 1994, March and December 1995). Minneapolis ARA published eleven (1996–1998); Chicago ARA published four (January, March, May, and August–September 1999); Maryland ARA published two (May–July and June–August 2000); and Toronto ARA published two (January and October 2001). After this, most political discussion between conferences was

held over email. The name of the publication varied: *The Midwest Anti-Fascist: The MAFNET Internal Bulletin, Anti-Racist Action Network Bulletin, anti-racist action bulliten* [*sic*], *ARA Internal Network Bulletin, ARA Bulletin*. We strive for accuracy when we cite the bulletin, therefore our citations will appear inconsistent.

19   *Anti-Racist Action Bulletin* no. 11 (c. Summer 1998): 67.

20   *Anti-Racist Action Network Bulletin* 2, no. 2 (March 1999): 16. In December 1999, *ARA News* was renamed *Anti-Racist News* and billed itself as a publication of the Columbus Institute for Contemporary Journalism (not Columbus ARA).

21   *Anti-Racist Action Bulletin* no. 9 (c. Fall 1997): 8.

22   Cited in "New Anti-Racist Network Formed," *ARA News* (Columbus OH), November 25, 1994.

23   *Workers' Struggle Supplement* no. 1 (1996).

24   KKK retreats in the Midwest," *ARA News* (Columbus, OH), September 9, 1994.

25   "Konehead Klowns Konfronted," *ARA News* (Columbus, OH), August 8, 1996.

26   Lois Beckett, "US Police Three Times as Likely to Use Force against Leftwing Protesters, Data Finds," *Guardian*, January 14, 2021.

27   Anna Stitt, prod., "Minneculture In-Depth: 'Fighting Back: The Rise of Anti-Racist Action In Minneapolis,'" KFAI Minneapolis, accessed April 4, 2022, https://www.kfai.org/minneculture-in-depth-fighting-back-the-rise-of-anti-racist-action-in-minneapolis.

28   Deepak Karamcheti, "The Day the KKK Came to Town: Klan Rally Unites Races," *New Pittsburgh Courier*, April 9, 1997; Gerry interview.

29   Karamcheti, "The Day the KKK Came to Town."

30   Gerry interview.

CHAPTER 4

THE CANADIAN CONNECTION

It was the night of June 11, 1993. Wolfgang Droege, leader of Canada's most successful fascist organization in decades, was on the pavement, blood on his face, under arrest. Earlier that evening, anti-racist protesters had caught his organization off-guard with an audacious public protest, trashing the home of a fascist spokesperson. Bent on revenge, Droege led fifty followers to find the anti-racists at their favored bars, but things went from bad to worse for him. Droege's organization, the Heritage Front, had been on an upward trajectory until that day, but it was all downhill from there.

In this chapter, we turn our attention north of the US-Canada border. Canadian anti-racist skinheads were connected to ARA from the early days of the Syndicate and joined with other youth to fight bonehead crews out of their youth scenes in the early 1990s. The strongest organizational ties between Canadian and American anti-fascists of the 1990s were forged in 1994, when representatives of Toronto ARA traveled to Columbus for the founding conference of the Midwest Anti-Fascist Network. Toronto ARA's victory over the Heritage Front, a story we will tell in this chapter, laid the groundwork for anti-racists in sixteen Canadian cities and towns to affiliate with the ARA Network, making the network truly international.

In Canada, it's a criminal offense to advocate for genocide, to publicly incite hatred, or to willfully promote hatred against an identifiable group. In the period covered by this book, it was also specifically prohibited to use telephones or the internet to promote hatred. (That section of the Canadian Human Rights Act was repealed in 2013.) These laws constrain fascist organizing in Canada, even though such charges are rarely laid and penalties are light, but, as in the US, ARA organizers in Canada did not generally advocate for state action against fascists. Like in the US, militancy was one crucial characteristic that set ARA chapters apart from other anti-racist efforts in Canada, along with open public organizing and a commitment to fostering a dynamic, authentic anti-racist youth culture. These aspects of ARA's organizing were key factors in turf wars against white-power boneheads, the collapse of the Heritage Front, and several successful campaigns against the far right thereafter; it was many years before the Canadian far right recovered from these defeats.

Threat Assessment

In 1990, the Canadian state besieged Kanehsatà:ke, an Indigenous community near Montréal, Québec. People of the Kanien'kehá:ka (Mohawk) Nation had stood up against developers in the neighboring town of Oka, Québec, who aimed to expand a golf course over a traditional burial ground. Images of armed Indigenous warriors filled television screens across the country, giving notice that after five hundred years of colonial rule, Indigenous people were still fighting for their land.

Soon thereafter, the New Democratic Party took office for the first time in Ontario, Canada's largest province. The NDP is one of two Canadian parties (along with the Greens) that are to the left of the Democratic Party in the United States on many social and economic issues and that win seats in government. During its term, the NDP challenged racism both in the job market, through the adoption of the Employment Equity Act, and in policing, through a wide-ranging Commission on Systemic Racism in the Ontario Criminal Justice System; that Commission was established after a Black Action Defense Committee march, called in the wake of the LA Uprising, erupted into rioting. The whole capitalist class, media, and police were determined to thwart these progressive steps.[1]

Joining in the right-wing backlash was the Heritage Front, a fascist outfit that had got its start in 1989, when seventeen far-right activists traveled together to Libya to attend the twentieth anniversary celebration of the Libyan Revolution. (Colonel Muammar Gaddafi, leader of the country, frequently invited European and North American radicals of all political stripes in order to promote his ideology among them.)[2] Among the Canadian far-right delegation was Wolfgang Droege, a past KKK organizer whose claim to fame was his role in the bizarre scheme to launch a coup on the Caribbean island nation of Dominica in 1981. Hired by a wannabe mercenary named Mike Perdue, he had joined the scheme and served as Perdue's lieutenant, envisioning an island paradise for cocaine smuggling and white supremacy. Instead, Droege got caught by US federal agents and served prison time, first for the Dominica scheme and later for cocaine trafficking, before making his way back to Canada.[3]

During the Libya trip, Droege laid the groundwork for the Heritage Front, meant to be a united front of Klan members and nazis. Little did he know that Grant Bristow, who was also part of the far-right delegation, and who soon became one of Droege's trusted colleagues, was already spying for the Canadian Security Intelligence Service (CSIS, Canada's civilian spy agency).[4]

By 1991, the Heritage Front was hosting rallies and events and publishing a newsletter, posters, and leaflets. One of their main organizing tools in these pre-internet times was a telephone hotline, which they publicized as widely as they could. Interested people could call to hear a racist or otherwise offensive outgoing message, as well as to leave their own message and receive a call back quickly if they wanted to get involved.

In private, the Heritage Front flew nazi and Confederate flags and celebrated racist terrorism. One prominent member was George Burdi, the leader of the Canadian chapter of the Church of the Creator (COTC),[5] which was explicitly white supremacist. He founded Resistance Records in 1993, a music label that distributed white-power bands from its base in Detroit. These included Burdi's own hardcore band called RaHoWa, short for "Racial Holy War," a COTC slogan.

For the outside world, the Heritage Front's slogan was "equal rights for whites," and they claimed to be advocating for white people just like other ethnic or racial groups advocate for themselves (an orientation known as "white nationalism" today). "Their strategic ends were to push the needle on any of their issues that they could, to exercise power, to have that influence, and, in their dreams, to elect some leaders—a party, a city, a mayor. They would have taken anything they could get," says Bill Dunphy, a reporter who covered the far right extensively during this period. He noted that this was happening during the rule of the Ontario New Democratic Party, which was denounced as "socialist" by the right wing. Dunphy adds:

> That's not a coincidence. That's when they can feel aggrieved, when
> they can feel victimized, when they can feel they are not being

heard. That's the extra big fat audience, their whole hope and their goal. Their strategy is to use the media to get to those people in those times. That's how you build power. And in other countries that's been successful.

We interviewed Dunphy in 2018, just a year after Donald Trump was sworn in as president of the United States, elected with the strong support of the racist right that had successfully organized during Barack Obama's eight-year presidency. We are commonly told that the far right grows in reaction to economic hardship, but the growth in the Heritage Front during the NDP's term in Ontario and, more critically, the surge of Trump's MAGA movement under Obama in the US suggest that the far right grows just as much in reaction to gains—or perceived gains—by people of color, Indigenous people, women, queer communities, poor people, trade unions, and so on. It's a powerful lesson.[6]

Expose and Oppose

One of the first anti-racist organizers to take action against the Heritage Front, and the person who inspired the formation of ARA in Toronto, was Rodney Bobiwash. A young Anishinaabe man from Mississauga First Nation, in northern Ontario, he was the race relations coordinator at the Native Canadian Centre of Toronto (NCCT) when he became alarmed by the emergence of the Heritage Front. In 1992, he filed a complaint against the Heritage Front's telephone hotline with the Canadian Human Rights Commission. Racists began to threaten him; he sought protection from police and support from allies both inside and outside the Indigenous community.[7]

Among those answering the call were anarchists and socialists, "a big collection of disparate people, but almost all from political backgrounds," remembers Harry, an early Toronto ARA member. Raised in an anti-fascist household in London, UK, Harry moved to Canada as a youth; he hooked up with ARA through the Love and Rage Revolutionary Anarchist Federation and spent almost a year in Minneapolis with the Anti-Racist Summer Project described in chapter 2. When Toronto ARA was founded in fall 1992, he got involved. Looking back, he describes the group as follows:

Almost all of the core group of Toronto organizers were people who were experienced and committed enough to accomplish the tasks

Hate slaying of gay man stuns Montreal

Police charge four neo-Nazi skinheads

BY ANDRÉ PICARD
Quebec Bureau

MONTREAL — Four youths, described by police as neo-Nazi skinheads, were charged with first-degree murder yesterday in the stalking and killing of a gay man in a Montreal park on Sunday.

GAYS MURDERED IN MONTREAL AT THE HANDS OF NEO-NAZIS

THEY ARE BASHING HERE TOO

RALLY AND MARCH
Saturday, December 19
7:30 PM

Cawthra Square Park
just beside 519 Church St., north of Wellesley
• Childcare available

TAKE BACK THE STREETS

Organized by **ANTI-RACIST ACTION**

• Endorsed by AIDS ACTION NOW •

Toronto, 1992.

that come with political organizing. With that also came a critique of the society in which we live. People were doing Indigenous solidarity already. They were either in, among, or doing solidarity work with various immigrant communities, or they had done anti-colonial solidarity work on matters of El Salvador or elsewhere.

Judith, another early ARA organizer, had years of experience with anarchist projects but "came to this more as a parent," she says. "I had a teenage son, and the Heritage Front was actively recruiting in high school." Judith remembers that many of ARA's organizers were connected to or part of the punk scene that had been battling nazi boneheads on the streets for years. "There were lots of fence-sitters," she notes. "There was a vouching system in place to try and keep information from getting back to the nazis."

ARA's first months in Toronto were a flurry of activity, beginning with a skirmish with Heritage Front members in September 1992 outside of a court hearing on the complaint brought by Rodney Bobiwash. Then, there was a protest at the German consulate against changes to refugee policies, a teach-in about the far right at the NCCT, a nighttime demo outside a downtown banquet hall hosting a Heritage Front rally with British Holocaust denier David Irving,[8] and a march with the LGBTQ community following the murder of a gay man by nazis in Montréal.[9] There were also trips to support anti-fascist organizing in both Montréal and nearby Kitchener-Waterloo, a protest denouncing the police shooting of a Latin American man,[10] and an anti-hate rally at a high school where the Heritage Front was trying to recruit.[11]

Throughout this period, meetings were held every week or two at a warehouse space run by the Kensington Youth Theatre Ensemble.[12] In this dusty, smoky, and dimly lit environment, the group crafted their mission statement: "ARA will expose and oppose organized racism and hatred through education, mass action and support of broader anti-racist action."[13] "For a group that was just pulling itself together in a period of weeks, it's pretty amazing that we had such a coherent mission statement that was arrived at really through a consensus process," remembers Judith. "It was very quick, very collaborative, and I think it was part of that early strength of the group."

Toronto ARA's character was established early on—including that it could include physical confrontation. At the David Irving/Heritage

Police attack anti-fascists to ensure safe passage for Heritage Front members, Toronto, 1993.

Front rally referred to earlier, while Heritage Front speakers exhorted their recruits, and George Burdi's band RaHoWa entertained, ARA members chanted and jeered outside, for hours, threatening Heritage Front members as they left the hall protected by police. "[This] demonstration was the first time where I actually felt it physically," says Judith. She explains:

> I had to ask myself: "Do I engage in a physical level with these folks when they come out?" Our side was chasing them into the side streets, and I had never been in that kind of situation. I was nervous, and I didn't want that type of engagement, but that was the turning point for me, where it was very clear that that was going to be part of it. That the physical confrontation part, that was going to go with the territory.

A second courthouse confrontation related to the human rights complaint filed by Rodney Bobiwash occurred in January 1993. Dozens of Heritage Front members rallied and marched, and over five hundred anti-racists counter-demonstrated first thing in the morning, despite freezing temperatures. To ensure that the Heritage Front supporters had safe passage to the courthouse, police on horseback beat back lines of anti-racists, injuring several, and arresting two.[14] Some anti-racists

NAZIS OUT OF OTTAWA!

DEMONSTRATE AGAINST THE RACIST GROUP, **"HERITAGE FRONT"**

MAY 29th at MINTO PARK Elgin at Gilmour

• 6:30pm •

Support **A.R.A.** (Anti Racist Action)

Help keep the Heritage Front out of Ottawa!!!

This event culminated in a midnight fascist march to the Canadian Parliament Buildings, Ottawa, 1993.

threw eggs and were otherwise aggressive, but police actions prevented any contact between the groups.

One of those in the crowd that day was Emmy. Emmy had lived on the streets and, as a mixed-race teenager, had many run-ins with racist boneheads. "Five hundred people now feels like nothing," she reflects, "but in that time, in 1993, it felt so powerful, so meaningful—like, you're not alone. So, I think that those big public expressions of coming together to show that we won't tolerate racism, or whatever it is, are very important, because they interrupt."

Throughout 1992 and 1993, tensions between racists and anti-racists were growing. Grant Bristow, the CSIS spy who had become the Heritage Front's head of security, had started the "It Campaign" against anti-racists (as in "you're it!"). Heritage Front members searched for phone numbers of anti-racists (sometimes by breaking into their first-generation answering machines by guessing their codes) and harassed them relentlessly.

In May 1993, a Heritage Front recruitment rally in Ottawa, Canada's capital city, culminated in a midnight march to the steps of Parliament Hill and assaults on anti-racists; George Burdi himself was charged for kicking a young skinhead woman who was a member of ARA Ottawa in the face.[15] Soon after came the brutal attack that for many epitomized the threat posed by the Heritage Front. Sivarajah Vinasithamby, a young father originally from Sri Lanka, was taking out the trash after his dishwashing shift at a downtown Toronto restaurant. In the alley, he encountered two racist boneheads heading home after a Heritage Front concert, again featuring George Burdi's band, RaHoWa. They beat Vinasithamby senseless; it was months before he could walk again.[16]

Taking the Fight to Them
By late spring 1993, ARA had decided to go on the offensive. Rather than confront the Heritage Front when they were organizing in public, a small group of ARA organizers planned a more ambitious demonstration on June 11, 1993. It turned out to be one of the most effective actions in Toronto ARA's decade of activism.

Through painstaking information gathering, which included going through people's garbage to find clues, ARA researchers had determined the address of one of the Heritage Front's operational centers—the home of Gary Schipper, who recorded the messages on the Heritage Front hotline. The ARA membership decided to march there but to keep the target a secret even from the majority of marchers, including members themselves, to make it more difficult for fascists to attack the anti-racist demonstration and for police to control it. The public meeting point was picked to give the impression that the target was the home and headquarters of Ernst Zündel, internationally known nazi propagandist. Harry was a demo marshal that day and remembers:

> Hundreds of people joined the demo, and then the organizers handed the marshals packets, but we weren't supposed to open the packets. And they managed to get us all onto these streetcars, and we took those streetcars into a residential neighborhood. When we turned the corner, and I opened it up, it was flyers about Gary Schipper.
>
> We marched there in a very loud and angry way. A lot of the youth that we had around us at the time, who were from a range of diverse backgrounds representing a cross section of Toronto, were enraged at the sight of the place that had been the hotline, spewing these vitriolic hateful messages. Our thing was about keeping the demonstration safe, it wasn't about policing what took place. And that was it. So, the house got "renovated."
>
> I was going door-to-door, handing out the flyer. While you could hear the crash-bang of what was going on, I was having actually really good conversations with people to keep them appreciative of the fact that no one was going to be harmed. They weren't going to be harmed; it wasn't about them. None of this was being "organized"; this just happened to be how these young folks responded to what they were seeing. And I didn't have anyone angrily react. The whole day was impressive. In my memory, nobody was arrested, nobody was hurt. To this day, I credit that with being one of the most effective mobilizations that I have ever been party to.

"The fact that you got everyone on the streetcars and left, that was just freaking brilliant," says Elizabeth Moore, a former Heritage Front member who now speaks out against racism. "Back then, I didn't think highly of ARA at all, but I know it left the police just scrambling. It was great. The whole thing just really shook people up, a lot. I don't think anyone expected Gary Schipper to be targeted. I didn't even know where he lived; he never had anybody over at his place."

The Saturday Sun, June 12, 1993

RAMPAGE ... Anti-racists
trash a home on Bertmount
Ave. last night.

- Veronica Henri. Sun

VANDALS ELUDE POLICE

Racist's home hit

By BILL DUNPHY
Toronto Sun

A rampaging mob of 300 anti-racists trashed the rented east-Toronto home of a prominent racist last night.

Organizers for Anti-Racist Action (ARA) pulled a fast one on Metro Police and racist security forces, who had expected them to demonstrate at the Carlton St. home of Holocaust denier Ernst Zundel.

Six officers stood by helplessly as hooded ARA thugs smashed windows and doors at the Bertmount Ave. home of Gary Schipper, the "voice of the Heritage Front."

Demonstrators tossed smoke bombs, paint bombs, rocks and bags of excrement through the front and side windows of the small, semi-detached Queen St.-Jones Ave. area home.

Schipper, who returned home soon after the 7 p.m. attack, said: "The communist rabble have shown their true colors.

"I'm never surprised by what they do.".

Schipper, who said he had no insurance, said he felt the worst for the owners of the house he rents.

"I planned on moving out at the end of the month anyway," said Schipper.

One of Schipper's neighbors, who watched the destruction from his front porch, expressed disgust at the demonstrators' action.

"There's no way this is going to get rid of the Nazis. They're behaving like a bunch of bloody children," said Ronald Hovbay.

A small group of racists led by a furious Heritage Front boss Wolfgang Droege promised revenge if the police fail to arrest the vandals.

Droege, his face clouded with fury, said: "The ARA has five of our addresses. We have 74 of their residences."

The mob, which arrived at Schipper's house via the TTC, hopped a westbound Queen St. streetcar and dispersed in the subway.

Story by Bill Dunphy in the *Toronto Sun*, the local tabloid newspaper, in 1993.

Meanwhile, Heritage Front members were gathered at a park far away, close to Zündel's bunker, which he had covered in plastic sheets. They were furious at what had happened. Reporter Bill Dunphy explains, "I was in Allan Gardens where they gathered. As I walked among them, I was told to fuck off or I'd get my head punched in. There was a real intense anger, and that was going to come out."[17]

Later that evening, Wolfgang Droege and George Burdi led Heritage Front members to Toronto's West End, where ARA members often met for drinks. That night, Janusz Baraniecki was waiting tables at Sneaky Dee's, a neighborhood bar.

> A group of people came in, kind of marched in, single file, more than fifty altogether.... It was comedic that they all without exception ordered Molson Canadian—which we carried, but it was not the beer of choice!
>
> These guys were looking for somebody, they came for some kind of confrontation, but that was the extent of it. They marched out, and, on their departure, we were kind of piecing it together. Oh, yes, these guys are Heritage Front people, and they were after the other guys, who we knew were visibly missing that day, because it was during that price war between Sneaky Dee's and the bar across the street for the prices of a pitcher of beer. Another fifteen minutes later or so, people were coming in saying, "There's a big fight going on on College Street." And you could hear the cops, the ambulance, the sirens.

Sure enough, about twenty anti-racists had come out from across the street to engage the Heritage Front members. Bottles, pipes, knives, and chains were used, and several people on both sides were injured. Droege sustained several slashes on the face, and he and two other Front members were arrested; he had broken the jaw of a teenage anti-racist with a heavy flashlight.

One condition of Droege's release from jail, pending trial, was that he not associate with the Heritage Front; this effectively deprived the group of its leadership.[18] Both the attack on Schipper's house and the subsequent street fight made local and national news.[19] After that, Droege was consistently described as "charged with aggravated assault," undermining the Heritage Front's credibility with the general public. (He was eventually convicted, receiving six months in jail.)[20]

While ARA members like Harry viewed the action as a total success, some anti-racists and left-wing groups criticized ARA. A number of organizers even launched a new organization, the Toronto Coalition Against Racism, which hosted a large (two-thousand-strong) anti-fascist demonstration before shifting focus to countering institutional racism.[21] The community radio station CKLN gave voice to some concerns in an interview with Ravi John, a representative of Toronto ARA. The radio show host, a woman of color, asserted that "the ARA actions are creating an atmosphere where there is retaliation against communities of colour." Ravi, who is South Asian, responded strongly: "The violence of the nazis is not initiated by action against them. They are not motivated to go out and attack people of colour because there is an anti-racist presence in the streets. Rather, that is their ideology, that is what they spend their time preparing for." He cited the experience of people of color in Germany, where fascist street violence had greatly increased since the fall of the Berlin Wall:

> Despite the anti-racist presence there in Germany, the brunt of the attacks are against people of colour. But that does not mean that people of colour should not take part in defensive actions against nazis. Actually, the strongest anti-racist youth are Turkish youth because they are the people who are targeted. They are much more militant than all the radical political activists. Day-to-day they fight the nazis in the street because that is a matter of survival for them.[22]

Despite the criticism, ARA stood strong through 1993 and 1994, as the Heritage Front suffered further bruising blows. George Burdi was tied up in court with the Ottawa assault charges. Elisa Hategan, groomed for leadership by Droege himself, decided to leave the group after meeting two ARA women. With the support of other ARA members, in particular a lesbian couple, she came out as gay, while continuing to spy on the Heritage Front for months, passing information about members and activities to Montréal anti-racist activist Martin Theriault.[23] "Her story is so emblematic of why ARA was effective," Judith remembers. "She relied on us 100 percent to leave the HF, and she helped do enormous damage to them once out." Eventually, Hategan publicly defected and her testimony was instrumental in more charges, convictions, and, eventually, jail time for Wolfgang Droege,[24] although the authorities declined to act on much of the information she had provided. She received no government support in this, relying completely on a network of safe houses established by Theriault, with support from Indigenous allies and the lesbian couple who moved out of Toronto to support her.

In August 1994, the reasons for this lack of state support for the defecting Hategan became clearer, and the terrain of struggle shifted yet again, when reporter Bill Dunphy exposed Grant Bristow as a CSIS agent.[25] Anti-racists were outraged that the government had employed Bristow, effectively paying a full-time organizer for the Heritage Front. Furthermore, Hategan had identified Bristow as the lead organizer of the harassment campaigns against anti-racists and a funder of its activities, with the result that CSIS had intervened to discredit her and deny her witness protection.[26] Meanwhile, the leader of the up-and-coming Reform Party, which was competing with the ruling Conservative Party, complained that Bristow had offered them the services of Heritage Front volunteers to do security, without disclosing their fascist affiliations, in a covert political operation to discredit Reform. Bristow's role was investigated by the government's Security Intelligence Review Committee,[27] but neither Bristow nor his handlers were ever held accountable for their dirty tricks. Bristow himself was given witness protection and a new identity.

Nonetheless, the exposure of Bristow, along with the criminal charges and relentless pressure by ARA, contributed to the decline of the Heritage Front. Former Heritage Front member Elizabeth Moore describes the collapse:

> I was there when things started unraveling and falling apart. From what I saw, it wasn't just Grant Bristow being uncovered. It wasn't just this charge or that charge. It really was a death by a thousand cuts kind of thing.... The Heritage Front would have been permanently crippled from Grant Bristow one way or the other, but I think they could have bounced back. But the fact that ARA was preventing them from having any meetings—they couldn't get people out, they couldn't get fundraising happening, they couldn't have concerts, they couldn't rally the troops, they couldn't have any cohesion. Canada Post was checking some of our mail. There were the mounting legal costs, people ending up in jail. Just everything.[28]

All in all, the Heritage Front never recovered.

Youth Against Hate: Growing the ARA Network in Canada

For many Toronto ARA members at the time, the Schipper demo was a high point of struggle. The Heritage Front never regained its former strength, after all. While many early ARA members left the group, a core of organizers remained committed.

On the street level, Toronto ARA led a successful boycott campaign against two stores specializing in Doc Martens and other street fashion, owned by a nazi father-and-son team. A sticker/graffiti campaign, ongoing vandalism, and a high-profile picket on one weekend during the height of the holiday shopping season were all tactics in the campaign; both stores closed down within two years.[29]

Toronto ARA also launched a neighborhood-based campaign against Ernst Zündel, the internationally known Holocaust denier and publisher who had scored a major win in 1992, when a conviction against him for "spreading false news" about the Nazi Holocaust was overturned at the Supreme Court of Canada.[30] ARA recognized Zündel not only as a publisher but also as an organizer who employed and convened local fascists, including many youth, and the ARA campaign focused attention on him at a time when the legalist strategies pursued by others were at a standstill. Ultimately, the Canadian state took its own action and deported Zündel to Germany, where he was born, but not before an arsonist severely damaged his headquarters, on May 8, 1995—the fiftieth anniversary of the Allied victory over Nazi Germany.[31]

Still, Toronto ARA may have lost momentum within a year or two, if not for the birth of the ARA Network. In 1994, representatives from ARA in Toronto traveled to Columbus, Ohio, for the first Midwest Anti-Fascist Network (MAFNET) conference. They were invigorated by meeting so many like-minded people with skills and experience. By 1996, Toronto ARA had decided to host its own conference, called Youth Against Hate, to bring together anti-racists and anti-fascists from across Canada. Two hundred thirty people attended.

The program included many skills-based workshops, while political discussion was framed by panel discussions focusing on the nature of the far-right threat and anti-fascist strategy. "I saw Youth Against Hate as a bid for the mainstream acceptance and support for anti-fascism, as messy as it was," says Judith. "It was an opportunity for us to defend that position that street violence needs a street-level response, and that, ultimately, the issues are much bigger, and that we're part of that movement."

ARA rallied outside a store called IXL, which had been a meeting point for a Hitler birthday celebration the year before, Toronto, 1995.

Logo of the Winnipeg ARA chapter, 1996.
Designed by Thomas Jay Bruyere.

An event of this kind needed money for travel, space rental, accommodation, and food. Toronto ARA applied for funding from Metro Toronto and the province, with the help of the Canadian Anti-Racism Education and Research Society (CAERS). Fromm, Zündel, and the remnants of the Heritage Front were able to stir up controversy in the right-wing media, and Toronto City Council debated the request for six hours before approving it.[32] Some in the ARA Network also criticized the Toronto chapter for seeking government funds. (Thereafter, Toronto ARA relied solely on grassroots fundraising.) Still, the conference served its purpose. Young people across Canada formed new ARA chapters, leading up to a high point of sixteen active groups across the country in 1999: in Brampton, Calgary, Fredericton, Kitchener-Waterloo, Kingston, London, Montréal, Niagara, Pickering, Peterborough, Sarnia, Sudbury, Toronto, Vancouver/Surrey, Winnipeg, and Oakville (where it was called "Youth Against Hate").[33]

Confronting the White-Power Music Scene

One major focus of ARA's work in Canada, one which connected ARA chapters across the Canada-US border, was white-power music. One of the biggest labels in racist rock was Resistance Records, run by Canadians from the Toronto area, although legally operating out of Detroit, presumably to avoid prosecution under Canadian law. As early as 1994, just a year after the founding of Resistance Records, Minneapolis ARA was already on their case, getting a racist ad for the label pulled from a tattoo magazine, which agreed to stop running such ads and printed a letter from ARA.

TRUE COLOURS

A PUBLICATION OF ANTI-RACIST ACTION NIAGARA

ISSUE # 5 ——————————————————*SUMMER 1997*

<u>WARNING</u>: MAY BE OFFENSIVE TO PARANOID RIGHT-WING CAB DRIVERS.

TAKE YOUR FUCKING RACE WAR AND SHOVE IT UP YOUR ASS

SAYING THAT ANTI-NAZIS ARE JUST AS BAD AS NAZIS IS LIKE SAYING THAT FIREFIGHTERS ARE JUST AS BAD AS ARSONISTS.

ARA zine, Niagara, Ontario, 1997.

A new chapter launches, Brampton, Ontario, May 1998. Courtesy of Norm Villeneuve.

In 1996, Detroit ARA convinced a local independent music store to stop stocking Resistance Records merchandise, a success that ARA tried to replicate in other cities and towns.[34] In November 1997, Canadian ARA chapters traveled together to Detroit to disrupt a Resistance Records concert. "That was wild," remembers Walter, founder of Montréal ARA.

> Driving the mini-van down from Montréal, stop in Peterborough, stop in Toronto, stop in Guelph, stop in Kitchener-Waterloo, picking up kids on the way. One kid got in, and he's got a giant pot leaf patch on his back. I was, like, "What, did you not have the jacket saying 'Customs Official, please search my anus?' You're not getting in with that. We're going to America." … Los Crudos were playing the Trumbleplex that night, and if you fucked up the nazis you got in for free. And they had a bunch of neighbourhood kids who came out, who had never been to a punk show before in their life.

Other white-power shows were canceled or disrupted simply by exposure made possible by inter-chapter information sharing and mentorship by more experienced members. A nazi show celebrating Hitler's birthday, in 1997, in Buffalo, New York, was disrupted through the combined efforts of Canadian and US ARA chapters.[35] A show in Kingston, Ontario, was similarly canceled.[36]

The ARA Network made it possible to achieve much more than any one chapter could achieve on their own. Walter remembers:

Community Alert!
Neo-Nazi Concert in Madison Heights
SHUT 'EM DOWN

On Saturday, November 29th Anti-Racist Action will expose and confront a Neo-Nazi concert in Madison Heights featuring local racist band Steel Cap. This is not just a harmless concert but a recruiting effort by organized fascists who are building a network in Southeastern Michigan. We can already see the results of their organizing with racist and homophobic leaflets in Ferndale, a Nazi youth club on the Eastside of Detroit (now shut down), racist attacks and vandalism in the Western suburbs, and openly Nazi record stores Downriver.

If left unopposed Metro-Detroit could see these random acts of hate grow into a more organized campaign of terror. Last week one only needed to turn on CNN each night to see Nazis shooting people in the streets of Denver to understand how real this threat is.

EXPOSE AND CONFRONT ORGANIZED HATE
Saturday   November   29th,   6PM
Gather @ 11 Mile and Lorenz (Madison Heights)
next to Madison High School- from here we will
go to the hall to confront the Nazis' concert.

Anti-Racist Action is a multi-racial direct action group dedicated to building a movement to fight white supremacy, sexism, and homophobia in the schools, workplaces and our communities.

Detroit Anti-Racist Action
313.796.0539
POB 321211
Detroit, MI 48232

Macomb Anti-Racist Action
pgr. 810.450.8716
POB 343
Richmond, MI 48062

ARA confronts a white-power music show, Detroit, 1997.

A local chapter that had maybe a dozen members could pick up a phone or get on the fucking ARA email list and say, "This is going on, on this date. We need people to back us up. Who can come?" and we would come. You would get at least a carload from every city. It was almost a social thing. You saw people you hung out with at the Columbus conference, at the camping trips.[37] Expose, oppose, and confront. We knew we were all at least down for expose, oppose, and confront. We weren't going to be with the "stay away, sway, and pray" crowd.

One great example is when people came together to shut down a white-power concert in Montréal, in February 1998. While local bone-heads had been holding secret concerts over the previous year, they had featured only local nazis. The February show was to be the first concert in some time with bands from the US and Ontario, which would potentially mean a much larger audience and cross-border networking opportunity.[38] Walter reached out to the network for help, and on the night of the show,

> We probably had 120 people ... but 60 of them were from ARA chapters from out of the province. And we were dealing with some violent motherfuckers that had murdered people in Montréal. They beat a gay man to death and bragged about it. They did bar attacks on us. So ... to have 60 people come from out of town made a huge difference.

The nazis' meeting point for the show was Jolicoeur Metro station. ARA people occupied the station, confronted would-be concert goers, and showered the nazis with spittle as riot police escorted them to safety. "We ran their point-person off the rendezvous spot for their own show, ran him out. He hid in a utility closet crying, until the police rescued him. That was a huge one. They were fucking so pissed. We got death threats from them that same night. It was fantastic," says Walter.

In 1999, multiple ARA chapters in Florida prevented a show in Tampa Bay, planned by Florida Hammerskins to raise money for eight Montréal boneheads on trial for a string of assaults. Montréal ARA sent an email to the network, lauding "the efforts of the ARA chapters in Florida and coordination from Columbus and intelligence work by SHARP Montréal."

White-power music was a significant fundraising and networking tool for the fascist movement in the 1990s, as detailed in the 1999 book

Soundtracks to the White Revolution: White Supremacist Assaults on Youth Music Subcultures, edited by researcher Devin Burghart.[39] Labels like Resistance Records gave organizational structure and support for the strategy that Tom Metzger had launched in the late 1980s to recruit rebellious white punks and skinheads into the fascist movement. Metzger's strategy was ultimately unsuccessful; punk as a counterculture is arguably more steadfastly left-wing and anti-oppressive today than it was in the 1980s and 1990s, but it could have gone the other way, and ARA's campaign against white-power music was critical to keeping fascists out of rebellious countercultural spaces. As Burghart remembers, ARA's work to build "mass opposition ... in music, when it was more contested terrain back then, was incredibly important." We'll talk more about ARA's broader cultural work in chapter 7.

Hounding Paul Fromm

Among the most intractable targets of anti-fascists in Canada proved to be Paul Fromm, the publisher of several racist and anti-Semitic newsletters and a self-styled free speech advocate who advanced racist and fascist positions within established political parties and institutions.[40] Based in the Toronto area, he also traveled often to host lectures in hotel meeting rooms and libraries. (He has remained active and is now based in Hamilton, Ontario.)

The Edmonton Anti-Fascist League had gone on hiatus after beating back the Final Solution Skinheads (boneheads) in the early 1990s, but was reinvigorated by news of Fromm's planned appearance at a local hotel in 1996. They sought out information and resources about Fromm from Toronto ARA, and organized a protest of 150 people, including "representatives from the Jewish Students' Association, the Muslim Students' Association, Food Not Bombs, the Anti-Fascist League, Skinheads Against Racial Prejudice, the University of Alberta New Democrats, the Edmonton Multicultural Society, the Student Organized Resistance Movement, and numerous punks, anti-racist skins, street kids, and concerned citizens."[41] When the crowd turned up at the hotel, ready to rumble, they found that the hotel had canceled Fromm's booking. Was the hotel convinced by the lobbying of more mainstream anti-racist groups or by the threat of a messy confrontation? Either way, Fromm was thwarted on that occasion.

In Toronto, Fromm booked regular speaking events at the Swansea Town Hall, a city-funded community center. Representing the

"If 'free speech', not bigotry, is the issue that Paul Fromm claims it to be, then all Canadians have the right and the obligation to counter lies, deceit, and hatred as vocally as the proponents of racism who espouse it. It is for this reason that we are determined to confront, disrupt, interfere with, and shut down the activities of Fromm and his ilk, no matter where they go."-Anti-Fascist League

Help us counter Paul Fromm's misinformation campaign. Meet us on Friday, March 15, 1996 at 7:30p.m. SHARP in the food court of Kingsway Garden Mall (109St. & 111Ave.). From there, we will proceed to where Fromm is speaking to find out how far he's willing to take his vision of "free speech".

PAUL FROMM

RACIST DORK!
Why He Sucks

brought to you by the Anti-Fascist League

Anti-fascists reorganized to confront fascist speaker Paul Fromm, Edmonton, 1996.

neighborhood was progressive city councilor David Miller. (He was later elected mayor of Toronto.) ARA approached him in late 1997 to complain about city resources being used by a white supremacist. Miller put his team on it, and within a year the City of Toronto had adopted a policy prohibiting city-funded institutions from hosting "hate" activities. With lax enforcement, however, the policy was not enough; Fromm continued to hold meetings at Swansea Town Hall. In February of 1999, ARA took direct action to stop one such gathering. "Dozens of anti-racism protesters descended on the Swansea Town Hall ... banging on windows and chanting. They made their way into the hall and tipped over tables.

ARA disrupts a speaking event with Doug Collins and Doug Christie at the Vancouver Public Library, on September 30, 1999. "The police wouldn't let us in, so we shut down the whole building, but then a smaller group of us snuck in in ones and twos through other doors and reconvened, shutting down the room itself." Credit: Denise from ARA Vancouver.

Eventually, a fire extinguisher was set off and the hall was engulfed in a chemical mist."[42]

Toronto ARA also flyered the neighborhood, urging residents to call Swansea Town Hall to complain about Fromm's meetings. Then the Cross-Cultural Communication Centre, a local anti-racist organization, gathered support for a letter to the hall, reminding them of their responsibilities under the City of Toronto policy. Miller remembers:

> Some of the ways that ARA drew attention to its cause are not ways that I would behave, but … ARA achieved a really important goal, not just through the policy being developed, but it actually being used. Once it's used, it's living and breathing. I believe that was the end of [Paul Fromm] there.[43]

The drive to prevent white supremacists and fascists from using public facilities, particularly libraries, to organize is common to anti-fascists across Canada and continues to this day.[44] In 1999, ARA Vancouver mobilized several hundred people against a speaking event at the

Vancouver Public Library, with Doug Christie, a lawyer who defended Holocaust deniers, and Doug Collins, a newspaper columnist who had been fined $2,000 by the British Columbia Human Rights Tribunal for having "exposed Jews to hatred."[45] Giles had been active in ARA in Toronto and Peterborough before moving to Vancouver. Thinking back, he's still pumped.

> It was obvious that people were waiting for someone to take the lead on these issues. People wanting to take some action. First, the police shut down the building, which was a victory in itself, because it kept others from going into the event. Then several of us snuck in and blocked the entrance to the room and basically shut the event down.... Christie and Collins held these events to legitimize themselves, to push their "free speech" line. By my memory, we were successful in labeling it a white supremacist event and changing the narrative.

Building Community in K-W

The last story in this chapter brings us to Kitchener-Waterloo ("K-W"), a small city one hour west of Toronto, and hearkens back to the early days of ARA and the grueling struggles for turf between racist and anti-racists. A K-W ARA chapter was first established in 1992, around the same time as Toronto ARA. Among the early members was Julian Ichim. "I got involved with ARA because I was walking to high school one day and a neo-nazi sieg heiled me, and I told him to fuck off, and I got beat up in front of my high school.... All the teachers and everyone sat around and did nothing," he says. The Heritage Front was active in K-W, recruiting skinheads, while Zündel had a close ally, the owner of a shop called European Sound, which hosted far-right events.

After organizing several demonstrations, activity slowed. The group was reenergized after the Youth Against Hate conference in 1996, but, still, "because of the very significant street presence of nazis at that time, people were afraid to be open about being a part of ARA," says Davin Charney, who joined a couple of years later. "There was the Tri-City Skins, the Canadian Ethnic Cleansing Team. The soft-sell group was the Canadian Heritage Alliance. Paul Fromm would come to town as well." K-W ARA participated in wider network events and patiently worked to build their local credibility. Things picked up in 1999, when a street-involved youth came to an ARA meeting and spoke up about harassment by private security and police. ARA decided to prioritize creating a safe space for youth downtown and started a new organization called the Youth Collective to achieve that goal. Membership grew, and after two years the Youth Collective had raised $10,000, enough to rent a second-floor warehouse space. This became the Spot, an independent, volunteer-run youth drop-in that operated from 2001 to 2004. Davin reckons that thousands of people participated in the Spot during this time. "All of the youth who were in the shelters or in and out of jail or involved in gang activity. Homeless youth." University students like Davin himself joined but were the minority. The Youth Collective became "like a family," says Davin. "We really brought together and unified and built this community that didn't exist before." The political organizing of the Youth Collective focused on policing and homelessness, conflicts with the Children's Aid Society and City Hall, and gentrification.

The Youth Collective also came into conflict with the street-level fash. Boneheads came to the Spot more than once to fight with people there. "We weren't pacifists," says Davin, "and we were very capable of defending ourselves.... To defend yourself using violence wasn't a foreign concept to many people." Their "weapons drawer," in a filing cabinet, was full of pipes and pieces of rebar.

One night in October 2002, a group of fifteen nazi boneheads were drinking at a bar near the Spot; observers thought they were looking for trouble and warned the Youth Collective. About twenty-five Youth Collective members prepared to defend the Spot. When a nazi broke a bottle on the front door, a young Black woman on the street, who was involved with the Spot, saw them. "She was tough," as Davin tells it. "By herself, she was screaming and shouting at them and confronting them. Someone came up to tell us, and we then emptied the weapons drawer, and all of us, we charged out of the Spot and followed these guys down the street." It was a busy Saturday night, and word had got around that something was up. The Youth Collective's group swelled as they followed the nazis for a couple of blocks. "My memory may be embellished, but it seemed like a hundred of us had gathered," says Davin, "and there was going to be a very violent confrontation with these guys." "We chased them all the way downtown," remembers Julian. "The police encircled us, and people from downtown actually came and joined us, and, at that point, the movement was born. The police had to drag the nazis out of the hands of the people, literally.... And that showed to the people the links between the police and right wing at the time."

For Julian, this was the turning point, "when the tide shifted," when the nazis realized they had lost control of the street. Davin agrees:

I like to say—and I don't know how people will take this—that we "out-violenced" them. That's not the only thing we did, but it's one of the things we did. And for many years after that there was no significant fascist presence in K-W, until more recently, I think, with Trump. It was one of the great successes of the Youth Collective and Spot, to drive out that far-right presence. We didn't end racism on that day. We certainly didn't end the racism from the police, institutional and systemic racism. But we did put a stop to that far-right fascist street presence, which I think is significant.

In sum, Canadian ARA chapters were responsible for, or made significant contributions to, some big wins in the anti-racist/anti-fascist struggle in Canada in the 1990s. The most critical, on a national level, was the collapse of the Heritage Front. The cancellation or disruption of white-power concerts and speaking events, taking back the streets in smaller cities, and the strengthening of anti-racist policy at the City of Toronto were also important. Each successful action or campaign had common elements: solid intelligence work, community outreach and alliance-building, and an openness to direct action.

Direct action also had consequences for ARA members. Several were seriously injured over the years. In Toronto alone, about forty people were arrested and charged—with members of color far overrepresented—although none were ever sentenced to jail time. Mid-decade, there were active investigations of ARA organizers across the country by the Canadian Security Intelligence Service and the Royal Canadian Mounted Police.[46] Facing those risks, some potential recruits were discouraged. "It felt like it would be a heat score, that there would be undercovers," says Soheil, a friend of Toronto ARA. "I remember going to a party at one ARA house and being shown a bulletin board with all the business cards of agents who had come knocking at the door. It was a place where it was hard to stay under the radar and still be active, at least that's [the] impression I got."

In reporter Bill Dunphy's view, Toronto ARA played an important role by highlighting—and sometimes provoking—the Heritage Front membership's more violent and criminal side, indirectly forcing the state to take action:

> Free society was able to recognize what they [Heritage Front members] were, talk about it, and deal with it, with the assistance of the state, because when they broke laws, those were the opportunities to grab them ... and that came about partly because—certainly because—of ARA, which flushed those actions out and made those actions more likely to happen, and, once [they] happened, less likely to be ignored.

Moreover, given the specific conditions in Toronto at that time, the Heritage Front wasn't able to defend itself politically from either the human rights complaint laid by Rodney Bobiwash of the NCCT or the notoriety associated with the criminal charges. Dunphy explains:

> The human rights complaints dragged them off their agenda, off their targets, away from their building. They didn't have the abilities, resources, timing to flip that, jiu-jitsu-like, to "see how the state is oppressing us." They weren't able to get away with that, because they also had the criminal things, which lost them support, ultimately. Those things in Canada still seem to be death for you, politically. You don't get to have thugs in the street as part of your [political] party.[47]

Having said that, fueling strong state action against the fash was never Toronto ARA's strategy; from ARA's point of view, direct action was valuable in and of itself. "Since 1994, the fash have been less inclined to plan public events in downtown Toronto.... They know we're on the prowl!" asserted the fall 1997, five-year anniversary issue of Toronto ARA's *On the Prowl*. Other observers agree. Asad Ismi is an award-winning writer and radio documentary maker. He is the international politics columnist for the Canadian Centre for Policy Alternatives publication *The Monitor*, Canada's biggest leftist magazine by circulation. Never a member of ARA, he nevertheless appreciates its work:

> They were not waiting for the city government, the national government, the provincial government. No, these were people in the neighborhood taking up the task of beating back nazism and racism.... Think about it. You are a member of a far-right group,

fascist group, and you think you can organize something just like that, as if you are in some bicycle club, as if it's a picnic. No, you can't. Once they see that, it's so much trouble to get people together, they don't do it. But you must make them pay a price, in physical terms. The price of going to jail or hospital or both. If you do that, they'll be finished. And they were. It was direct action, physical action, that led to the decline of nazis…

Who is ruling [in 2020] in the United States … in India … in Brazil? A fascist.… If you don't have citizen action at the city level, you'll get fascism at the national level. You don't have a fascist government in Canada today … partly because of groups and movements like ARA, who made sure it didn't happen.

Former Heritage Front member Elizabeth Moore says: "With my current perspective, I have a lot of respect for people who physically put themselves in harm's way and stood outside in the rain and the snow and whatever elements and took whatever risks that were thrown at them to shut down these meetings and to call the venues and pressure them and do that kind of work. That took a huge amount of guts." At the same time, Moore encourages anti-fascists to pursue all strategies to counter the far right today. "When I look at anti-racist organizing now, they're all fighting. 'No, we should be doing it this way.' 'No, we should be doing it that way.' Actually, no, do everything. We need everything."

In our first four chapters, we have described the interplay between street-level anti-fascism and ARA's more public organizing against the nazis, the Klan, and the white-power music scene in the US and Canada. As the Kitchener-Waterloo story illustrates, ARA could integrate their militant anti-fascism into broader organizing against racism and poverty. In our next chapters, we'll examine ARA members' thoughts on such intersections to get a more complete picture of the ARA Network.

NOTES

1   Anthony Morgan, *Populism and Racism in Two Ontario Elections*, Canadian Centre for Policy Alternatives, April 23, 2018, accessed April 5, 2022, https://policyalternatives. ca/publications/monitor/populism-and-racism-two-ontario-elections.

2   Canadian fascists were invited to Libya twice. On this trip, they traveled from Malta to Tripoli on the same boat as left-wing activists and revolutionaries. In the words of a government report, "The right wing racists had to be separated from the left wing

anti-fascists for the formers' protection. After the ship docked, the NPC [Nationalist Party of Canada] group were not allowed to disembark and only after several days of complaining were they allowed to reside in Camp Kadhafi some miles from Tripoli"; *The Heritage Front Affair: Report to the Solicitor General,* Security Intelligence Review Committee, December 4, 1994, accessed April 5, 2022, https://www.publicsafety.gc.ca/lbrr/archives/jl%2086.s4%20s43%201994-eng.pdf.

3   See Stewart Bell, *Bayou of Pigs: The True Story of an Audacious Plot to Turn a Tropical Island into a Criminal Paradise* (Hoboken, NJ: John Wiley and Sons, 2008). Among the coconspirators was Don Black, a KKK leader and member of the American Nazi Party, who founded Stormfront, the first significant fascist website, after his release.

4   Bill Dunphy, "STIR IT UP. Spy Unmasked: CSIS Informant 'Founding Father' of White Racist Group," *Toronto Sun*, August 14, 1994.

5   The Church of the Creator renamed itself the World Church of the Creator in 1996. For more information on the group's later efforts, see chapter 9.

6   Robin D.G. Kelley makes this point more strongly in the prologue to *No Fascist USA! The John Brown Anti-Klan Committee and Lessons for Today's Movements*, saying that that book challenges "the prevailing wisdom that racist terrorism rises in response to economic downturns, because of white downward mobility, or in a vacuum created by a lack of progressive alternatives. On the contrary, the Klan's resurrection [in the 1970s] was a *reaction* to the radical insurgencies of the era: Black and Brown rebellions, struggles for gender equality and sexual freedom, the defeat of U.S. imperialism from Vietnam to Tehran – real movements for democracy and social transformation"; see Hilary Moore and James Tracy, *No Fascist USA! The John Brown Anti-Klan Committee and Lessons for Today's Movements* (San Francisco: City Lights Books, 2020), 14.

7   Catherine Dunphy, "Rodney Bobiwash: Mild-Mannered, but Not One to Back Down from a Fight," *Toronto Star,* January 31, 1993.

8   Scott Burnside, "Racists Ripped," *Toronto Sun*, November 14, 1992.

9   André Picard, "450 Protest Gay Bashing, Rise in Racism," *Toronto Star*, December 20, 1992.

10   "Protesters Decry Police Shooting," *Globe and Mail* (Toronto, ON), January 4, 1993.

11   Tim McCaskell, *Race to Equity: Disrupting Educational Inequality* (Toronto: Between the Lines, 2005), 175.

12   Later Toronto ARA meeting venues included the offices of an AIDS service organization, a halfway house for people being released from federal prisons, an immigrant-serving organization, a local union office, and a bar (outside of opening hours).

13   *On the Prowl: News Bulletin of Anti-Racist Action* no. 1 (November–December 1993), 4. The wording changed over time. *On the Prowl* no. 3 (Fall 1994) included this version: "ARA will expose, oppose and confront organized racism and hatred through education, mass action and support of broader anti-racist struggles". *On the Prowl* no. 10 (Fall 1997) replaced "hatred" with "the far-right agenda" and also included this description of the group: "ARA Toronto came together in September 1992 to show the strength of our opposition to fascism, as well as our commitment to a multi-racial, multi-cultural, sexually diverse, liberated and fun society." That wording had been used in leaflets and pamphlets since 1993.

14   Michael Tenszen and Moira Welsh, "3 Protesters, One Officer Hurt in Anti-Racist Clash," *Toronto Star*, January 25, 1993; Jack Kapita and Rudy Platiel, "Heritage Front

Hearing Ends in Muddle; Police on Horseback Clear Path through Protesters Outside Courthouse," *Globe and Mail* (Toronto, ON), January 26, 1993.

15   Mike Shahin, "Neo-Nazis, Opponents Clash," *Kitchener-Waterloo Record* (ON), May 31, 1993.

16   Peter Small, "Beaten Tamil Slowly Rebuilds His Life," *Toronto Star*, September 4, 1993.

17   Dunphy interview.

18   Henry Hess, "Forbidden On-Air Interviews, White Supremacist Complains," *Globe & Mail* (Toronto, ON), October 2, 1993.

19   Jennifer Lewington, "Anti-Racists Vent Anger on White Supremacist; Demonstrators Vandalize House While Outnumbered Police Look On," *Globe & Mail* (Toronto, ON), June 12, 1993; Gail Swainson and Jim Wilkes, "Anti-Racist Mob Trashes Home," *Toronto Star*, June 12, 1993; "Racist's Home Hit," *Toronto Sun*, June 12, 1993; "Protesters Trash Supremacist's House," *Edmonton Journal* (AB), June 13, 1993; "Racist's Home Attacked in Toronto," *Kitchener-Waterloo Record* (ON), June 13, 1993.

20   "Heritage Front Founder Gets Six Months in Jail (Wolfgang Droege)," Canadian Press NewsWire, Toronto, March 9, 1995.

21   Toronto ARA participated in and contributed to this broad coalition led by Black, Latine, and Asian organizers, even though the organizing group included many members of the International Socialists (IS—affiliated to the International Socialist Organization in the US) who had been voted out of Toronto ARA by a two-thirds majority some months before. The IS had argued against ARA's focus on the far right and its openness to physical confrontation. Debates about Toronto ARA within the left are described in more detail in the Arm the Spirit archives; see Lola, "On the Prowl—Notes on Anti-Racist Action and Developing Anti-Fascist Strategies in Toronto, June 11, 1993," accessed June 2, 2022, https://armthespiritforrevolutionary resistance.wordpress.com/2017/04/19/anti-racist-action-on-the-prowl-1993.

22   CKLN 88.1, "Interview with a Member of Anti-Racist Action: Toronto Anti-Racist Action June 11, 1993," *Arm the Spirit* (Toronto), accessed April 5, 2022 https:// armthespiritforrevolutionaryresistance.wordpress.com/2017/04/17/toronto-anti-racist-action-june-11-1993.

23   Elisa Hategan, *Elisa Hategan, Race Traitor: The True Story of Canadian Intelligence's Greatest Cover-Up* (Toronto: Incognito Press, 2014).

24   Rudy Platiel, "Front Played Dirty, Court Told Ex-Member Witness in Contempt Case," *Globe and Mail* (Toronto, ON), March 17, 1994.

25   Dunphy, "STIR IT UP."

26   Jon Milton, "Police, Spies and White Supremacy: A Brief History. Law Enforcement Focuses on "Left wing gangs" while keeping ties to the extreme right," Ricochet, July 25, 2018, accessed June 2, 2022, https://ricochet.media/en/2276/police-spies-and-white-supremacy-a-brief-history.

27   Security Intelligence Review Committee, *The Heritage Front Affair*.

28   Elizabeth Moore interview.

29   *On the Prowl: News Bulletin of Anti-Racist Action, Toronto* no. 10 (Fall 1997): 4.

30   Sean Fine, "Top Court Quashes Zundel's Conviction: Back in Business, Publisher Says," *Globe and Mail* (Toronto, ON), Aug 28, 1992.

31   Bob Brent, "Some Cheer Zundel Home Blaze (but Many Condemn 'Vigilante Justice')," Toronto Star, May 8, 1995.

32   Donovan Vincent, "Metro Okays $8,000 Grant for Anti-Racist Group Meeting," *Toronto Star*, July 5, 1996.

33   *On the Prowl: News Bulletin of Anti-Racist Action, Toronto* no. 13 (Spring 1999): 8.

34   Public statement by Mr. Musichead Management, November 14, 1996; *Anti-Racist Action Bulletin* no. 4 (c. January 1997).

35   "Concert Marking Hitler's Birthday Is Canceled," *Buffalo News* (NY), April 1997.

36   J. Calugay, "Racist Concert Cancelled, but Activists Still Vigilant," *Kingston Whig-Standard* (ON), July 3, 2000.

37   In the late 1990s, Kitchener-Waterloo ARA and Toronto ARA organized three campground retreats for nearby chapters, involving up to seventy people.

38   Montréal ARA, "ARA Ruins Nazi Concert in Montreal!" February 1998.

39   Devin Burghart, *Soundtracks to the White Revolution: White Supremacist Assaults on Youth Music Subcultures* (Chicago: Center for New Community, 1999).

40   Stanley R. Barrett, *Is God a Racist? The Right Wing in Canada* (Toronto: University of Toronto Press, 1987), 189–204.

41   Edmonton Anti-Fascist League, "Anti-Fascist League Shuts Fromm Down!" *Antifa Info-Bulletin*, Supplement, March 25, 1996.

42   Eric Volmers, "Down into the Darkness; Matt Lauder's Inside Look at Canada's Racist Groups Wasn't Pretty," *Guelph Mercury* (ON), March 19, 2005.

43   David Miller interview.

44   "Libraries and Hate in Canada," Canadian Anti-Racism Network, accessed April 13, 2022, https://stopracism.ca/content/libraries-and-hate-canada.

45   Shane McCune, "Collins-Christie Session Draws Protesters, Cops to Vancouver Library," *Province* (Vancouver, BC), October 1, 1999.

46   Jim Bronskill, "CSIS Targeting Anti-Racists, Annual Report Reveals: 'Potential for Violence': Foreign Conflicts Could Bring Trouble Home to Canada, Spy Agency Adds," *National Post* (ON), June 9, 1999.

47   Dunphy interview.

CHAPTER 5

FIGHT THE POWER: ANTI-RACIST SOLIDARITY

While punks and anti-racist skins first formed ARA to counter the specific threat of nazis within their scenes, their political commitments generally went beyond this. "The big event that would have brought people together would have been the LA riots," remembers Matt from Cincinnati, speaking of the five days of popular revolt in 1992 sparked by the acquittal of police officers who had brutalized Black motorist Rodney King, caught on amateur video that went viral.[1] "There were forums, there were teach-ins, demonstrations and all that stuff. A bit like George Floyd. LA wasn't just in LA. It got people mobilizing all around. It helped introduce ARA to lots of different people and ideas."

The year 1992 also marked the five hundredth anniversary of the fateful voyage of Christopher Columbus and his crew of invaders. Indigenous people across the Americas reframed that anniversary as "five hundred years of resistance" to racism and genocide through widespread ceremony, protest, political action, and artistic expression, with a lasting impact on the political consciousness of people on the left. In 1994, in resistance to the imposition of the North American Free Trade Agreement, the Zapatista Army of National Liberation (EZLN), an alliance of Indigenous farmers and leftist militants in southern Mexico, pushed representatives of the Mexican government out of their territories, declared themselves autonomous, and ignited hope that farmers, Indigenous people, and poor and working people could resist this neoliberal assault with creativity and passion. Furthermore, the EZLN uprising helped catalyze the wave of protest against neoliberal globalization, which hit US shores, in Seattle, in 1999.[2]

This was the broad political context of the 1990s as ARA was hitting its stride. While anti-imperialist and anti-colonial movements in North

ONLY YOU CAN FUCK SHIT UP FOR THE RICH

Fight against racism, sexism, homophobia, imperialism, and other forms of oppression

ARA

No reliance on the cops or the courts   Non-sectarian defense of arrested anti-fascist activists
Same time, same place direct action against fascist mobilizations

A 1990s ARA poster depicting Emiliano Zapata, hero of the Mexican Revolution, whose name was repurposed by the Zapatista Army of National Liberation, or EZLN. In January 1994, the Zapatistas expelled agents of the Mexican state from parts of the State of Chiapas and launched a grassroots revolution. Their influence loomed large for anarchists and anti-authoritarian leftists of the time, and continues to do so today. Original artwork by Arturo Garcia Bustos, 1953.

America and around the world appeared in retreat during the 1980s and 1990s compared to the heady previous decades, the spirit of resistance to oppression is never snuffed out, and ARA chapters and individuals were involved in struggles against systemic racism throughout the 1990s. Condemning police abuse was natural for many ARA members, particularly those with an anarchist orientation. When US activists launched the October 22 Coalition to Stop Police Brutality, Repression and the Criminalization of a Generation in 1996 (still active today),[3] many ARA chapters organized or participated in local events. Along the same lines, many ARA chapters carried out prison support or prison abolition projects and joined in the campaign to free US political prisoner Mumia Abu Jamal when he was first scheduled to be executed in 1995.

In this chapter, we examine two key interrelated themes of ARA and its broader political milieu(s). First, after originating in multiracial skinhead scenes, ARA became whiter as it expanded into the broader punk counterculture and beyond. Still, it never defined itself as a white organization, and members and organizers of color were key players in some chapters, the network, and the whole antifa scene. We'll examine ARA's

ARA joined with the Partisan Defence Committee, Friends of MOVE, and others to organize in support of Mumia Abu Jamal, Toronto, August 14, 1995. Photo credit: David Maltby, RIP. Courtesy Toronto ARA archive.

At the Millions for Mumia march, Philadelphia, April 24, 1999. Courtesy Toronto ARA archive.

Millions for Mumia march, Philadelphia, April 24, 1999. South Jersey ARA was one of many ARA chapters represented. Courtesy Toronto ARA archive.

membership in terms of race, nationality, religion, and ethnicity. Second, while ARA was perhaps most at home directly confronting fascists, many members advocated for working against broader systemic and institutionalized racism. Their success in, and approaches to, fighting systemic racism depended significantly on each chapter's membership and the relationships forged with people of color (POC)–led organizations in local campaigns. We will explore five ARA chapters' anti-racist work in this chapter, as well as potential lessons from ARA's successes and failures in fighting systemic racism, both in society and within the network.

Rival Vanguards?

Steve, a white member of Lansing ARA, recalls, "There was always conversations about the whiteness of the ARA groups and the ARA Network; not to pretend that it was all white, but I think it was fair to say that nearly all the chapters were majority white." To many people, including Steve, it was a "glaring limitation" for an anti-racist group.

As we saw in chapter 3, other members didn't necessarily agree that ARA's whiteness was a problem. Matt, a white member of Cincinnati ARA, viewed ARA as in "competition" with the Klan; every white kid in ARA was a white kid not in a fascist group. He thinks that "that perspective of

trying to concretely compete for the very people the fascists are trying
to compete for is an essential thing that part of the left has lost.... That
orientation toward white people is obviously not something that a Black
person should have to have—we're not gonna ask it of everyone—but the
anti-racist movement must have that in its arsenal." Furthermore, ARA
was perhaps able to do what it did because of many of its members' white
privilege. As Judith reckons: white ARA organizers "took our share of beat-
downs and arrests, [but] looking to Black activists on the daily I don't think
it is comparable," and moreover, "the access to resources that ARA chapters had was partly as a result of our racial privilege—cars, printing, etc."

Discussion about the heavily white makeup of ARA's membership
and ARA's scope of activity took place in local chapters, via email, in
the *Bulletin* and, crucially, at the annual conferences and delegate meetings. For example, as the network was building momentum, the 1995
Columbus conference featured Lorenzo Komboa-Ervin, a Black Panther
Party veteran who had turned to anarchism. Komboa-Ervin gave a workshop on "Building the Movement against Racism and Police Brutality,"
participated in the conference plenary, and convened a People of Color
caucus. He wrote a follow-up letter to the Columbus conference organizers, reprinted in the *Bulletin* at his request. His voice was one among
many, but he presented a succinct summary of criticisms and conversations consistently raised about ARA's demographic makeup and political
orientations. He believed:

> Too much emphasis is being placed on the rise of the white
> rightwing paramilitary movements, and not enough on racist para-
> military agents of the state, i.e. the police; as well as the rightward
> and openly racist drift of the capitalist state and all its institutions
> which has resulted in budgets cuts and layoffs; mass imprisonment
> of African American and other racially oppressed youth; police
> brutality; repression of our social reform movements; and the
> economic devastation of urban minority communities which has
> resulted in all of today's social problems.

Furthermore, he alleged that ARA was "an all-white movement with just
some token non-white participation." Such a movement, in his view,

> cannot begin to deal with racism and fascist organizing in North
> America. It is a serious fallacy to have a movement directed toward

the right-wing vanguard elements (the "bad" whites) and just fought by the vanguard elements of the Liberal-Left (the "good" whites). History has proven that such a movement will fail and may in fact do harm to the anti-racist fight back overall.

Komboa-Ervin proposed that ARA foster inclusivity through creating an outreach committee and a People of Color caucus, feeding into "a formal structure, i.e., a Coordinating Committee should be created to plan future meetings, administer the organization on a daily basis, and invite other organizations to join the ARA coalition." This is a common strategy for addressing issues of representation within left organizations: ensure that people directly affected by an issue are represented in leadership.

Delegates at the 1995 Conference voted unanimously in favor of guaranteeing representation for people of color—as well as women and queer people—in whatever governing body ARA eventually ended up deciding to establish.[4] However, after two years of discussion about establishing a steering committee, the network decided against forming one. Instead, network-wide decisions would continue to be made at the annual conferences. While agreement was reached that caucuses could select delegates to vote on their behalf, no caucus ever did. In the end, this route to formally foster leadership by people of color at the network level was closed off.[5]

What prevailed instead was a decentralized, anarchist-influenced perspective. Kieran, a member of the Love and Rage Revolutionary Anarchist Federation and ARA's Minneapolis chapter, advocated for this approach, which he describes as follows:

> [Minneapolis] ARA/L&R argued that movements can't be made more multiracial by edicts from above.... In general, the way that perspectives, strategies, and tactics became major areas of work was not by passing a resolution mandating the work within the network but by experimenting with an area of work and publicizing and popularizing it. Leadership in ARA was, therefore, by example and based on action, and not via any hierarchy or proclamation.

Minneapolis ARA had come to the 1995 conference with their own proposal about ARA's scope of work, advocating that the network and chapters focus on three areas: a campaign against the white-power

DIRECT ACTION AGAINST all forms of RACISM

Fight Back!

We're here to protest the racism of the government we live under. We're here to protest the racism of Bill Clinton and the Democratic Party. The Democrats and their so called "liberal" agenda are no less corrupt than the Buchanan- influenced Republican Party. The Democrats, with Clinton at the helm, have created some of the most racist and anti-poor legislation in recent history. The Crime Bill and Welfare Reform are examples of how the racism of the Democrats works. We're here to support groups that have organized against the DNC in Chicago and we hope to build alliances with other anti-racist groups in the Midwest. We're also here to protest the woman-hating agenda of the Christian Coalition and the activities of groups like Operation Rescue. We're here to participate in clinic defense and take a stand against anti-abortion forces that try to organize and shut down clinics during the convention.

Minneapolis ARA

Anti-Racist Action(ARA) is a youth based group committed to fighting all forms of racism: the racism of the state/institutional racism such as cops, and the racism of organized fascist groups such as the KKK and nazi skinheads. We organize a biweekly COPWATCH that intervenes in police abuse and harassment, we participate in anti-klan rallies, and we organize against the nazi music scene. We are also committed to fighting homophobia and sexism and believe that these forms of oppression should be taken just as seriously and fought just as rigorously.

The Anti-Racist Action Network

We are part of a growing network of ARA's that are taking root all across the U.S. and Canada. We think it's important to get organized on a grassroots level to fight racism. We don't believe that the government is going to fight racism for us, in fact quite the opposite, so we find people to work with who want to take responsibility to do it ourselves. We don't rely on politicians and party platforms and their empty promises.

GOVERNMENTS DON'T FIGHT RACISM! WE DO!!!

Minneapolis Anti-Racist Action
POB80239,MPLS,MN 55408 HOTLINE:612-649-4586

Minneapolis ARA encouraged ARA chapters to start Copwatch programs as a form of direct action against racism.

1990s. Courtesy of Anna Stitt.

music scene; establishing "Copwatch" programs to counter police abuse, described later in this chapter; and "pro-women, pro-queer" organizing. While no vote on the proposal took place, many ARA chapters did undertake all three proposed areas of work over the following years. ARA seemed to indeed be, as Kieran said, "based on action," not "hierarchy or proclamation."

In the years that followed, members and chapters continually advocated for more focus on systemic racism, both practically—e.g., by supporting political prisoners or Indigenous campaigns like that of Black Mesa/Big Mountain Diné (Navajo) against relocation—and "by proclamation." In 1996 and 1997, Chicago, Baltimore, and Minneapolis chapters proposed amending the points of unity to commit ARA to fighting institutional racism; in 1999, the small ARA affiliate Class War Cartel proposed including a definition of racism as "a form of economic control over ALL peoples."

During the June 1997 delegates meeting in Chicago, stark differences between individuals and chapters were revealed in a debate about ARA's second point of unity: "Don't rely on the cops and on courts to do our work. That doesn't mean we don't ever go to court. But we must rely on ourselves to protect ourselves and stop the fascists." Minneapolis ARA, supported by the Chicago A-Zone chapter, proposed ARA recognize that "police are our enemies," arguing that only such an explicit position could make ARA more attractive to people of color. In opposition, delegates from Montréal and Buffalo argued that ARA could, "sometimes," "use them [the police] to our advantage" against nazis. Meanwhile, a Toronto delegate characterized the Minneapolis proposal as "rhetorical and coming from a mostly white background.... We are alienating people of color who need recourse to the courts at times." A few others expressed fear that by denouncing the police ARA would invite repression. Delegates from Los Angeles, Ann Arbor, and Montréal suggested that a focus on police brutality rather than the police as an institution was a good starting point for ARA. This debate would be revisited a couple of years later, when two ARA members were murdered, and ARA organizers had to face practical questions about how to relate to the police investigation.

ARA never did amend its points of unity to commit the network to challenging institutional or systemic racism; it remained united as a specifically anti-fascist network. However, when the majority-POC Detroit chapter brought a resolution to the 1999 conference that the network "broaden anti-racist activity" (described later in this chapter), it was adopted by a large majority.

What follows are profiles of five chapters that each pursued different strategies to engage with broader anti-racist work and the racial demographics and politics of their own chapters and communities.

Columbus

One organizing strategy was replicated in several ARA chapters over the years: Copwatch. It was based on the same values and ethics underlying ARA's anti-fascist work: an independent, direct-action strategy to interrupt racism, carried out by people willing to put their physical safety on the line. Columbus was among the ARA chapters that took up the challenge of organizing a Copwatch program.

Young women in Minneapolis ARA first came across the idea, inspired by the Black Panther Party and reinvented in 1990 by activists in Berkeley, California. As they explained to the ARA Network in their 1995 proposal, "Cops, 'the arm of the state,' are given power to enforce racist laws and use their own personal racist bias to determine who to harass and detail, and often beat and kill, on the street." Copwatchers could intervene by observing and recording police interactions with people, the goal being "to make the pigs feel watched, and self-conscious. Copwatch

You're Never Fully Dressed Without a Smile

SOUTH CAMPUS-STUDENT NEIGHBORHOOD OR PENAL COLONY!?

A few observations from Friday night May 17, the last in a series of Police incited riots in the Campus area:

1.   Police officers purposely shove Shomas Jones, a third-year criminal law major over a chain enclosed planter . Defenseless and on the pavement, they mace him and deliberately smash the camera he had been using to tape arrests. They then detain him for four hours without charge. Chris Wisniewski a fourth year journalism student is beaten to the ground, maced and arrested for complaining about Jones' treatment.

2.   Another OSU student is attacked and maced by police in riot gear ON HIS FRIEND'S FRONT PORCH. He suffers lacerations to his face and a possible broken nose. He is also detained, without care, for two hours.

3.   Detainees, cuffed and reasonably upset, ask questions of an officer to which he responds sarcastically. A fellow officer says: "That's it, get them riled up so I can mace them again!"

4.   A woman, also an OSU student, is arrested when she checks on her car to make sure that there is no parking ticket.

5.   At present, it is not a crime to have a party. Indeed, area residents complied with earlier requests by police to use plastic fencing to contain their guests and even made an announcement over a P.A. to cooperate with police.

6.   There was no provocation for police to charge the crowd. No bottles thrown, nothing set on fire *until* the indiscriminate use of knee-knockers and random arrests. Make no mistake this was a POLICE RIOT.

7.   IT HAS HAPPENED BEFORE. In Autumn Quarter 1995, police fired tear gas canisters and knee-knockers into residences and on the streets making a four square block area unbreatheable and then arresting those trying to find fresh air. IT WILL HAPPEN AGAIN.

UNLESS WE DO SOMETHING...

COORDINATE: ON FRIDAY, MAY 31, COPWATCH WILL SPONSOR A FORUM TO DISCUSS POLICE BRUTALITY. IF YOU WERE ARRESTED, FEEL YOU WITNESSED SOMETHING, OR ARE JUST INTERESTED PLEASE COME. TOPICS WILL INCLUDE LEGAL ACTION AND OTHER MEASURES WE CAN TAKE FOR WHAT HAPPENED MAY 17 AND HOW TO PREVENT IT FROM HAPPENING AGAIN. LAWYERS WILL BE PRESENT. 4:30 P.M. BROWNING AMPITHEATER (NEAR MIRROR LAKE).

DEMONSTRATE: SHOW THE C.P.D. THAT WE WON'T LIVE IN FEAR. JOIN COPWATCH IN A PEACEFUL DEMONSTRATION ON THE NORTHWEST CORNER OF 12TH AND HIGH (CAMPUS SIDE) FRIDAY MAY 31, 5:30 P.M.

COPWATCH
A DIVISION OF ANTI-RACIST ACTION

PO BOX 82097
COLUMBUS , OHIO
43202

(614) 424-9074

"A few observations from Friday night May 17, the last in a series of Police incited riots in the Campus area," and future events by Columbus Copwatch. From *ARA News*, 1996.

INVI̶ ̶IGATIVE/INFORMATIONAL REP
INTELLIGENCE BUREAU

░ect COPWATCH P.O.BOX 83097	Project # I-96-5	Activity Classification 138, Left wing	
░urce Printed Flyers	Source Evaluation X Rel. _ Unrel. _ Uneval	Date Typed 11/26/96 je	
░formation Personal Knowledge X Documents _ Conversation		Information Evaluations X Verified _ Unverified	
░vestigator T. Woodland # 956	Supervisor *I'L *Tim Warren	_ Further Inv. Required X For File	

░semination Authorization:
░y Bureau Commander   _ To Cols. Div. of Police   x Any Authorized Agency

░semination: _Cmdr Mincum, Zone 4 , Cmdr Eckles - Zone 3_
Cmdr Rod - Zone 2 , Cmdr Mattel - Zone 1.
D/C Durcier - Patrol Cnt · D/C Kean Patrol West

Summary:

Attached are printed leaflets that were being distributed in the campus

(OSU) area during the OSU v. Michigan football weekend. COPWATCH is an

off-shoot or sister organization of A.R.A. (ANTI-RACIST-ACTION). Both

organizations are loosely comprised of student activists, some youthful,

some more seasoned. The primary leadership seems to be ████████████

professor, ████████████ and local attorney and long-time activist,

████████████

Detective Terry L. Woodland # 956
Intelligence/Investigative Unit

962169

An internal report on Copwatch from the Columbus Police Department's Intelligence Bureau, July 14, 1997; names redacted by the authors.

may also prevent potential police brutality, and in cases where violence and brutality does occur Copwatch intervenes and records the incident by taking notes and using a camera/video camera."

The Columbus PD was "often involved in egregious acts of violence and unnecessary arrests and a lot of pepper spray," says Josh, a white Columbus ARA member core to its Copwatch program. Black students in the neighborhood around Ohio State University and residents of the adjacent working-class Black neighborhoods bore the brunt of this. "We saw, and heard reports of other times, police firing tear gas canisters through windows," Josh remembers. "They had a police helicopter, and they flew that almost nonstop through the second half of the 1990s, I swear. They would use it to intimidate, to come down real low, shine a spotlight on people, and use a PA system. There was just a general heavy police presence and repressive behavior."

As discussed in chapter 3, Columbus ARA was traveling to protests at Klan rallies all over the Midwest. But, says Josh, "We were seeing all this going around us with the police. And we were, like, 'obviously, they are doing more damage on a regular basis than these hate groups, so let's see what we can do about that right here, in our backyard.'"

Columbus ARA got a video camera and some still cameras, created a *Know Your Rights* pamphlet about what to do when stopped by police, and started going out to monitor the police. "Every Saturday night for a couple of years," says Josh. They used a police scanner to listen for incidents and would rush to the scene.

> We were constantly going out confronting the Klan and nazis, so we might have been a little too brash in our approach, a little too confrontational perhaps. We'd show up, we'd see someone getting arrested and their friends shouting "This is bullshit!" and we'd jump in, camera rolling, and say, "What's going on? Is this person being detained?" And we'd sort of push the line to see how we could help the person.

They would collect information from friends and witnesses, stay in touch, and refer people to lawyers when necessary. It was also an opportunity to collaborate with the nearest Copwatch chapter, the one being run by Kent State University students, two hours north of Columbus. Together, the two Copwatch chapters would attend each other's events when they thought backup was needed, trade *Know Your Rights* literature for distribution (same state, same laws), and generally check in on what methods were or were not working.

The annual African American Heritage Festival, a weekend of student educational and arts events, followed by socializing in the evenings, was a particular target of police, who would "go ballistic," says Josh.

> We went out to patrol as Copwatch, and we'd see things where there'd be a group of young Black people just hanging on the corner, just talking. A cop would walk by with a container of pepper spray like a small fire extinguisher, and just cloud it around the people, so they're in a cloud of pepper spray. At some point, the cops decided they wanted to clear out a 7-11 parking lot. They used wood knee knockers—wooden dowels. They'd fire them at people at chest height as they're running away.

Columbus ARA members met with the African Students Union, which organized the Heritage Fest. "We enjoyed a decent relationship with them. It wasn't a bad relationship, but we didn't do a lot of work together," says Josh. He attributes this to ARA's "punkity rockity nature," the cultural gap between student groups and community groups like ARA, and political differences. Rath, another white Columbus ARA member, is more self-critical:

> We always wished that we were more multiracial. We were trying to be more conscious of that by making alliances with marginalized groups, largely that were POC groups. So we formed a relation-ship with the African Students Union; we had a relationship with the Native American Center. Part of reaching out to those groups was probably hoping some would come to ARA, but they saw right through us.

She attributes Columbus ARA's whiteness to several factors, among them: "Speaking for myself, consciousness. It's one thing to believe in anti-rac-ism, to believe that a person is equal to me, but it's far different to do a deep level of work to break down racism. It just wasn't enough to form alliances with people when we didn't talk about the struggles of our lives, what it means to be a white person and a person of color." Rath is Jewish and queer but found those "big identity pieces" were "always sort of on the back burner in ARA." She also notes that during the period she was involved in Columbus ARA, none of the initial core group of young

Columbus ARA taking part in their local October 22 Coalition Against Police Brutality National Day of Protest, October 22, 1999.

Columbus ARA pictured on the steps of the Columbus Police Department headquarters, with the October 22 Coalition Against Police Brutality and community members, October 22, 1999.

Original artwork by Heather the bike messenger, Columbus, c. 1999.

Columbus, c. 1999.

organizers, herself included, was actually from Columbus. "I was invested in ARA, but I wasn't invested in Columbus per se.[6] And I wonder how much that played into us being unable to recruit more non-white people." She remembers, for example, that one of the few people of color in the chapter, an Asian-American, was part of a crew of punk kids who had grown up in a suburb of Columbus and who joined ARA together.[7]

In chapter 3, we talked about how ARA's anti-Klan work could be alienating for people of color. As Rath observes, "Not that many people of color are that interested in showing up to a white supremacist rally and wondering if they are going to make it out alive." The Copwatch program also involved risks for those who participated and was a tough sell to new members. Josh himself was arrested and injured during one Copwatch patrol, when attempting to intervene in an arrest; he eventually won $10,000 in a lawsuit against the police.

By 1999, several of the key people in Columbus ARA's Copwatch had become new parents and backed away from that kind of intense activism. The Copwatch project petered out. Copwatch had "felt like the right thing to be doing," Josh remembers, "but it didn't feel like enough, and it didn't feel real sustainable." Aside from burnout, there were hard costs. "We needed these little VHS-D cassettes. My partner, she shoplifted when we were broke and didn't have the money for it.... Sometimes it came down to petty theft to keep it going, I guess is the point."

A sticker and poster produced by local and non-local ARA members who participated in the Cincinnati rebellion of 2001. Cincinnati exploded in protest and rebellion in April and May of 2001, following the April 7 police killing of nineteen-year-old Timothy Thomas, the fifteenth African American man under the age of fifty to be killed by Cincinnati police between 1995 and 2001. It was the largest disturbance in the city since the ghetto rebellion of 1967 and the largest in the US since the Rodney King riots of 1992, in Los Angeles.

Justice for Edmond Yu
為余偉康討回公道

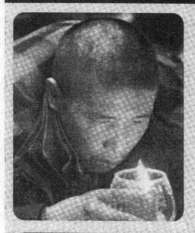

DEMO 示威

To protest the brutal killing of Edmond Yu by Louis Pasquino, police officer at 52 Division. Edmond Yu, 35 years old, was shot on Thursday, February 20.

二月二十日警察開鎗殺死余偉康，死因未明。只有透過公眾壓力，開庭聆訊，真相才會水落石出。

齊來參與三月一日〔星期六〕下午一時在中區華埠舉行之示威行動，我們將會遊行至警察總部。

SAT MARCH 1
Assemble 1pm
Dundas & Huron

March through Chinatown, along College St. to Police HQ.

VIGIL   公祭

A vigil will be held for Edmond Yu at the site of his death on Thursday February 27 7:00pm.

二月廿七日〔星期四〕是死者的頭七，

當晚七時在死者過害地點 (Spadina & Lakeshore)

將會舉行公祭悼念，超渡亡魂。

Meet at the "Spadina Loop", Spadina & Lakeshore.

Please bring a candle.

Did Yu deserve to die?

DEMONSTRATION ENDORSED BY: THE 519 • ABORIGINAL LEGAL SERVICES • ACROSS BOUNDARIES: ETHNO RACIAL MENTAL HEALTH CENTRE • AFRICAN-CANADIAN LEGAL CLINIC • AFRICAN RESOURCE CENTRE • ANTI-RACIST ACTION • ASSOCIATION OF CHINESE-CANADIAN SOCIAL SCIENTISTS • BLACK ACTION DEFENCE COMMITTEE • CANADIAN UNION OF PUBLIC EMPLOYEES - ONTARIO DIVISION • CHINESE-CANADIAN NATIONAL COUNCIL (TORONTO CHAPTER) • CHINESE INTER-AGENCY NETWORK • COALITION OF AGENCIES SERVING SOUTH ASIANS • COALITION OF VISIBLE MINORITY WOMEN • DEJINTA BISHA • ETHNO RACIAL MENTAL HEALTH COALITION OF METRO • ETHNO RACIAL PEOPLE WITH DISABILITIES COALITION OF ONTARIO • HISPANIC DEVELOPMENT COUNCIL • HONG FOOK MENTAL HEALTH ASSOCIATION • JAMAICAN CANADIAN ASSOCIATION • JUSTICE FOR FARAZ SULEMAN • LABOUR COUNCIL OF METROPOLITAN TORONTO & YORK REGION • LAW UNION OF ONTARIO • NEW SOCIALISTS • METRO TORONTO CHINESE & SOUTH EAST ASIAN CLINIC • MIDAYNTA • ONTARIO COALITION AGAINST POVERTY • ONTARIO FEDERATION OF LABOUR • ONTARIO PUBLIC INTEREST RESEARCH GROUP (YORK) • OPSEU REGION 5 HUMAN RIGHTS COMMITTEE • PARKDALE ACTIVITIES & RECREATION CENTRE • PARKDALE COMMUNITY LEGAL SERVICES • PRISON NEWS SERVICE • STREET HEALTH • STUDENTS OF TORONTO AGAINST RACISM • TORONTO COALITION AGAINST HOMELESSNESS • TORONTO COALITION AGAINST RACISM • WOMEN'S ACTION AGAINST RACIST POLICING • • • PRINTING DONATED BY CANADIAN LABOUR CONGRESS - ONTARIO REGION

Stop the Police "Shoot to Kill" Policy!
COALITION AGAINST RACIST POLICE VIOLENCE

for more information: Chinese-Canadian National Council (Toronto Chapter) 596-0833 • Black Action Defence Committee 656-2232
Anti-Racist Action 631-8835 • Toronto Coalition Against Racism 530-0262 • OPIRG-York 736-2100 ext.30323

Protest in Toronto in 1997 organized by the Coalition against Racist Police Violence. Poster by Toronto ARA. Courtesy of Toronto ARA Archive.

Aside from the occasional lawsuit, Copwatch's clear-cut victories were perhaps rare, but Columbus ARA members had contributed to the broader community effort against local racist police. Consequently, the federal Department of Justice investigated the Columbus PD, suing in 1999 to implement a "consent decree" with the city and to force police reforms. Although the Department of Justice abandoned the effort some years later, Josh calls it a victory and says, "That felt good, to be a part of that."[8]

Toronto

While Toronto ARA had come out of a majority-white left/anarchist milieu, "the initial ARA people were much more racially mixed, I think," says Judith, who is white, with a Jewish background. According to Harry, another early white member:

> As it grew in prominence and effectiveness, you started to get even a wider base, when we started to collect a lot of young folks who were coming out of high schools, who were great, amazing organizers, but [who] didn't necessarily have the deep political roots and background. And, quite frankly, that's when ARA became much more diverse and more reflective of Toronto at the time.[9]

Several Toronto ARA members of color took the fascist threat seriously, because they had seen firsthand the revival of the far right in Europe. For example, two young sisters named Nadia and Saba, refugees from Iran, had lived in Germany where Saba had witnessed extreme racist violence, and their whole family had participated in anti-fascist protests. When they learned that nazis were organizing in Canada too, Saba felt compelled to act. Neither Nadia nor Saba felt able to risk arrest by participating on the "front line"—"I can't afford to have anything on my record. In the body that I'm in, we're already racialized, we're going to face other barriers in life," says Nadia—but they attended several protests, and Saba felt "everyone had their autonomy to decide where to place themselves physically—literally—in proximity to the action." Nadia took on organizing the Rock Against Racism shows, while Saba, an "early adopter of online chatting systems," promoted ARA widely.

In a 1997 edition of Toronto's ARA newsletter, members described their motivations for being involved. C, "a 15 year old biracial female punk rocker," wrote:

Outside the courthouse during the trial of Kenneth Deane, the OPP officer charged with the murder of Dudley George, in Sarnia, Ontario, March 11, 1997. The judge concluded that Deane had knowingly shot an unarmed man and concocted a story to cover it up and convicted him of criminal negligence causing death. Deane was sentenced to two years less a day, served in the community.

> The nazis are the epitome of the racist society. They hate people like me and call us "mud people." For this reason I have chosen to get involved in the fight against them. Racism doesn't end with the fight against fascists, it extends beyond to other aspects of society: such as governmental policies, schools, religion, media and KKKops.... The ARA is a more exciting and interesting anti-racist group than most of the other mainstream ones.

"N, a 24 year old Filliipina" [*sic*] wrote:

> We are the anti-fascist youth who are self-educated and have learned the consequences of what hateful violent sick mother fuckers who would try to destroy lives of us diversified people, such as Native Peoples and people of colour, and our race mixing counterparts can do. This is why I love ARA.

On another tip, as an anti-fascist group, Toronto ARA prioritized good relations with both local Jewish organizations active against anti-Semitism and the far right and with individual Holocaust survivors. This wasn't without challenges. In the early days of Toronto ARA, the

Illustration by Gord Hill, poster design by Joanne Kewageshig, Toronto, 1997.

Jewish Feminist Anti-Fascist League (JFAFL) formally criticized the group after an ARA speaker declined to name Jews as victims of the German Nazis, calling Jews "the group that everyone knows about." The individual involved and ARA as a group accepted responsibility for the error, and ARA members with Jewish backgrounds formed a caucus to build solidarity.[10] The two groups, ARA and JFAFL, continued to work together.

Other, more mainstream Jewish advocacy organizations were harder to find common ground with. A speaker from Toronto's Simon Wiesenthal Centre, for example, invited to Toronto ARA's 1996 Youth Against Hate conference, said that anti-fascists must work with police to organize orderly counter-protests, and show "the silent majority … that you are trustworthy."[11] This difference in perspective could not easily be bridged.

Toronto ARA had its own basis of unity, which prioritized anti-fascist work but also committed the group to "support for broader anti-racist struggles." From its earliest days, the group worked closely with a local grassroots Black community organization, the Black Action Defense Committee, to mount protests against police shootings. Over the years, the group maintained relationships with other Black, Indigenous, people of color (BIPOC)–led community organizing efforts, including the Canadian Alliance in Solidarity with Native People, the Anti-Racist Response Network, the Toronto Coalition Against Racism, the Robert Gentles Action Committee, the Coalition Against Racist Police Violence, and Friends of MOVE. In this rich ecosystem of resistance, Toronto ARA was "not trying to do everything," says Judith. "Not trying to do all the work that other groups are doing around systemic racism, around poverty, [but instead] letting the groups do what they did and seeing ourselves as doing something different [that is, anti-fascism] and taking on that piece."

Indigenous peoples' struggles for self-determination and land are fundamental to social and economic justice campaigns within Canada. One campaign in which Toronto ARA took on a politically significant role concerned the police murder of Anthony O'Brien "Dudley" George of the Aazhoodenaang Enjibaajig ("Stoney Point People"), an Indigenous community on Lake Huron, west of Toronto and north of Detroit. The government of Canada had taken a large tract of their land in 1943 for use as a military training base during World War II, supposedly as a temporary measure. Despite the persistent efforts of the Stoney Point people, the government had never returned it.[12] In 1993, however, Stoney

In Toronto, in 1998, ARA collaborated with the Ontario Coalition Against Poverty and Active Resistance, a radical gathering, to put on a thousand-strong march with street youth who were being targeted by police for panhandling and squeegeeing. Poster design by Toronto ARA.

Pointers began to move back onto the military base in tents and trailers. Dudley George was a key person in this grassroots effort before being shot by a police sniper during a midnight raid.

Toronto ARA participated in the Coalition for a Public Inquiry into Ipperwash and formed relationships particularly with the members of Dudley George's family, who had participated in the land reclamation alongside him. In a common colonial dynamic, the direct-action tactics of the Stoney Pointers had not been supported by the First Nations leadership recognized by the government of Canada, and the political divisions within the community were reflected among those doing solidarity as well, with ARA choosing to align with those who were more oriented to (in this case, nonviolent) direct action. ARA chapters around Ontario worked together to organize speaking events and tours, a benefit concert, and protests in Toronto, London (Ontario), and Sarnia, the nearest city to Stoney Point. Eventually, ARA members helped to ensure that family members had independent standing and legal representation in the Ipperwash Inquiry, a formal and wide-ranging investigation called by the Province of Ontario in 2004.[13]

For many Toronto ARA members, this was among the most meaningful work that they did in the late 1990s; for some, the connection felt personal. John Bueno was an ARA member, a punk with Mexican background, who was also active in Zapatista solidarity. He had served with the Canadian Armed Forces Army Cadet program, and in the early 1990s had trained at Camp Ipperwash, during the summer camps that brought together cadets from around Ontario.[14] "Dudley George was probably there," he remembers. "I didn't see them [Stoney Pointers] up close; they were far. But I was there when they were occupying the thing. And then, later, I got exposed to all that stuff through ARA, and I went back to Ipperwash with you guys. Like, I was there. I remember sitting there and waiting in line for the mess hall. That was a crazy thing for me." For John, ARA was about way more than nazis.

> Honestly, it was police, Mumia, Dudley George, Stoney Point. All of that stuff really resonated to me. For me, it was learning about racism, about colonialism. I didn't know what the fuck fascism was.... For me, it was very much more like a right and wrong kind of thing. Racism is bad, simple. Police shouldn't shoot people. Native people should have their shit and have their land.

Event in Toronto in 1999. Poster by Toronto ARA. Courtesy of Toronto ARA Archive.

While there were certainly Black, Indigenous, and people of color who were dissatisfied with or outright critical of Toronto ARA's internal culture and politics, the range of activities and issues that the group participated in and the visibility of people of color in all types of roles contributed to the group's appeal to a relatively broad range of people and to its longevity and success as a chapter overall.

Detroit

Detroit ARA had a lot of the classic features of Anti-Racist Action chapters. They traveled to Klan rallies and opposed nazis in the area. They defended abortion clinics threatened and harassed by anti-choicers. They had strong connections with their local punk and countercultural scenes. However, Detroit ARA was also atypical in two key, closely connected ways: one, they organized not only against outright fascists but also around local economic issues, to fight broader institutional racism; two, they were a strongly multiracial, majority-POC chapter. ARA had, very broadly speaking, a cultural background of (primarily white) "anti-authoritarian youth culture" and a definite focus on anti-fascism, but Detroit ARA was uniquely successful in going beyond that mold.

Involved from 1997 to 2000, Charles joined an already established Detroit ARA chapter—members had been around continuously since early enough to help plan the 1994 MAFNET conference—but he saw it become bigger during his time. In particular, as a Black man, Charles wasn't the only person of color in the group when he joined, but he saw the group become significantly more multiracial over the years he was involved.

Charles explains that Detroit Anti-Racist Action "was kind of existing in the same space as a bunch of other groups that were made up of similar people with similar politics." There were prison support groups like Anarchist Black Cross or Books for Prisoners, the food salvaging Food Not Bombs, and the radical environmentalist Earth First! He explains:

> But all of those groups were almost, like, 100 percent fucking white, not even kidding—in Detroit, which I already told you is, like, 80 percent Black.... A lot of [them were] suburban-type people.... They weren't thinking about, "Well, let's talk to people in the community and try and get them involved." But Detroit ARA was, definitely. That was, like, one of our main goals, was bringing in people that weren't white punk rockers, you know what I'm saying?

And, of course, I'm a Black punk rocker, so they didn't get too far with me with that.... As opposed to Anarchist Black Cross or Books for Prisoners, which is helping some white dude in prison in Oregon, you know what I'm saying—not to say I'm not down with the white dude in prison in Oregon, but I'm in Detroit, you know? And I think we definitely had a very Detroit-centric aspect.

As we've seen, Black revolutionary Lorenzo Komboa-Ervin had questioned if ARA was an organization of "vanguard" leftist whites fighting "vanguard" fascist whites. During the late 1990s, Detroit ARA defied that description by working to address issues of importance to their local communities, namely, economic issues. A 1996 flyer from Detroit ARA includes demands around education, employment, social services, and public transportation—fairly uncommon causes among ARA groups. They demanded a bold rise in the minimum wage, then $3.35, to $7 an hour. They opposed cuts to summer youth employment programs in Detroit. When the city of Detroit and the Detroit Tigers, the city's Major League Baseball team, began construction on a new stadium, ARA demanded "a fair share of the jobs" for Detroit youth.[15]

While Detroit ARA sought to fight institutionalized mechanisms of racism like poverty, they also continued anti-fascist organizing. Charles explains that the different fields of work blended together:

> They were building a new jail, like, a juvenile detention center type of thing, so we protested that.... I'm looking at this flyer [and it asks], "Whose city is this anyways?" "We're against racist and elitist redevelopment." This is before people said gentrification, you know ... and then on the same flyer it has something about "Smash the Klan," you know what I'm saying, on the bottom. So it's kind of how we were, you know—we had that thing, and then we had this next thing, and then ... it might have been some clinic defense after that.

Detroit ARA was also particularly multigenerational. Charles and Kieran (the Baldie and founding Minneapolis ARA member) were in their mid- to late twenties, already older than many in the ARA Network. A few key "older white guys," as Charles called them, included Mike, the long-time anti-fascist, autoworker, and Love and Rage member who helped plan the 1994 MAFNET conference, and Bill, described by Kieran as a

Detroit Drum no. 3 (1999), published by Detroit ARA.

To: Mike Ilitch, Mayor Dennis Archer, The Detroit City Council, and The Big "3" Auto Plants:

1. Do not cut the summer youth employment programs.

2. Include Detroit youth in the Tiger Stadium Construction Programs, give us a fair share of the jobs.

3. Raise the minumum wage in Wayne, Oakland, and Macomb County to $7.00 per hour

4. Equal wages at all fast food restaurants in the Tri-County Area to at least $7.00 per hour.

WHAT IS DETROIT ARA?

Detroit ARA is a group of people from many different ethnic backgrounds that came together to fight against the problems we face. Problems like racism, sexism, anti - gay bigotry, anti - Semitism. We also fight for jobs for everyone that wants to work. A raise in minimum wage to $7.00 per hour. No cutbacks in Child Nutrition Programs, Food Stamps, Medicaid, or A.D.C. programs. No attacks on Affirmative Action programs or laws.

ANTI - RACIST ACTION
P.O. BOX 321211
DETROIT, MI 45232
(313) 730 - 3555

Detroit ARA flyer, 1990s.

"longtime radical and anti-fascist." Bill mentored an activist club at the all-Black high school where he taught; according to Kieran, maybe six to ten students "from working-class and impoverished Detroit neighborhoods, and *not* from the alternative subcultures [that so often fed ARA], frequently participated in ARA because of this relationship."

Altogether, Detroit ARA was uniquely diverse to the point that both the chapter and other ARA chapters knew it. After Charles "went to one or two of [the network conferences], that's when I realized that what we had in Detroit was kind of different and special, in terms of the makeup of the chapter and some of the stuff we were working on."

> I think other chapters had ... white punk rockers that were in their, you know, early twenties to early thirties, if they were even thirty. That was the general dynamic of [ARA]. But when *we* showed up, it was always a lot of people of color, and people of different generations. And, you know, sometimes they'd be, like, "Who are these old motherfuckers?" and then we'd be, like, "Well, your whole group's white."

Detroit ARA was one of the chapters pushing the network to have a broader anti-racist lens. In 1999, they submitted a formal proposal, mirroring some of their community-focused activism:

1) Take on Institutional and Economic Racism:
    a) Community and schools issues...
    b) Immigration issues...
    c) Issues of incarceration and genocide...
2) Give our anti-racist politics an internationalist application...
3) Strive to make ARA's membership more multiracial and international.

Unlike other proposals on similar themes presented by majority white chapters (Minneapolis and Chicago), Detroit's proposal was adopted by a strong majority.

Detroit was not the only chapter in which people of color made important contributions to Anti-Racist Action. It was not even the only chapter that had a large number of people of color. But after the decline of ARA's founding multiracial skinhead crews, Detroit ARA had uniquely strong contributions by people of color, with a focus on opposing systemic and economic racism and fostering multigenerational organizing.

Lansing

Ninety minutes northwest of Detroit is Lansing, the capital of Michigan and the home of Michigan State University (MSU). As we saw in chapter 3, a founding member of Lansing ARA, Steve, got involved in Anti-Racist Action early on, opposing the Klan all over the Midwest and helping plan the 1994 MAFNET conference. Steve started Lansing's chapter in 1992 as an explicitly anarchist group called Active Transformation (AT). Starting in 1996, AT and Lansing ARA were sometimes two different groups, at least in name, and sometimes not. Because the division was often porous, when it existed at all, we will use the name ARA here.

Lansing ARA strikes an instructional contrast with Detroit. Lansing also participated in broad campaigns against institutional racism; however, while the Detroit chapter was multiracial, Lansing was a mostly white chapter that worked in and helped grow an informal but very real multiracial coalition of activist groups united by anti-austerity and anti-racist politics. Importantly, it bridged campus student and local community organizing. Most members were students at MSU—that was why many of them had moved to town—but there were also students who were from the area. As Todd, one of those non-ARA locals, says, the story of Lansing ARA's coalition "doesn't start with ARA. It just starts with a bunch of kids realizing that they all agreed on a bunch of stuff; like, they all agreed that the cops were fucked up, and they all agreed that this shit that the university was doing was stupid." Their coalition demanded actions and policies from MSU's stagnant administration, organized against their city's racist police, and opposed Michigan's Republican governor John Engler in his never-ending quest to cut education funding, affirmative action, and general social spending.

Dr. Ernesto Todd Mireles, now a professor at Prescott College, was a student at the time and a founding member of the group that would build what was probably the closest relationship to Lansing ARA: the local chapter of MEChA, the Movimiento Estudiantil Chicano de Aztlán/ Chicano Student Movement of Aztlan. Since its founding in the late 1960s, MEChA has been an important organizing node within the larger movement for Xicane and Latine liberation, particularly among young people. Lansing's chapter was always something of an outlier within these broader circles, not least because it was an early adopter of the alternate spelling "Xicano," instead of "Chicano"—the two are pronounced the same—and, thus, went by the acronym MEXA. (The traditional endings,

-*o* or -*a*, reference the Spanish masculine and feminine; to avoid unnecessary gendering and the gender binary, some people use -*x*, while we
have opted to use -*e*.)[16] Xicane is a sort of chosen political identity of
Mexican Americans, whether they or their ancestors immigrated to the
US or lived in what is now the American West ("Aztlan") before the border
crossed them after the Mexican-American War of 1846–1848. Compared
to Chicane, Xicane generally implies more affiliation with a pre- and
anti-colonial, Indigenous-aligned identity.

MSU MEXA formed in 1992 and soon began calling for the
university to create a "Chicano/Latino Studies Center" offering a full
bachelor's degree and to join a grape boycott led by the national United
Farm Workers.[17] By April 1994, they had the capacity to organize a rally
featuring speakers from the United Farm Workers and the Farm Labor
Organizing Committee and attended by students from MSU and at least
five other colleges.[18] A year later, they organized a sit-in at MSU's administration building. Individuals attended from MSU's Black Student Alliance,
the Student Environmental Action Coalition, and Lansing ARA,[19] but
the budding ties among groups went deeper than that. Todd credits an
organizer named Jay, of the radical environmentalist Earth First! and a
radical feminist organizer named Nicole for first introducing MEXA to
the sort of confrontational and direct-action tactics that made a sit-in
make sense.[20] By 1995, Todd recalls, MEXA members were "absorbed
in" *Ecodefense*, the Earth First! manual of nonviolent direct action. In
October 1995, ARA, MEXA, and other activists disrupted MSU's annual
homecoming parade and pep rally, in support of the grape boycott and of
maintaining financial aid (such as Michigan's tuition waiver for Native
American state residents) and affirmative action.[21]

Lansing's anti-racist coalition, thus, went back years, but Todd labels
1996 a "watershed."[22] On February 13, 1996, MEXA members began a
hunger strike, lasting a week, to "recapture the grape boycott issue."[23] Todd
believes that without a variety of non-Xicane (specifically, white) comrades
in support roles, the hunger strike "wouldn't have been anywhere near as
successful as it was."[24] While MEXA continued its campaigns afterward,
the hunger strike won "a mechanism for removing grapes" from student
dormitories and a "No Grapes Day" every March 31. Steve remembers the
hunger strike as a major milestone. That was when he "had really started
to get to know several people," when inter-group solidarity "was starting
to become less of an abstract thing. It was like there was a … culture of

State of the People Organizing Committee

Makes a Call to Action...
End Engler's War !!!

Contact Numbers for the State:

Lansing - 517.374.6646   Email- Engler.Watch@umich.edu
Ann Arbor - 313.973.3031   Detroit - 313.965.0074
                Kalamazoo - 616.372.9527

Stop Welfare Cutbacks
Civil Rights
Homeless Crisis
Reproductive Rights
Tenant Rights
Police Brutality
Bilingual Education
Stop Union Busting
Financial Aid
Health Care
Livable Minimum Wage

All out in Protest Jan. 17 for the State of the State Address!!!

Partial list of Endorsers:
"Justice not Just-Us"

Alianza de University of Michigan, MEChA de Michigan State,Michigan Anti-Poverty Coalition,Homeless Action Committee, Social Work Action & Change Coalition, Joe Summers - Pastor Church of the Incarnation Thomas Saffold - Pastor, Bethelehem United Church of Christ, Jodi Atwood - Pastor, Guild House Campus Ministry, Michigan Welfare Rights Union, Minister Malik El Shabazz. New Marcus Garvey Movement. Universal Contact Center Church. Tom and Sue Ness, publishers, Jam Rag Magazine*. Economic Justice for All. Millie Hall, President, Metro Detroit Coalition of Labor Union Women*. National Lawyers Guild, Detroit chapter. David Sole, president, UAW 2334*. Job is a Right Campaign, Workers World Party, National Peoples Campaign, Alliance for Justice, La Onda Latina, Patricia Clair, President, Oakland County NOW, Latin American Student Organization(LASO) Wayne State, Active Transformation,Reverend David Kid, First United Methodist, Reverend John Rohde, First Congregational United Church of Christ.
(* organization listed for identification purposes only).

The list of endorsers for this January 1995 event, in Lansing, demonstrates the breadth of the anti-racist coalition that Active Transformation/Lansing ARA was involved with. Courtesy of Steve.

resistance, where we rally around each other all the time," and "the boundaries that exist with solidarity were starting to come down."

Soon this "culture of resistance" was drawn beyond the campus. In the span of four months, Lansing police killed Edward Swans, an unarmed Black man, in the Lansing City Jail; another Black man, named Rex Bell, died in police custody, and the city announced plans to build a new precinct on the north side of Lansing, a predominantly Latine part of town.[25] In the aftermath of the police killings, Steve recalled, at first, "we were not attached to anybody in the community ... not amongst the people who are really facing any of the [police brutality]. We were kind of trying to do our thing, instead of listen." But when the police raided a party at the local the Latin American Cultural Club, arresting or citing all hundred-plus people attending,[26] Steve says, "That was when we started to think about 'How do we organize in the community outside

STRIKE BACK AGAINST POLICE BRUTALITY!

STOP RACIST COPS!

NEVER

ANTI·RACIST ACTION

FORGET

STATEWIDE RALLY AND MARCH

SUNDAY MAY 12 *   3 PM

LANSING CITY HALL

REMEMBER BELTRAN'S RAID!
NO TO NORTHSIDE PRECINCT!

SPONSORED BY **ACTIVE TRANSFORMATION**
MEXA, AND ANTI - RACIST ACTION

A demonstration protesting the deaths of Edward Swans and Rex Bell, as well as the heavy-handed police raid of a local Latine nightclub and the city's proposed construction of a new police precinct in the primarily Hispanic and Latine northside of Lansing, 1996. Courtesy of Steve.

of campus?'"[27] In response to the quick string of events, ARA and MEXA organizers in particular began to engage communities off campus.

MEXA and ARA started going door-to-door together. According to Steve, "It was basically a kind of facilitated letter-writing campaign; go to houses, ask people their thoughts, if they wanted to fill out the card for where they would rather see the money spent ... and we'd send 'em in." They conducted a survey of community attitudes toward the new proposed police precinct, and about seven hundred out of a thousand respondents said they'd rather see the precinct's proposed budget, around $600,000, spent on other things: roads, speedbumps, a conflict resolution program, recreational centers for kids. Steve remembers a "general unpopularity of the police across racial lines."[28]

On September 26, 1996, less than six months after the city first announced the idea, the Lansing city council voted not to approve the police station[29]—to both Steve and Todd's enduring surprise. "Even to this day, I'm fucking shocked," Todd remembers. He reckons some city councilors might have been happy to have a reason to ax the proposal, and Todd thinks, "We provided them with the information that they needed, through the community survey that we did, that justified them being able to say, 'No, we're not going to build this.'" Steve explains:

> We were used to fighting and never winning.... That [the police precinct] was something that we organized to make ... not happen, and it literally didn't happen, and that was weird. [laughs]...
>
> The level of community organizing we did for that was also new ... moving the origin of our work from campus to different neighborhoods in the city ... [and] we didn't get a lot of people saying "blue lives matter." People were, like, "No, we do need to spend less money on the police."[30]

The precinct was eventually built a few years later. As Steve put it, "They just waited until the movement had dissipated, and then kind of snuck it through.... Without building some long-term political institution that could defend the gains, you know, we just lost them."[31]

On September 28, 1996, two medical students of color, only ever publicly identified as "a twenty-three-year-old Latino man and a twenty-two-year-old Black man," were attacked by members of the Theta Chi fraternity after accepting an invitation to a party at their house. The two victims alleged the attack was racially motivated.[32] Anti-racist students, including MEXA and ARA, picketed the frat house for at least five days straight. One day, "all of almost thirty protesters were given noise violations ... a misdemeanor that carries a $115 fine."[33]

The pickets and protests perhaps raised some awareness and added some pressure to those institutional processes, but they also had an energy of their own. Steve explains Theta Chi's significance for ARA specifically:

> We had already kind of started to get to know each other, but I think because we were there, and we were ready to throw down, that was meaningful, and it set the tone for later things. Developed, just, our closeness. We weren't just standing with signs at a building; we were out there ready to fight back against these, you know, frat boys who had done this hate crime.

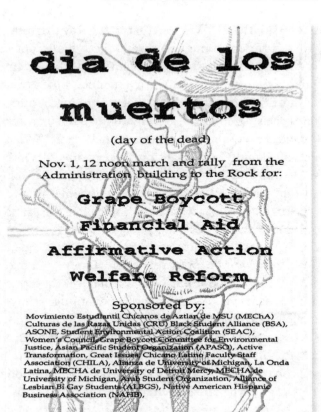

dia de los muertos

(day of the dead)

Nov. 1, 12 noon march and rally from the Administration building to the Rock for:

Grape Boycott
Financial Aid
Affirmative Action
Welfare Reform

Sponsored by:

Movimiento Estudiantil Chicanos de Aztlan de MSU (MEChA) Culturas de las Razas Unidas (CRU) Black Student Alliance (BSA), ASONE, Student Environmental Action Coalition (SEAC), Women's Council, Grape Boycott Committee for Environmental Justice, Asian Pacific Student Organization (APASO), Active Transformation, Great Issues, Chicano Latino Faculty Staff Association (CHILA), Alianza de University of Michigan, La Onda Latina, MECHA de University of Detroit Mercy, MECHA de University of Michigan, Arab Student Organization, Alliance of Lesbian Bi Gay Students (ALBGS), Native American Hispanic Business Association (NAHB),

Collaborating with MEXA was central to Lansing ARA's work during the 1990s, as in this 1996 event. Courtesy of Steve.

By late 1996, the activist milieu in and around MSU had the politics, network, and motivation to organize a march on the Day of the Dead, November 1, from MSU's administration building to the Capitol Building. A flyer promoted the march as a call for a grape boycott, financial aid, affirmative action, and welfare reform; Steve remembers one of the main motivations being potential cuts to the American Indian Tuition Waiver program. The flyer showed endorsements from *eighteen* different groups, including MEXA and Lansing ARA. Steve remembers the march as a "culmination" of the Lansing/MSU coalition. "In that moment, it was a dynamic and interesting thing," he says, which "tied campus to the city.... It was an anti-racist thing, against the right-wing governor, and it was against poverty."

The Lansing/MSU coalition involved multiple different student groups, but ARA's closest relationship was probably with MEXA. We asked Todd why MEXA and ARA worked together in the way that they did, and why they were different groups working together and not a single, harmonious, multiracial organization. Todd notes, "There were way more white students than there were Brown students. Like, thousands and thousands more." Thus, many white students grouped around specific issues, like anti-racism, feminism, and environmentalism, while Xicane students had control over their own organization. In short, "What we had *was* a very well-oiled multiracial coalition," he explains. "[White activists] brought something to us that we didn't have in terms of thinking through strategy and tactics, right, and we brought something to them … a certain type of, like, legitimacy around things like the grape boycott and Xicano studies."

Steve credits a large part of the coalition's success to MEXA's "openness" to contributions from white people. As he told Todd, "You had patience with people when they came around. I think that over time [one can get] less patient with some people … but in the beginning, I think [there] was … a real openness to that."[34]

ARA and other activists showed up for MEXA's events, while MEXA began endorsing and attending anti-Klan and other anti-fascist events— by Steve's memory, probably "all" of Lansing's events in this period. Todd caught an arrest at a rally against Michigan's National Socialist Movement. In fact, Lansing MEXA grew to have relationships with ARA well beyond their fellow Lansingites. In 1997, they hosted the national MEChA conference. Now thoroughly enmeshed in militant organizing, they wrote a proposal for, as Todd paraphrased, "a national MEChA structure that trained organizers to go out into communities to begin direct-action campaigns that centered around things like immigration and all this other stuff." Three members of Chicago ARA attended the conference to give a guest presentation: "Surviving a Radical Demo: A Workshop on Demonstration Survival Tactics, Self Defense and How to Keep Aware and Safe When Things Get Hectic. Tactics for Before and After Arrest, Dealing with the Legal System While Maintaining Solidarity." At the end of the conference, the hosts, Lansing MEXA, were kicked out of the national MECHA structure.

Other attempts by Lansing ARA to support POC-led organizing were less successful. Steve remembers that in trying to support Black student activism "the feeling was very different.… There was a handful of people that were very inviting and very supportive about [my] coming around …

[and] a lot of people were really opposed." For example, Steve was invited by some MSU's Black Student Alliance members he had gotten to know fairly well to speak at a Black Power rally. Steve recalls:

> It's in an auditorium, so there's, like, eight hundred people. And so, when I get up to speak, and people see who I am, there's a mixture of, like, you know, quietness, when they introduce me maybe a little bit of clapping, but then there's also some people, like, "get him off the stage!"...
>
> I think when I started talking about shit [support for political prisoners and the exploitative conditions of prison labor], people stopped booing. But when they [first] saw a white person come up on stage at the Black Power rally, I think there was some—like, "What the fuck is this shit?" Which, you know, is fair.[35]

The successful relationship between Lansing MEXA and ARA owed a lot to their members' personal relationships. Steve reckons "the road to developing strong multiracial solidarity in the fight against racism and other things, all the stuff we're talking about, was based on ... showing up time and again, being able to be relied upon, and building trust with people versus, like, a campaign where you move on to the next thing." To this day, Steve is "friends with a lot of those people.... [They're] almost like family now."

While Steve reckons ARA managed better than many, they couldn't completely escape the challenges of student organizing. Lansing ARA member Heather summarized this period this way:

> That kind of transient environment in a city like Lansing—where, you know, people come and attend college for a few years, and then move onto something else—was both a benefit and a deficit.... People could kind of come up politically in ARA and get more and more involved in the work and get really fueled by the work we were doing. But, then, as their tenure at the university [ended], they would kind of migrate to different places ... which helped to fuel movements [in] other places, but, then, at the same time ... worked against us in Lansing, in that there was kind of an ever-changing body of people.

Nonetheless, Lansing ARA has things to teach us, both good and bad, about relationships to place and student and community activism.

The coalition that ARA, MEXA, and other groups built sought to connect campus organizing with struggles in the city they lived in and the state Capitol Building they were so close to.

Los Angeles

The long-running ARA-LA, aka People Against Racist Terror (PART), and its founder Michael Novick embodied two crucial themes. First, although PART has always been a small group—two or three dedicated activists, including Novick, or sometimes just Novick—it "punched above its weight" by helping to build broad, diverse coalitions of anti-racist organizing. Second, Novick consistently published political analysis and education and influenced young activists in a network that often didn't focus on political theory.

Introduced in chapter 2, Novick was an experienced anti-racist when he founded PART in 1987 to oppose a speaking event by J.B. Stoner, a white supremacist newly released from three and a half years in prison for bombing a historic Black church in Birmingham in 1958.[36] Stoner was now coming to southern California "to do some talks on why AIDS was God's gift to the white man."[37]

In 1990, Michael attended the first ARA conference in Portland, Oregon.[38] The ARA model was attractive to him as a "grassroots, locally based, off the books, direct-action, anti-racist type organization." "I think one of the critical choices for us," says Novick, was that "around the time we formed PART, there were these other small anti-racist groupings that were starting that went the route of being nonprofits, that had 501(c)(3) status. We didn't want to do that. I felt like it was the kiss of death to become established in that way." Instead, Michael chose to remain connected with younger activists and based on the streets.

A central strategy of PART was to support, and often help build, political coalitions: the Pro-Immigration Mobilization Coalition, a coalition against the first Iraq war, Neighbors Against Nazis in Simi Valley and Ventura County, and the Crack the CIA Coalition. This last one was "a significant formation," says Novick, coming together after journalist Gary Webb published a series of articles documenting how the CIA had, at best, turned a blind eye to drug trafficking carried out by the contras, who were CIA allies fighting Nicaragua's left-wing Sandinista government—while the highly addictive product they brought into the Black and Brown neighborhoods across the US fueled the destructive crack

TURNING THE TIDE
ANTI-RACISM NEWSLETTER
Vol. 5, #5 - Sept.-Oct. 1992 - $1.00 at newsstands

People Against Racist Terror/P.O. Box 1990/Burbank 91507
24-hour Anti-Klan

Journal of Anti-Racist Action, Research and Education

TURNING THE TIDE
Volume 13 Number 2   Summer 2000 $2.50/newsstands
ISSN 1082-6491
INSIDE THIS ISSUE: Combat the Colonial Criminal Justice System
Land Struggle on Guam*Capitalism and the Iroquois*Vancouver 5
Demonstrate at Republican, Reform & Democratic Conventions

STOP BORDER VIGILANTES!
People Against Racist Terror*PO Box 1055*Culver City 90232*
310-495-0299* <part2001@usa.net>

Journal of Anti-Racist Activism, Research & Education

TURNING THE TIDE
Volume 8 Number 2   Summer 1995 $3.95/newsstands

Inside this Issue: Affirmative Action*Native Land Struggle
Mumia Abu-Jamal*Hiroshima Pilgrimage*German Fascism

MILITIAS:

ROOTED IN
WHITE SUPREMACY

Journal of Anti-Racist Activism Research & Education

TURNING THE TIDE
Volume 8 No. 4 Winter 1995-96 $3.95/newsstands

Inside This Issue: Anti-Asian Violence*Mexico
Police Brutality*Political Prisoners Speak Out

WOMEN PRISONERS RESIST!

Burbank CA 91507

Journal of Anti-Racist Activism, Research & Education

TURNING THE TIDE
Volume 11 Number 2   Summer 1998 $3.95/newsstands

INSIDE THIS ISSUE: YEAR 2000 & CHRISTIAN FASCISM*ALOHA MARCH ON D.C.*
PRISONS & THE GLOBAL ECONOMY*GAY NAZIS*COMMUNITY CONTROL OF POLICE*

Independence for Puerto Rico Now!
Free All Puerto Rican
P.O.W.'s and Political Prisoners!
People Against Racist Terror*PO Box 1055*Culver City CA 90232
Tel: 310-288-5003 ISSN 1082-6491 E-mail: <part2001@usa.net>

A Journal of Anti-Racist Activism, Research & Education

TURNING THE TIDE
Volume 8 # 3   Fall 1995 $3.95/newsstands

Inside This Issue: Free Mumia - No Let-up!
Europe *Tahiti*Canada*Militias*Affirmative Action*Calendar

BLUE BY DAY, WHITE BY NIGHT

POLICE AS AN OCCUPYING ARMY
PRISONS AS SLAVE LABOR CAMPS

Covers of
Turning the Tide,
publication of
People Against
Racist Terror.
Courtesy of
antiracist.org.

cocaine epidemic. Crack the CIA, according to Novick, "called for the abolition of the CIA and reparations to the affected communities and had significant Black, Nicaraguan, and Chicano/Mexicano leadership and participation and drew two thousand people to a downtown LA march and rally in a period when there were few large-scale protests." He also highlights the protests against the Democratic National Convention in 2000, when PART was "instrumental" in protests drawing six thousand young people demanding an end to police brutality, mass incarceration, and the prison industrial complex, as well as the abolition of the death penalty and freedom for all political prisoners.

Through *Turning the Tide* and other writings, Novick also published political perspectives influential in a network with young activists who didn't always come in with strongly defined political ideologies. Although they also sometimes used the name ARA-LA, Novick explains:

> We took the name People Against Racist Terror, I think, because we wanted to identify that the problem was terror. That terror was not something that took place, you know, in foreign countries, but terror was something that took place in the long history of the Klan and the Night Riders and racists who were trying to terrorize particularly Black communities and other communities of color.

Novick writes from an anti-imperialist and anti-colonial perspective that draws from both the contemporary and the more historical. Compared to ARA's beginning in the Reagan years, and its heyday in the post–Cold War "end of history" 1990s, Novick remembered more politically dynamic traditions. He explains:

> I came up doing anti-racist politics in a period when, you know, we had the Black Panther Party, we had the Revolutionary Black Workers, you had national liberation movements around the world and all kinds of Afrikan struggles for liberation, Afrikan Liberation Day in the United States.... ARA came up in a different context, where that was not as pronounced.

Through *Turning the Tide*, Novick promoted the revolutionary legacies of Martin, Malcolm, and others, alongside ongoing movements, from Puerto Rican nationalism through Hawaiian indigenous sovereignty to the Zapatistas. He taught younger activists, like coauthor Mike, about Martinican intellectual Aimé Césaire's analysis of fascism as the crimes of colonialism brought home to the metropole.[39] To go beyond simplistic models of "allyship," Novick's analysis of privilege is useful:

> It's a method of social control. If you look at prisons, they explicitly use privilege as a mechanism. If you're a teacher or parent you see it, which I've been both. Privilege is the flipside of oppression. If you're not oppressed, you're in some way privileged by virtue of not being oppressed, but it's still social control. If it's a privilege, it's not a right. Internationalism and solidarity are the road to liberation. If you want to be liberated, if you want to be free from a system that gives out privileges to control you, you need to fight that system alongside the other people who are fighting that system.

Novick wrote a book published in 1995, *White Lies, White Power*, analyzing the presence of organized white supremacists in prisons and the military, links between the Christian right and the racist right in the anti-abortion movement and anti-queer violence, different racist and right-wing responses to the environmental movement, anti-immigrant organizing, and other arenas of far-right organizing. The book was widely read within the ARA Network and, while Novick and his wife traveled across the country in the summer of 1998, he connected with and spoke to several chapters in an informal book tour.[40]

ARA was united by tactics and a militant attitude against fascism rather than by ideology or questions of political analysis. Novick was thus able to make a meaningful contribution to the network by being a voice—only one in a diverse crowd but a consistent one—for political analysis that was often less emphasized elsewhere in the network.

Turning the Tide, still published and extremely insightful, is available at antiracist.org.

These five stories illustrate similarities and differences in ARA membership and how different chapters approached anti-racist struggles beyond anti-fascism. There are many more stories to tell. ARA in Louisville, Kentucky, for example, a relatively diverse chapter, established a youth center that we'll cover in chapter 7, which addresses youth culture. At their height, Minneapolis and Chicago ARA were very racially diverse. On a different tip, Baltimore ARA explored the politics put forward by *Race Traitor*, a journal well-known for its tagline "treason to whiteness is loyalty to humanity" and the notion that racist capitalism also harms working-class white people. The Baltimore chapter was heavily involved in prisoner support and prison abolition work, getting its monthly anarchist newspaper *Claustrophobia* into prison facilities across the country between the late 1990s and 2002.[41]

Although this chapter couldn't be exhaustive, we can draw a few loose conclusions. First, for each ARA chapter highlighted, campaigns around broader anti-racist issues were important, even defining those chapters' activities. Second, today's discourse about BIPOC leadership and accountability to communities of color was uncommon within ARA circles, especially where ARA was focused on anti-fascism. Nevertheless, in broader anti-racist struggle, many ARA chapters sought to network with majority-POC groups with shared political ideals (like in Lansing or Columbus), fostered involvement of people of color (like in Detroit), or did both (like in Toronto). Furthermore, when people described successes or victories against systemic or institutionalized racism, they all highlighted relationships with a larger array of organizations and social forces.

Working against systemic racism was not the only way that Anti-Racist Action evolved over time. Though women in ARA had been fighting sexism, both within and beyond the network, since its beginning, the network evolved in the 1990s to fight in earnest for reproductive freedom and against the Christian right, the subject of our next chapter.

NOTES

1   The LA Uprising left in its wake almost fifty deaths, two thousand people injured, and nearly six thousand arrests of people accused of looting and arson. It took a combined fourteen thousand National Guardsmen, regular infantry, and marines, armed with tanks and live ammunition to take back control of the city from residents sick and tired of racism, poverty, unemployment, and mistreatment by cops and courts; see Anjuli Sastry and Karen Grigsby Gates, "When LA Erupted In Anger: A Look Back at the Rodney King Riots," NPR, April 26, 2017, https://www.npr.org/2017/04/26/524744989/when-la-erupted-in-anger-a-look-back-at-the-rodney-king-riots.

2   The literature on the Zapatistas is extensive. One good starting point is Gloria Muñoz Ramírez, *The Fire and the Word: A History of the Zapatista Movement*, trans. Laura Carlsen, with Alejandro Reyes Arias (San Francisco: City Lights Books, 2008).

3   The core of the original National Coordinating Committee was: Pam Africa (International Concerned Family and Friends of Mumia Abu-Jamal), Akil Al-Jundi (Community Self-Defense Program), Angel Cervantes (Four Winds Student Movement), Omowale Clay (December 12th Movement), Carl Dix (Revolutionary Communist Party), and Keith McHenry (Food Not Bombs).

4   According to "Structure Proposal for Anti-Racist Action Network (ARA-Net) submitted by the Trotskyist League" (c. Fall 1994), "at least 25% women, 25% people of colour, and 10% lesbian, gay, bisexual, or transgendered (l/g/b/t people) on whatever leading

bodies ARA-Network decided on. If that quota could not be achieved by including the specially oppressed from particular areas as representatives to the leading body, then one or more of those seats from the locality or region would remain open until the mandate could be achieved."

5 Komboa-Ervin did not participate with ARA after 1995, although several ARA chapters maintained friendly relations with him and groups he helped organize.

6 In fact, after a couple of years of hard work in the Columbus ARA office, Rath went on the road as "Nomadic ARA," living in an RV and traveling to towns and cities to support ARA folks and other activists.

7 Coauthor Lady, who joined Columbus ARA after the initial core group of organizers Rath mentions, *is* originally from Columbus.

8 Fast-forward to 2021, when twenty-six people injured during the 2020 Black Lives Matter protests sued and won a federal injunction prohibiting the Columbus PD from using tear gas, pepper spray, or wooden bullets against nonviolent protesters. Their legal team included Mac, who sees a "clear lineage" from the 1990s Copwatch work to this success; see Marc Kovac, "Federal Injunction Prevents Columbus Police from Using Tear Gas, Wooden Bullets," *Columbus Dispatch*, April 30, 2021, accessed April 5, 2022, https://tinyurl.com/ytk35hjn.

9 Several of these high school organizers had been trained in an innovative program called Students of Toronto Against Racism, developed by activist and writer Tim McCaskell, who was working with the Equity Unit at the school board. He later wrote about his experiences, including with ARA; see Tim McCaskell, *Race to Equity: Disrupting Educational Inequality* (Toronto: Between the Lines, 2005).

10 Among themselves, members called it the "Mischling caucus," *Mischling* being a word used by the German Nazis to categorize people of mixed heritage, "Aryan" and non-Aryan.

11 Anti-Racist Action Toronto, *Youth Against Hate Conference Report*, 1996, 17.

12 The lands were formally transferred from the Department of National Defence to the nearby Chippewas of Kettle and Stony Point First Nation in 2016, although full return is pending an environmental cleanup expected to take 25 years; see Tyler Kula, "Quarter-Century of Remediation Work Left at Former Military Base: DND" *Observer*, accessed May 16, 2022, https://www.theobserver.ca/news/local-news/quarter-century-of-remediation-work-left-at-former-military-base-dnd.

13 For more background, see *Aazhoodena: The History of Stoney Point Nation*, July 2006. https://www.attorneygeneral.jus.gov.on.ca/inquiries/ipperwash/policy_part/projects/pdf/Aazhoodena_history.stoney.point.pdf.

14 John remembers regular fights between racist skinhead cadets from Ottawa and the predominantly Black and Brown cadets from Toronto; white supremacist organizing within the Canadian military was a major issue in the 1990s; see, for example, Bruce Wallace, "Too Few Good Men: An Inquiry Reveals Ugly Truths about Peacekeepers," *Maclean's* 106, (September 13, 1993): 16–17.

15 "To: Mike Ilitch, Mayor Dennis Archer, the Detroit City Council, and the Big '3' Auto Plants," ARA flyer, date unknown.

16 See Andrea Merodeadora, "Latino, Latinx, Latine," Puentera (blog), Medium, August 7, 2017, accessed April 6, 2022, https://puentera.medium.com/latino-latinx-latine-a3b19e0dbc1c.

17 Ernesto Todd Mireles, "The Struggle for Xicana/o Studies," in Jerry Garcia, ed., *We Are Aztlan* (Detroit: WSU Press, 2017), 113.

18   Central Michigan, Eastern Michigan, University of Michigan, Oakland Community College, and Wayne State; Tony Scotta, "Hispanics Rally for Rights," *Lansing State Journal*, April 1, 1994.

19   Art Aisner, "Students Sit In for Grape Boycott," *State News* (East Lansing), February 13, 1995.

20   Ernesto Todd Mireles interview; Mireles, "The Struggle for Xicana/o Studies," 107.

21   The governor was scheduled to speak at the pep rally after the parade but didn't. (Todd reckons he was just "too rattled."); see Amy Snow, "Angry Crowd Protests Engler at Pep Rally," *State News* (East Lansing), c. October 7, 1995; Bob Allison, "MSU Parades Its Spirit, but Protesters Block Governor's Pep Rally Speech," *Lansing State Journal*, October 7, 1995.

22   Mireles interview.

23   Ernesto Todd Mireles, "'We Demand Xicano Studies,' War of the Flea at Michigan State University," *Latino Studies* 11, no. 4 (October 2013): 576. While the Delano Grape Boycott of the 1960s was more widely known, the United Farm Workers union promoted a grape boycott from the mid-1980s until 2000; see James Rainey, "Farm Workers Union Ends Sixteen Year Boycott of Grapes," *Los Angeles Times*, November 22, 2000, accessed April 6, 2022, https://www.latimes.com/archives/la-xpm-2000-nov-22-mn-55663-story.html.

24   Mireles interview.

25   Heather Morgan, "Swans' Death Haunts Community," *Lansing State Journal*, February 2, 1997; Betsy J. Miner, "Group Fights Police Station," *Lansing State Journal*, May 29, 1996.

26   Jodi Upton, "After-Hours Club Raided; 23 Arrested," *Lansing State Journal*, March 25, 1996; Jodi Upton, "Panel: 2 Sides Share Blame in Latin Club Raid," *Lansing State Journal*, July 16, 1996; Mireles interview.

27   Steve (Lansing ARA/Active Transformation), interviewed by Ernesto Todd Mireles, December 21, 2016; quotes from Steve not noted in this way come from interviews conducted by the authors of this book.

28   Ibid.

29   Chris Golembiewski, "Northside Precinct Proposal Dies," *Lansing State Journal*, September 27, 1996.

30   Steve interview.

31   Steve interview with Mireles.

32   Kelley L. Carter, "Police Investigate Alleged Attack," *State News* (Lansing), October 17, 1996; Kelley L. Carter and Rebecca E. Eden, "Activists React to Alleged Attack," *State News* (Lansing), October 22, 1996.

33   Kelley L. Carter, "Group May Penalize Fraternities: Interfraternity Council to Examine Allegation, Police Continue Inquiries," *State News*, October 25, 1996; Steve interview.

34   Steve interview with Mireles.

35   Steve interview with author.

36   "J.B. Stoner, 81; White Supremacist Bombed Black Church," *Los Angeles Times*, April 28, 2005, accessed April 6, 2022, https://www.latimes.com/archives/la-xpm-2005-apr-28-me-passings28.3-story.html.

37   A thousand people attended the rally against Stoner, according to Novick: "Glendale police shut the freeway offramps to prevent more people from arriving, brought out a water cannon (though they didn't actually fire it), and declared it an illegal assembly,

dispersing it after some teenage boneheads who showed up got their asses kicked before they could get into the meeting held at the Holiday Inn."

38   See "Portland Resists Racist Terror," *Turning the Tide* 3, no. 6 (October–December 1990).

39   See Aimé Césaire, *Discourse on Colonialism* (New York: Monthly Review Press, 2001 [1950]).

40   Michael Novick, *White Lies, White Power: The Fight against White Supremacy and Reactionary Violence* (Monroe, ME: Common Courage Press, 1995).

41   See the Claustrophobia Archive, accessed April 6, 2022, https://claustrophobia collectivearchive.blogspot.com.

CHAPTER 6

OUR BODIES, OUR CHOICE

"Girls Kick Ass" was a popular patch distributed by ARA, challenging sexist stereotypes and promoting women's courage, leadership, and agency. And women did kick ass in ARA, on all levels. They not only executed plenty of vital behind-the-scenes work to keep ARA groups strong, like facilitating meetings, keeping track of money and contact lists, and constant networking, they also took on roles as organizers, public speakers, graffiti writers, spies, strategists, and physical fighters. One way that women shaped the ARA Network was by mobilizing ARA's energy in defense of abortion and reproductive freedom. A key demand for people with uteruses is the right to decide whether or not to have children, and when. That right and access to abortion services (as well as contraception and reliable information on sexuality and reproduction) was under attack in the 1990s, as it is today.

Over the course of the 1990s, Anti-Racist Action defended access to abortion and fought for other pro-choice causes. Pro-choice work, in fact, became one of the foremost arenas of ARA's organizing because of a strong overlap with the street-level organizing and direct-action tactics that the movement was best at: ARA members and chapters physically defended abortion clinics, escorted patients to abortions, countered far-right anti-choice organizing, and more. The broader struggle for reproductive freedom encompasses more than just abortion access; many BIPOC women and poor or working-class women in general are at least as interested in protecting and expanding their ability to have children as they are in terminating unwanted pregnancies. Fighting the Christian right's attacks on abortion access on the ground was well within ARA's tactical wheelhouse, while advocating for more comprehensive supports for parents was not.

The cover of an Anti-Racist Action internal bulletin, 1997.

In this chapter, we'll look at how ARA chapters did this work, we'll connect it to campaigns for LGBTQ rights and freedom, and we'll trace how the ARA Network decided to incorporate a commitment to defending abortion rights and reproductive freedom into the points of unity—arguably the most significant political development within the ARA Network during the period covered by this book.

Abortion Wars

The right to have an abortion has been legally protected in the United States since 1973, when the Supreme Court ruled that people have the right to make their own medical decisions in the landmark *Roe v. Wade* case. In Canada, it took until 1988 for the Canadian Supreme Court to rule definitively that abortion is a medical service and not a crime. Access to abortion is declining in the US and is uneven in Canada,[1] and anti-abortion activists have never given up trying to limit or shut down abortion services altogether. The largest part of the anti-abortion movement, made up of conservative religious and political organizations, has been focused on supporting anti-abortion political candidates, lobbying elected representatives, advocating for restrictive regulations, and large-scale public protest. That part of the movement has had huge success in many American states and in 2022 achieved its goal of overturning *Roe v. Wade* at the US Supreme Court.

Beyond these legislative and legal tactics, in the 1980s and 1990s, "antis" directly targeted abortion providers and patients, harassing them outside of clinics and physically blocking access to medical facilities where abortions were performed. They committed acts of vandalism and property destruction, even arson and bombings. Most chillingly, they targeted doctors and clinic staff with extreme violence, including kidnapping and murder. According to statistics compiled by the National Abortion Federation, in the US and Canada together,

> between 1977 and 2008 there have been 7 murders, 17 attempted murders, 41 bombings, 175 arsons, 96 attempted bombings and arsons, 385 cases of invasion, 1,358 cases of vandalism, 1,833 cases of trespassing, 100 Butyric acid attacks, 658 anthrax attacks, 171 cases of assault and battery, 399 death threats, 4 kidnappings, 140 cases of burglary, and 506 stalking cases. The highest number of murders (4) and attempted murders (8) for any single year took place in 1994, during the Clinton era when the abortion wars were at their peak.[2]

The perpetrators justified these acts of terror against women and their support systems by referring to the Christian Bible and fundamentalist theologies. The Pro-Life Action League, founded in 1980 by Joe Scheidler, and Operation Rescue (OR), founded in 1986 by Randall Terry (later renamed Operation Save America in 1999), were at the forefront of very damaging mass campaigns in the United States. OR popularized mass physical blockades of clinics, intimidating both patients and staff; between 1986 and the early 1990s, "tens of thousands" of anti-abortion zealots participated in these attempts to deny women health care.[3] They were guided by the *Abortion Buster's Manual*, which further advised anti-abortion activists on how to collect personal information of providers and use it for harassment. For Randall Terry, ending access to abortion was just the first step in a moral overhaul of the nation:

> Once we mobilize the momentum, the manpower, the money and all that goes with that to make child killing illegal, we will have sufficient moral authority and moral force and momentum to get

the homosexual movement back in the closet, to get the condom
pushers in our schools back to the fringes of society where they
belong.[4]

Terry stopped short of endorsing murder of abortion providers.
Rescue America, founded in 1980, the Missionaries to the Preborn
(1990), and the American Coalition of Life Advocates (ACLA, 1994)
had even fewer scruples. Some of their members signed the "Defensive
Action" statement, which justifies the murder of abortion providers,
and the ACLA published the Nuremberg Files, a website sharing private
information about clinic staff, clinic owners, and pro-choice activists.
Meanwhile, the anonymous *Army of God Manual* provided step-by-step
instructions on vandalism, using butyric acid, making bomb threats, and
bomb-making.

Direct Action in Minneapolis

The first ARA chapter to really prioritize pro-choice work was Minneapolis
ARA. By the mid-1990s, the group had "done a really good job of pushing
overt nazis and organized white supremacists out of the urban areas,
so it wasn't something that people were having to deal with," explains
Katrina. The group began having more political discussions and doing
readings together, figuring out how to up their game and stay relevant
and effective.

> We still wanted to confront nazis and take that seriously, but as an
> organizing tool and a strategy, we were looking around and asking,
> "What is affecting the people in our community, in our neighbor-
> hoods, and in our city?" And we decided that police violence and
> harassment and access to health care were affecting people in a
> more obvious way in the day-to-day life.

At the ARA Network conference in 1995, Minneapolis ARA proposed
that ARA groups "start to embrace anti-racist and anti-fascist work that
more explicitly confronts patriarchy and homophobia" and suggested
focusing on "reproductive freedom (clinic defense and intelligence
gathering on the Christian right), welfare rights, exploitation of female
immigrant labor, anti-queer initiatives, queer bashing, and hate speech."[5]
Their first big opportunity to put their pro-choice and queer-positive
politics into practice came when they learned that the Catholic far-right

organization Human Life International (HLI) had planned its annual conference in neighboring St. Paul, Minnesota, in April 1997. "As ARA Minneapolis, we decided that they fit the definition of fascism to us," says Katrina. "They were really trying to limit the rights of women and queer people, so we decided to take them on with the same kind of energy and strategies that we were using against white supremacists."

ARA partnered with District 202, a queer youth community center, and other activist groups. They held a queer kiss-in at the St. Paul Cathedral where HLI opened their conference (the archbishop of Saint Paul and Minneapolis condemned HLI).[6] With this tactic, inspired by queer direct-action movement ACT UP and Queer Nation, "young queers felt excited and empowered to use public displays of affection to confront our enemies and make them uncomfortable, while we were celebrating our community. It was taking a stand, that queer couples should not be afraid and would be protected and supported," says Katrina. "Straight ARA members, especially cis-men," were strongly encouraged to participate. "Standing by wasn't enough; we needed them to kiss each other, and maybe wear a dress to the action also. Confronting homophobia in the system and the streets also helped us, as a group, challenge internal homophobia and toxic masculinity, and made space for more cis male affection." The action against HLI "went really well. It was incredibly positive. There were no arrests," says Katrina. "I was really young at the time, but there were just a ton of people even younger than me getting really energized and radicalized by this action. We decided to keep the energy going and asked ourselves, 'What else do we have to work on locally?'"

Minneapolis ARA identified over a dozen "fake clinics" that claimed to offer medical information, support, and services to people dealing with unplanned pregnancies. "Young women in our group would go into the fake clinics and pose as a woman who might be pregnant," Katrina remembers. "I did it and so did others, so that we would know exactly what was going on and confirm that they were definitely going to push religion on us and show us pictures of aborted fetuses [to discourage abortion]." Next, ARA followed up with action, with about a dozen members demonstrating outside a fake clinic in Robbinsdale, a working-class suburb of Minneapolis. They wheat-pasted posters over the windows of several fake clinics, exposing the fact that these facilities were not providing a medical service but were engaging in dangerously deceitful behavior.[7]

...You thought you wanted a pregnancy test, but that's not what they want to give you....

THE ATTACK OF THE...

FAKE CLINICS!!!!

If you were a good person, you wouldn't even think about abortion!

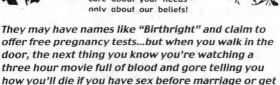

Remember, we don't care about your needs— only about our beliefs!

They may have names like "Birthright" and claim to offer free pregnancy tests...but when you walk in the door, the next thing you know you're watching a three hour movie full of blood and gore telling you how you'll die if you have sex before marriage or get an abortion. You've been fooled by the fakes!

Real clinics respect your needs. Real clinics will help you find prenatal care, adoption, a gynecologist, birth control—or an abortion. Real clinics leave your religion up to you, and they never try to scare you. You can find a real clinic by asking your doctor or by calling organizations like Planned Parenthood. * (612-823-6300)

This message brought to you by ANTI-RACIST ACTION
*ARA is not associated with Planned Parenthood

ARA chapters pursuing pro-choice work often sought to educate against "fake clinics" that have the air of being medical pregnancy clinics but are, in fact, counseling centers offering limited resources other than pressure not to get an abortion, Minneapolis, 1990s.

ARA joined the pro-choice movement to confront the anti-abortion movement's annual protest of the *Roe v. Wade* decision. "It was in January, so it was always really, really cold," remembers Katrina. "It was this intense action or event that was hard to do, but we felt that we needed to hold some space against these anti-choice people." Over the years, turnout would vary from a few dozen people to a few hundred.

The anti-abortion movement was also engaging in a cultural struggle against abortion, particularly among young people. To counter that in its scene, Minneapolis ARA produced a zine of abortion experiences. "We asked for stories from people, from the network of ARA and others we had connections to. We wanted to offer support and to normalize abortion and give young women the chance to feel okay about it or explore their feelings about it," says Katrina.

Minneapolis ARA's pro-choice work also gave them new tools for standing up to street fascists. When a nazi bonehead committed a gay

An action
cosponsored by ARA,
Minneapolis, 1996.

bashing, ARA and their allies brought two hundred people to the lawn of his home for a queer kiss-in. One of the survivors of the attack attended and told a local newspaper, "I felt a lot better ... to know that there was a really strong showing, more than I anticipated. Any sense of isolation that I might have had from the incident was washed away."[8]

A Pro-Choice Network

Minneapolis ARA was by no means the only chapter concerned with abortion rights, LGBTQ rights, and the Christian far right. Some Cincinnati ARA activists attended pro-choice events as early as 1990. The 1994 MAFNET conference had featured a workshop called "Fighting the Right" by Stonewall Union, the Columbus LGBTQ organization that had originally formed to oppose Jerry Falwell's (failed) attempt to establish a Moral Majority headquarters in Columbus,[9] and the 1996 ARA Network conference had featured Russ Ballant, a researcher on the Christian right, as a keynote speaker. Lansing ARA's first action as an official chapter, in

ARA Network Bulletin cover (1999)

1996, was against a fake clinic. Detroit ARA declared, "We are fighters for women's reproductive rights," in a 1996 flyer. Toronto ARA's 1996 Youth Against Hate conference featured a workshop sharing ARA's research on "specific and documented neo-Nazi and far-right connections to anti-choice and anti-queer activism and terror." Also speaking at the conference was educator and AIDS activist Tim McCaskell, who described homophobia as an ideological pillar of fascism.[10]

Minneapolis ARA took a further step to ensure that the ARA Network as a whole adopted a consistent pro-choice position. This wasn't a given. "I remember encountering vegan eco-warriors in the punk scene who wanted to be a part of ARA but were explicitly anti-choice," says Katrina. "Punks, vegans, and graffiti writers were pretty nomadic, going from city to city, and we didn't want them joining ARA chapters in other cities, and then affecting the strategic politics of Anti-Racist Action. We felt that we needed to make a stand and say that they could not claim Anti-Racist Action."

At the 1997 delegates meeting in Chicago and going into the ARA Network Conference in Columbus, Ohio, Minneapolis ARA proposed to amend the first point of unity to include "the Christian right" as fascists that ARA pledged to confront.[11] During the conference itself, Minneapolis teamed up with Kent ARA to propose that the points of unity be amended "to include the specific assertion that ARA is pro-choice." Toronto countered with a proposal to "leave the points of unity alone but develop a publication outlining the specific work chapters are involved in."

The debate was on. Anti-choice ARA members were a tiny minority, but some delegates opposed adopting a pro-choice amendment for other reasons. Some expressed hesitation about using the term "Christian right," fearing that ARA would alienate anti-racist supporters who identified as Christian. Others argued that reproductive freedom was not core to ARA's mandate. Still others feared endless debate on the points of unity, period, and pushed back on that basis. Delegates voted on a motion to open up the points of unity for amendment; the motion received 58 percent support. Because a motion to amend the points of unity needed a two-thirds majority to pass, no changes were made that year. Many supporters of the pro-choice amendment were frustrated, and some even felt betrayed by the chapters that voted no.

Throughout the next year, discussion continued by email, over the main list, and on a women's list, with excerpts printed in the *Network Bulletin*; here's one pro-choicer's response to an anti-choice email, which succinctly combines a variety of the arguments being made on both sides:

> People can be anti-racist/anti-fascist without needing to be pro-choice or a "right to lifer" ... one of our principles is, "Non-sectarian defense of other anti-fascists."
>
> [response] Pro-lifers are fascists! it's non-sectarian defense of OTHER ANTI-FASCISTS. If I saw an ARAer protesting at a clinic and blocking access to it, I would beat the living fuck out of him!
>
> ARA-NET should not alter their principles, because the chapters have already agreed on a set of previously defined principles, and modifying them to fit views that certain persons/groups may disagree with is unfair to the chapters that suffer losses.... [T]he changing of the principles for ARA-NET possesses a high probability of being a chaotic and somewhat costly decision for ARA-NET.
>
> [response] I'm sorry, but you seem very confused. Our vagueness and ambiguity causes chaos and I would argue it is costly in our fight against fascism. We are not adequately building a movement

against sexism, like the principles state. We're barely doing shit about sexism. If we take up the battle for reproductive freedom that would be a gigantic step forward. To me, fence-sitters on women's issues are in the same category as fence-sitters on race issues. It's impossible to not take a stance on an issue. Failing to take a stated position is to tolerate the current condition. Failing to fight for reproductive freedom is standing on the sidelines allowing fascist pro-lifers to scale back women's rights more and more. If this was a race issue, there wouldn't be any debate whatsoever, thus again proving that ARA as an organization needs to come to terms with it's [*sic*] sexism.

A year later, at the 1998 conference, delegates voted overwhelmingly in favor of taking a clear position on the issue (69 in favor, 3 opposed, and 2 abstentions) and formally agreed to expand the fourth point of unity by adding: "We support abortion rights and unrestricted reproductive freedom for all."[12]

After that, ARA organizers could more easily draw the line with anti-choice people or groups that wanted to join ARA. Josh, a Columbus ARA activist who continued to serve as a contact with ARA chapters all over, even after Columbus's de facto "national office" formally closed around 1999, remembers a lot of work "trying to get people to understand that, yeah, we're against racism, *and* we're against the anti-choice movement. One particular example that I remember, I think was in West Virginia ... [members of a would-be ARA chapter] were adamant about being pro-life and we were, like, 'No, you just can't.'" The issue was decided: after the amendment passed in 1998, ARA was always officially and explicitly pro-choice.

"I remember being demoralized that first year [1997], that it didn't happen," says Katrina. "But we were, like, 'We're going to keep doing this work and pushing for it,' and the next year we did get it passed, and it was even more explicit. We felt really good about it, that we had helped shape the direction of the network in a really positive way."

Columbus and Clinic Defense

By the time the 1998 pro-choice amendment passed, Columbus ARA was also incorporating pro-choice work into its regular activities, alongside the ongoing anti-Klan work, with the same dedication and conviction.

For coauthor Lady, just getting involved with Columbus ARA at the time, the pro-choice work of the chapter ended up being "the thing that stuck with me the most, and that I feel I put the most *emotional* investment into." She says, "I personally have always considered people who try to restrict abortion rights and reproductive freedom for everyone a form of violence against women.... It didn't seem like that big of a jump to me," from opposing fascists "to stand up against that."

In Columbus, as in many cities and towns, anti-abortion activists regularly harassed patients and staff at local health care centers that provided abortions. Churches and right-wing groups would take turns "to show up and shame women," says Lady. "Anti-choicers would come with really graphic signs that [were] factually inaccurate and doctored up to seem more horrendous.... They would physically block women from going into the clinic, push them. I've seen anti-choicers stand on rooftops and throw things at the women going in."

Columbus ARA members took part in clinic defense training offered by the clinics, and accepted shifts to "physically escort the person who was getting the procedure, so they wouldn't get hurt," or to offer rides. Other ARA members would

> hang back and look for safety issues.... And we would try to have some sort of presence to stop that from happening or to just send a loving and supportive message to the women who needed the health service. So it takes different responses to stop stuff like that from happening, especially [for] people who don't rely on police.

Like in Minneapolis and other chapters, Columbus ARA challenged the false information about abortion put out by fake clinics: "We just followed all that stuff around and tried really hard to tear it down.... Where billboards would come up, we'd try to take them down." And they contributed to intelligence gathering about the anti-abortion movement. When a friend and ally, Daryle Lamont Jenkins, joined a Columbus anti-abortion group to gather information, ARA offered concrete support. Says Daryle:

> I infiltrated those anti-abortion activists and found a cell of the Army of God which was calling for the killing of not just abortion activists but also of the LGBTQ community. I went in and IDed everybody. The guy running this particular cell was Chuck

Spingola. He was a nasty anti-gay activist. At the Ohio State House, he took down the Rainbow Flag and set it on fire. I would go to Chuck Spingola's house to have a weekly dinner and Bible study. ARA members would be outside waiting for me to get out. In case something went down, they would be there, literally guns a-blazing.

Columbus ARA was simultaneously defending a clinic on a weekly basis and secretly acting as a security detail for Daryle.[13] The infiltration ended when he was asked to not come to dinner anymore: "a few weeks later, they saw me doing clinic defense and they were sooo pissed."[14]

In July 2001, Columbus ARA members traveled to Wichita, Kansas, to participate in the defense of Women's Health Care Services operated by Dr. George Tiller. The anti-abortion group Operation Save America (formerly Operation Rescue) had planned for a week-long protest at the gates of the clinic, dubbing it their "Summer of Mercy Renewal" tour, after their successful "Summer of Mercy" event ten years earlier at the very same clinic plus two other locations.[15] Dr. Tiller—the man whose motto was "trust women"—was one of only three US doctors providing abortions after twenty-one weeks of gestation.

The anti-abortion movement focused on these very rare procedures to erode support for all abortion and targeted Dr. Tiller in every way possible. According to the *New York Times*, anti-choice activists

> blockaded his clinic; campaigned to have him prosecuted; boycotted his suppliers; tailed him with hidden cameras; branded him "Tiller the baby killer"; hit him with lawsuits, legislation and regulatory complaints; and protested relentlessly, even at his church. Some sent flowers pleading for him to quit. Some sent death threats.[16]

His clinic was bombed in 1986 (no arrests were made). Rachelle Shannon tried to kill him in 1993, firing five shots while he was in his car, wounding him in both arms. Shannon served a prison sentence and was released in 2018.[17] When the clinic was severely vandalized in early May 2009, Tiller reportedly asked the FBI to investigate the incidents.

Lady was among the Columbus ARA members who traveled to Wichita to take part in the defense of Tiller's clinic. Throughout the days of protest, hundreds of protesters on both sides vied for position surrounding the clinic gate, the only entrance for vehicles carrying

This image of ARA and local pro-choice activists, in Wichita, in July 2001, appeared on an abolish abortion website, hence the title it was given. When anti-fascists took a break from the human wall, a few anti-choicers would always come to "comfort" us.

patients. "The jostling began as early as 5 a.m.," reported the *Wichita Eagle*. "Tension escalated as more and more people from both camps squeezed into areas on both sides of the clinic driveway, bordered by temporary fencing to keep back protestors."[18]

Columbus ARA's Josh remembers being surrounded by "hundreds, if not a thousand, people around this clinic." He says:

> So it was, like, a driveway, right, into the clinic, and both sides
> had, like, barricades so that people couldn't block the driveway.
> So anti-choicers would get there early and stand at the barricades
> and just be a menacing group of assholes as women drove into the
> clinic. And so we hadn't got there early enough that day to beat
> them to it, so then we had to try and get up to the front—and I did
> that as gently as I could.

That didn't work out great for him, though. Josh wanted to bring his sign to the driveway and show the passing women who were seeking medical services a sign of support among the overwhelmingly anti-choice signs.

The Siege

of

Wichita

by
Peggy Jarman

© 1994

To Sam + Refuse +
Resist et al.
We drew the line in
Wichita "Summer of Renewal"
2001 July 15-21
You Rock!!
Ramona
7/21/01

An unpublished 1994 manuscript gifted to Columbus ARA by a local pro-choice activist after defending Dr. Tiller's clinic together, in Wichita, in July 2001, at Operation Save America's "Summer of Mercy" demonstration. The manuscript, written by the tenacious champion of reproductive freedom Peggy Bowman Jarman, was a firsthand account of Operation Rescue's first descent upon the same clinic in the summer of 1991. Peggy never sought a publisher; she wrote in her Acknowledgments: "I wrote this book primarily for me. It was my therapy, my survival. But it contains my heart and soul and I want to share it with people who are closest to me." Peggy passed away in 2016 at the age of seventy-five.

When he entered the crowd of anti-choicers, though, a woman called out to police that he was assaulting her. Josh explains:

> So then I was dragged out of the crowd by the cops and then taken downtown. I spent the afternoon in jail. I got bailed out. And then Planned Parenthood ... got me representation.

In the end, Josh's case was dismissed, because he was the only party that showed up to court.

Just as they did back home, Columbus ARA buddied up with locals to take their lead, showing up before the events and staying after, according to Lady. This often meant putting aside political differences with other groups, as long as they confronted the bad guys and defended the clinic. For example, Lady was incorrectly identified by local media as a member of a Maoist organization that ARA joined in the streets; given that they were aiming at the same target, though, the misidentification didn't trouble her.

More fundamentally, connecting with locals meant building relationships that are often profound in shaping and sharing our political identity and human existence. A local pro-choice activist, a stranger to Columbus ARA before fighting alongside them during Tiller's clinic defense, invited members to stay at her home to rest up. "I have a keepsake that Ramona gave me before ARA left town," says Lady, "a signed manuscript of a book Peggy Jarman was writing on the violence endured by the very clinic we were defending. It was an eye-opening experience, an emotional time for me."[19]

Dr. George Tiller was assassinated by an anti-abortion zealot on May 31, 2009.[20] He was wearing a bulletproof vest while serving as an usher at his church.

Emergency in Ontario

Up in Ontario, ARA groups were also taking on the fight against the Christian right and for reproductive freedom. In 1998, ARA learned of an upcoming tour of eighteen Ontario cities by the US-based anti-abortion group Missionaries to the Preborn (MTTP), headed by Matthew Trewhella, described by *NOW Magazine* as "one of America's most extreme anti-abortionists, a booster of the militia movement and someone who has publicly condoned the killing of an abortion doctor."[21] (Fast-forward to 2020, when Trewhella advocated against masking during the COVID-19 pandemic, comparing mask mandates to the Holocaust.)[22] Toronto ARA spread the word to other chapters and allies, who sprang into action. Giles, with Peterborough ARA at the time, remembers their action as "one of the great moments" of their chapter.

> We went in person to the local pro-choice clinic to warn them and put the word out to all the mainstream feminist groups and the older respectable left-wing people in Peterborough. It's one of

those issues that everyone's on board with. I felt proud that we were the ones who pulled it all together. Involving the more institutional and mainstream groups in a direct action, on the street. And, in the meantime, some of the more punk-ass members were finding the MTTP vehicles and slashing their tires.

The next day, MTTP was in Toronto. There too they were confronted by a hundred pro-choicers, in a demo hurriedly called by ARA. "[Anti-choice] organizers say they have never met with the kind of hostility displayed by the ARA counter-protesters, some of whom wore masks and carried signs affixed to baseball bats," according to an article in an anti-abortion newsletter.[23] ARA's actual tactics that day mainly consisted of unplanned acts of civil disobedience, sitting in the street and blocking traffic to limit the number of people who would see the MTTP and their signs. Police arrested eleven people, some roughly. "I was charged with assaulting police," says Giles, who had come into Toronto for the demo. "I was tackled, bleeding, and had my shirt ripped all the way off, so I guess they had to charge me with that. A young member got his nose broken." There were dozens of court hearings before the charges were "stayed" because of unreasonable delay in bringing those arrested to trial.

Following the demonstrations organized by ARA and allies, Canada's national television broadcaster, the CBC, aired a documentary highlighting Trewhella's support for murder of abortion providers and his involvement in the militia movement. Campaign Life Coalition, the main Canadian anti-abortion network, responded by distancing themselves from Missionaries to the Preborn,[24] and there is no sign that MTTP ever returned to Canada. ARA's determination to expose, oppose, and confront the MTTP had an impact.

Next, Toronto ARA learned that Human Life International (the same Catholic far-right organization protested by Minneapolis ARA in 1996) would be hosting its annual conference in Toronto in March 1999. Among the speakers was Joan Andrews-Bell, a friend and former employer of James Kopp, who was suspected of shooting three Canadian abortion doctors: Dr. Garson Romalis, in Vancouver in 1994, Dr. Hugh Short, in Hamilton, Ontario, in 1995, and Dr. Jack Faiman, in Winnipeg in 1997.

The HLI event was planned at a suburban venue, inaccessible by public transit. With plenty of time to prepare and a commitment to building the largest protest possible, Toronto ARA approached the Ontario

ARA at the annual Pride march, Toronto, 1999. Banner slogans included: "Pro Sex Pro Queer Pro Choice No Fear." "Support Your Local Prostitutes." "Rainbow Flags for Mumia."

Coalition for Abortion Clinics (OCAC). Both groups knew challenges could arise in working together, given ARA's more provocative public image and confrontational tactics. To maximize cooperation, while minimizing friction, the two groups decided that the OCAC would organize a demo on the conference's first day, while ARA would lead a demo on the "Youth Day." There were still disagreements, though. Jane, an ARA organizer, laughs as she recalls one coalition meeting:

> We were doing the artwork, and they didn't like the artwork. I think at one point there was a penis on one of the posters, and they made us take it off. So that was a lesson in diversity of tactics. It took a lot of effort to work with people who were coming from such a different kind of political organizing background than we did. Things that we just didn't care about, they cared deeply about. I'm making fun of them about the penis, but I'm not making fun of them for having a different perspective. You put these two groups together, and they are going to be baffled by one another.[25]

Mainstream media ran several stories in the days leading up to the HLI conference and the protests, often giving voice to the pro-choice and anti-racist organizers about anti-Semitic comments by HLI's founder, the overt homophobia of the conference program, and HLI's links to anti-abortion terrorism.[26] There was also a lot of hand-wringing in the media about the potential for confrontation between HLI and pro-choice protesters. The last HLI annual conference held in Canada, in Montréal, in 1995, had been the target of militant protest. The organization's US president Richard Welsh told media that "his group faces more hostility in Canada than any other country,"[27] but he hoped police security would be more effective at the Toronto event. Fears of the pro-choice mobilization had already forced a change in conference planning. Theresa Bell, the head of HLI Canada, admitted publicly that the organization had decided against staging their customary public march from a cathedral to the conference venue to avoid protests.

Jane stepped up to attend the HLI Youth Day undercover: "I grew up going to mass. Yes, I could blend in as a person from a Catholic family, and as a person with normal hair." She went inside with 150 young anti-abortion activists and a pocket full of quarters to make payphone calls and found it a very strange event. "All the speakers were treated like complete rock stars by the teenagers who were there," she remembers.

> Someone would go up—someone I had never heard of in my life— and the other youth would freak out, cheering and screaming. Most of the speakers were older, and it was all very finger-wagging: don't have sex; don't masturbate. If you want to date, that's fine, but if you have sex with the person you are dating—that's abuse.

The Youth Day activities took place on the ground floor of a hotel. Meanwhile, four hundred pro-choice protesters had gathered outside. Many pro-choicers had come in from out of town for the showdown, from as far as Montréal (including Montréal ARA). Riot police were there in force, some on horseback.[28] With info from Jane, ARA organizers marshalled the crowd away from the police lines to just the right spot, directly outside the venue with only tinted windows separating the demo from the HLI youth inside. Jane says attendees could hear the ruckus outside and the loud banging on the windows. The effect was dramatic. "I remember people being so scared that they literally knelt and prayed," she says. "They were not just intimidated. They were completely afraid." The day ended memorably, with protesters picking up horseshit and chucking it at police.

ARA didn't know it at the time, but HLI Canada was already on its last legs. Just a few months later, in July 1999, the HLI Canada board

In a mailing sent out by Austin ARA, 1997.

A rather famous design from Louisville ARA, c. 2000.

of directors announced the dissolution of the organization, due to the Canadian government's decision to revoke its status as a "charity" and, thus, reduce tax incentives for supporter donations.[29] This was the last HLI conference held in Canada. However, hundreds of Canadian anti-abortion groups with charitable status still existed.[30]

ARA had succeeded in obstructing some of the American anti-abortion groups bringing terror tactics to Canada. Meanwhile, ARA Kitchener-Waterloo and its affiliate the K-W Youth Collective focused their efforts locally. Abortions were performed weekly at the local Grand River Hospital, and anti-abortion activists held a regular "vigil" outside the hospital on that day. ARA K-W decided to disrupt their activities. "We did that for a long time, probably a couple of years," says Davin Charney, who believes that ultimately ARA's efforts were successful. "I think they stopped. I think we demoralized them and just made it unpleasant for them to be out there standing on the sidewalk. There were confrontations. After they'd have big prayer sessions, and they'd form a circle, and we'd be all around them."

These examples of ARA's pro-choice work are inspiring, but they don't tell the whole story: ARA groups defended reproductive freedom in towns and cities all over North America. "I feel like it was really good for ARA to bring this young, unfunded, direct-action-oriented energy to the pro-choice movement," says Katrina from Minneapolis ARA. "And, culturally, we made space for people to talk about reproductive health care if they needed it." Coauthor Lady agrees:

> I always felt it was more effective when we did use a diversity of tactics against people who are refusing to acknowledge the freedoms that all women should have, health care being one of them.... I really believe that the fight for reproductive freedom—from abortion rights to social justice—would be more effective if anti-fascists would take this cause up again.

The pro-choice focus was important within the ARA Network as well. "You have a bunch of women doing this anti-fascist work, and we saw the links between overtly fascist organizers and these far-right Christian groups. That was really important for me as a feminist," says Jane. "I think there was a lot of appetite for organizing work that was specific to our bodies." The pro-choice focus of ARA emerged from and further enhanced women's organizing within ARA.

NOTES

1　In Canada, typical abortion services are more easily obtained in urban centers than small towns and rural areas. They are covered by public medical insurance and, therefore, completely free to citizens, permanent residents, and refugees (undocumented people do not have insurance).

2　Aaron Winter, "Anti-Abortion Extremism and Violence in the United States," in George Michael, ed., *Extremism in America* (Gainesville: University Press Florida, 2013), accessed April 6, 2022, https://tinyurl.com/2u8xme6m.

3　Patricia Baird-Windle and Eleanor J. Bader, *Targets of Hatred: Anti-Abortion Terrorism* (London: Palgrave MacMillan, 2001), 88.

4　From www.orn.org, unavailable April 13, 2022, cited in ibid., 8.

5　Minneapolis ARA, *Structure and Strategy Proposal for an Anti-Racist Action Network*, c. October 1995.

6　"Minneapolis ARA Report," *Anti-Racist Action Bulletin* no. 6.

7　Fake clinics are still a problem today; see Lady Elaine, "Confronting 'Crisis Pregnancy Centers,'" Idavox, 2018, accessed April 6, 2022, https://idavox.com/index.php/2018/04/09/confronting-crisis-pregnancy-centers.

8　Rachel Gold, "Bias Case Goes to Court," *Focus Point* (Minneapolis, MN), September 25–October 1 1996; cited in *ARA Network Bulletin* no. 2, 1996.

9　"Stonewall Union History," 2, accessed April 6, 2022, https://kb.osu.edu/bitstream/handle/1811/47123/EA.2.225.xxx.pdf.

10　Tim McCaskell differentiated between the "religious world" up until about 1600 and the "racist world" that Europeans created alongside genocidal colonialism and chattel slavery. Said McCaskell, "In a religious world, non-reproductive sexuality can be seen as a sin or something weird and therefore gets treated differently in different times. But in a racist world, non-reproductive sexuality is not a matter of immorality. It's a matter of betraying the race. And therefore lesbians and gay men are seen as race traitors.… Homophobia becomes a logical and central outcome of fascism's notion of race and the importance of race in this world". Anti-Racist Action Toronto, *Youth Against Hate Conference Report*, 1996, 26.

11　They also proposed to add the phrase "direct action" and two entirely new points, one addressing "state and institutional racism" and another encouraging "equal participation of all our members." These proposals were discussed at the delegates meeting but were never brought to a vote.

12　*Anti-Racist Action Network Bulletin* 2, no. 1 (January 1999).

13　For more about the info gathered from the infiltration and clinic defense work in Columbus c. 2000–2001, see Daryle Lamont Jenkins, "Clinic Defense," Idavox, 2001, accessed April 6, 2022, https://idavox.com/index.php/2001/06/16/clinic-defense.

14　Daryle later founded the One People's Project, was interviewed repeatedly as an expert on "antifa" during the Trump presidency, and has been involved with film projects, including an Oscar-nominated film; Guy Nattiv, dir., *Skin* (Beverly Hills: New Native Pictures, 2018). It's unlikely that he'd be able to successfully infiltrate any far-right group again!

15　At the 1991 Summer of Mercy event, which lasted six weeks, over 2,600 anti-choicers were arrested, attracting considerable media attention.

16　David Barstow, "An Abortion Battle, Fought to the Death," *New York Times*, July 25, 2009.

17   Associated Press, "Rachelle 'Shelley' Shannon, Activist Who Shot Abortion Doctor George Tiller, Released from Prison," *Washington Times* (DC), November 7, 2018, accessed April 6, 2022, https://www.washingtontimes.com/news/2018/nov/7/rachelle-shelley-shannon-activist-who-shot-abortio.

18   Tim Potter and Lillian Zier Martell, "Two Protestors Arrested at Abortion Clinic Gates," *Wichita Eagle*, July 1, 2001.

19   Peggy Jarman, *The Siege of Wichita*, 1994, remains unpublished.

20   Scott Roeder was given a more lenient sentence in 2016, after serving seven years; Roxana Hegeman, "Man Who Killed Wichita Abortion Provider Is Resentenced," Associated Press, November 23, 2016, accessed April 6, 2022, https://www.kansas.com/news/local/crime/article116655173.html.

21   Scott Anderson, "Deadly Inspiration: The Brain Behind the Roving Anti-Abortion Demos About to Hit Ontario Says Killing Doctor Is Sometimes Ok," *NOW Magazine* (Toronto, ON), July 2–8, 1998.

22   Eddie Morales, "A Milwaukee Pastor Compared Mask Mandates to the Holocaust at a Brookfield Common Council Meeting," *Milwaukee Journal Sentinel*, July 24, 2020, accessed April 6, 2022, https://tinyurl.com/yvrsxjk5.

23   "Bat-Wielding ARA Protestors Beat Assault, Obstruction Rap," *Interim* (Hamilton, ON), October 28, 2000, accessed April 6, 2022, http://www.theinterim.com/issues/pro-life/bat-wielding-ara-protestors-beat-assault-obstruction-rap.

24   "CBC Documentary Alleges Pro-Life Links to US Extremists," *Interim* (Hamilton, ON), February 15, 1999, accessed April 6, 2022, http://www.theinterim.com/issues/cbc-documentary-alleges-pro-life-links-to-u-s-extremists.

25   Jane interview.

26   Jane Gadd, "Toronto Abortion Clash Expected; Jewish Organizations Blast 'Racist Rhetoric,'" *Globe and Mail* (Toronto), April 6, 1999, A7.

27   Louise Surette, "On Wednesday, Hundreds of Pro-Life Advocates Will… ," *CanWest News* (Don Mills, ON), April 5, 1999.

28   "Acting Our RAGE against HLI," *On the Prowl, News Bulletin of Anti-Racist Action, Toronto* no. 14 (Summer 1999): 4.

29   "Two National Pro-Life Groups Shutting Down," *Catholic Insight*, September 1999, 27, Academic OneFile.

30   Joyce Arthur, Anita Krajnc, and Nancy Zylstram, "Defining Charity," *Peterborough Examiner*, May 3, 2004.

CHAPTER 7

BE YOUNG. HAVE FUN.
SMASH RACISM.

The title of this chapter was one of ARA's most common unofficial mottos, and it says a lot. Since founding skinheads defended their scenes in Minneapolis's Uptown, on Chicago's Belmont, and around Cincinnati's Short Vine Street, ARA promoted militant anti-racism as a natural and attractive course of action for young people. As Walter, of Edmonton and Montréal ARA, put it simply, "We were the cool kids." He explained:

> We put forth that, hey, we should be having a good time, *and* we should be *explicitly* anti-racist, and we had a lot of success with that. That became a source for recruitment, for funding, but also to [be] the cool kids in our scenes … to challenge [fascists in youth scenes] and, you know, build up a more authentic anti-racist youth scene that was just better…. We did it because this was our scene, this was where we came from, and we were sure as fuck not gonna let nazis come in and fuck it up for us.

As ARA grew, it stayed connected to youth culture, which we use as a sort of catch-all term for young people's music and art scenes and general pastimes; we use the term counterculture to refer more specifically to noncommercial or antiestablishment music and arts. The ties between ARA and youth culture went both ways. Punks, skins, and other rabble-rousers built and continually joined ARA, bringing political ideas, countercultural aesthetics, and DIY attitudes that were significant parts of what ARA did and how it did it. At the same time, ARA strove to introduce politics into youth cultural scenes, both to keep fascists out and to carve out space for young people to do progressive political work with

A graphic including one common ARA motto. This ad is taken from an issue of *Arise!* (Winter 1997–1998), a Twin Cities–based anarchist periodical.

Stencil by Toronto ARA's "agitprop crew," 1990s.

their peers. Anti-racism was not consigned to a distant realm of "politics" but embedded in regular life.

ARA was closest to punk, broadly defined: skinheads, ska kids, skater kids, and hardcore kids might delineate between themselves, but they were realistically in the same overarching milieu of shared venues, zines, and interpersonal networks. (The boundaries between punk and metal, hippie, and other countercultures could be similarly thin.) ARA's connections to punk in particular went so deep that some members and outsiders viewed ARA as the "political wing" of punk. Columbus ARA member Josh described ARA as "omnipresent" in the punk and hardcore scene. Crucially, this does not mean that everyone in ARA was a punk,

An example of the Hobbes
design motif often borrowed
by ARA, Toronto, 1993.

cared about punk, or was even particularly aware of punk, but ARA was
viewed by punks and by lots of alternative youth as the place to go for
political activism. This very important point helps explain a massive
proliferation of small-town chapters between 1996 and 1998; small-town
misfits looking to become politically active saw ARA as the way to do it.

ARA especially seemed like "the place to go" for *white* alternative
youth. As previously discussed, after the movement's early multiracial
skinhead era, ARA was predominantly white, paralleling the youth scene
where it was so present; punk, at least in North America, is often seen
as a heavily white counterculture. However, nuance is crucial. In LA and
Orange County, for example, ARA was influenced by and drew members
from the predominantly Xicane, Mexicane, Central American, and Asian
punk scene; in Chicago, as we'll see later in this chapter, a few key Xicano
punks/hip-hop DJs helped to build one of the network's most multiracial
chapters.

Anti-fascism has important parallels with the punk ethos. Neither
defer to experts or professionals, and both uphold direct action as the
way to get things done. As Minneapolis ARA members often stated, "We
believe that the only way to smash racism is by doing it ourselves!" ARA's
background in youth scenes was, thus, closely tied to its militant, popular
organizing tactics, setting it apart from mainstream anti-racist liberals and institutions. It wasn't a coincidence that one of ARA's earliest

WARNING!

RACIST ASSHOLES ARE TARGETTING THE METAL SCENE

Nazi skinheads and other "white power" groups are recruiting in the heavy metal scene. These racist organizers are trying to play you like fools and use you as pawns for their race war.

In the eighties, these scum did the same thing in the punk scene. They tried to wreck the scene with their racist bullshit, but anti-racists united and chased them out.

Racist bands like Bound For Glory and labels like Resistance Records are trying to use the metal scene to recruit for neo-nazi organizations that want to wage war on anti-racist white kids, People of Color, Jews, gays and lesbians, and anyone else that doesn't support their fucked-up views.

It's funny that they are trying to recruit from the Metal scene. Three years ago they talked shit about "long-hairs". Don't be a sucker.

Not only do their ideas suck, but so does their music. Have you listened to some of the bullshit they think passes for metal? They need to make a trip down to Music Tech to see that you have to first take the guitar out of your ass before you can play it.

There is a bunch of great anti-racist metal/hardcore bands. And they stand up to the racists in the scene and speak out against bigotry everywhere. Check out Sepultura's new CD, Roots. Or listen to Biohazard, who have been fighting the racist bullshit in the New York scene for years. Or Napalm Death, who have some of the fiercest anti-racist lyrics around. On the local scene, Inveigh is down with fighting racism, and they say it at their shows. There's probably more bands who would be anti-racist if more people supported them.

We need to make every scene everywhere a Nazi-Free Zone. Anti-Racist Action is committed to that struggle, and if you want to check out our ideas more, and maybe help out, give us a call or write us at the address below. **We can only do it together!**

KILL RACISM DEAD

ANTI-RACIST ACTION · P.O. BOX 80239 · MINNEAPOLIS, MN 554308 HOTLINE #: (612) 649-4586

A flyer produced by ARA for the local metal scene and shared in the ARA internal bulletin, Minneapolis, 1996.

defining tactics was "physical confrontation, which is fighting them and kicking the shit out of them," which was Kieran's description of the Baldies' conflict with the white supremacist White Knights. Likewise, Judith, in Toronto, remembers that ARA's confrontational strategy and tactics were really "coming from the punks—the politics in the punk community around spaces, cheap spaces to get together and hang out and drink and so on.... It was really between the bonehead punks and the anti-racist punks that the war on the street began." Thus, there is a clear legacy and philosophical through line from the Baldies' early self-defense to ARA's generally confrontational approach to fascists.

For all this, we want to emphasize that ARA's ties to youth culture weren't all about keeping nazis out. A huge part of the connection was about positive, constructive, and proactive organizing. This chapter seeks to illustrate how ARA organized within youth cultures to make anti-racism an organic part of the experience of an entire generation and to show both the power of organizing youth and the power of youth to organize.

Rock Against Racism

Used throughout its two-decade history and across North America, one of the most consistent tools in ARA's arsenal was both a way to organize in youth scenes and a reflection of the reality that ARA was already there: Rock Against Racism (RAR).

ARA borrowed the name "Rock Against Racism" from Britain's anti-fascist movement, just like it modified Britain's "Anti-Fascist Action" to "Anti-Racist Action." RAR was a highly successful movement in Great Britain, begun by a group of Socialist Workers Party (SWP) members in 1976. Later joining forces with another SWP initiative called the Anti-Nazi League, RAR hosted large festivals, tours, and local gigs of musicians playing as a public statement against racism in music, as well as against Britain's rising fascist movement. Rock Against Racism "emerged on the back of the 'punk rock' youth movement,"[1] though it later nodded at broader genres.[2] ARA's very first members thought it was a great idea, so they took it. Not every show necessarily used the name, but the idea was consistent: to organize fun local shows to explicitly assert an anti-racist conception of one's local scene and promote anti-racism.

Chicago organized some of ARA's earliest RAR shows, when the city's chapter was still synonymous with skinheads. A show at a local church in April 1989 benefited an AIDS clinic run by Chicago's radical nationalist

Puerto Rican Cultural Center, because AIDS "and its sufferers are the victims of the same kind of lies, stereotypes, and misconceptions that fuels racism."[3] Another show, five months later (Rock'n'Reggae Against Racism, this time), was a benefit for ARA directly.[4] Shows continued to be a major and consistent ARA activity throughout its existence. A show was often a good early step for a new chapter, a way to announce their presence on the scene, to recruit members, and to make connections with like-minded groups, make some cash, and bring politics into what ARA members already liked doing. Shows are fun.

Some ARA members who weren't coming from youth culture backgrounds still viewed ARA's connection to youth culture as an explicit strength. Columbus ARA's Mac, for one, was introduced to ARA by his son who was in the punk scene—Mac "was the cool dad." When planning the first Midwest Anti-Fascist Network conference in 1994 (renamed the ARA Network in 1995), Mac believed that acknowledging the importance of youth scenes would be essential to building the previous few years' groundswell of militant anti-racism into a mass movement. He suggested one, "in our view essential," part of the conference "should be a social event, with live music." He was not the only one saying so, and it's not a revolutionary concept to want to include fun things at your political gathering. Still, this was a recognition that many anti-racist groups were *in* youth scenes, because so many members of those groups were coming *from* youth scenes. Thus, a certain explicit, though organic, commitment to youth scenes was embedded into ARA's network conference; every year, the conference included shows featuring acts playing punk, hardcore, ska, reggae, hip-hop, and more.

As the ARA Network became more established, Toronto wrote a primer pamphlet on getting started and running a chapter, explicitly including the basics of organizing a Rock Against Racism show. Most were small affairs, as underground shows generally are; they might attract twenty people in a smaller town or a few hundred people in bigger cities. However, some grew to be much bigger and were nearly professional festivals. Columbus ARA organized Anti-Festival from 1995 to perhaps 1999,[5] showcasing a potpourri of genres and styles. Toronto had some of the biggest successes. It hosted annual Ska Ska Oi! shows, as well as a techno-based "Anti-Racist Music Movement." One climax was the "ARA 2000 Urban Culture Jam," featuring three stages and ska, punk, house, and techno acts; a thousand people attended.

ARA puts on a benefit concert for the Stoney Point Legal Fund, Toronto, 1997.

Flyer advertising a 1999 benefit concert, in Toronto, featuring the Street Troopers, affiliated with Montréal SHARP. SHARP was a critical player in the anti-racist resistance in Montréal through the 1990s.

John Bueno remembers how shows were an integral part of Toronto ARA's organizing: "Sometimes with my friends, I couldn't get them to come out to a protest, but I could get them to come check out a show … and that's kind of a cool thing about the group, is that we had different ways of engaging with politics for different people." Organizing shows was also empowering. According to John, "There you are, a teenager, and you're involved with putting on shows where hundreds of kids, and sometimes more than a thousand, would go out and party and have fun. It's about politics, but it's fun."

ARA was able to use shows to advertise to future members, fundraise, and build ARA, and by putting on shows to attract people, they also built the power to influence the scene. In Toronto, for example, the head of the Rock Against Racism crew was Nadia, who had come to Canada as a refugee from Iran while still a teenager. She remembers that at the Rock Against Racism shows she helped organize:

> Some of the acts were quite sexist in their comments in between songs. So I made a commitment to not book them again, or at least talk to them about it. I remember [Toronto ARA members] talking to [one artist] and saying, "You can't say these things if you want to work with us. We won't tolerate it." So I saw it as living up to that aspect of being against sexism. That part for me was very important. When you're a woman, a racialized woman, an immigrant woman—you're aware of it. So that was important to me.

A similar dynamic emerged in Louisville, where most members of ARA were drawn in through their links to the punk scene. Many members were involved with *Brat* magazine, a local publication that gave a voice to youth concerns about gentrification and policing and in 1999 received a grant from the city to open the Bardstown Road Youth Cultural Center, or "BRYCC House."[6] BRYCC House prohibited racist, sexist, and homophobic bands. It was enough to generate some controversy from punks who accused BRYCC of censorship, but dozens of local and national hardcore bands performed there over many years and at multiple similar locations.[7]

The BRYCC House ran a computer lab, a radio station, and hosted several political conferences, including the 2000 Southern Girls Convention, an annual gathering dedicated to feminist activists of the American South.[8] (ARA members hosted a workshop on "gun safety

A fundraising seven-inch put out by Columbus ARA in 1999, in partnership with a local distro called Retribution Records. Courtesy of Josh.

NO JUSTICE NO PEACE

PARTY FOR ANDRE!!!

proceeds go to Andre Madison's appeal

LIVE HIP HOP

Andre Madison, 38 year old life long resident of North Mpls, is in prison for something he didn't do. He was framed. Andre was shot twice in the neck and the arm, during a police raid. Police fired 500 rounds of ammunition from both sides of the apartment. This left a cop injured by another cop's bullet as Andre, also shot by a cop, lay bleeding on the floor. Outside, his sister was denied information about what was going on. Meanwhile, racist insults were hurled at Andre and medical attention was delayed him while they rushed the wounded cop to the hospital.

Andre is alive but the community is outraged that he was charged with felonies and is now serving time in State Prison. Andre is a victim of the racist "war on drugs" being waged in inner cities all across the country. Andre needs at least $5,000 to hire an attorney for his appeal. Andre should be with his family and his community where he belongs! No Justice! No Peace!

• **Q-Bear** •

• **Native Ones** •

• **The One and Only Buggin'** •

• **North Side Hustlerz Clique** •

• **Final Chapter** •

members of
• **FWUAS** •

MARCH 17, 8:30pm
Red Sea Bar • 320 Cedar Ave S • West Bank
$5.00 donation at the door
• **All Ages • ID to drink** •

Freedom For Andre Madison!
Prosecute The Police!

Sponsored by:
People For Justice For Lawrence Miles and Andre Madison

Minneapolis ARA helped organize this 1998 benefit show for the legal defense of Andre Madison, a black man convicted of second-degree assault when Minneapolis police raided his home. Shared in ARA's internal bulletin, along with an account that noted that Minneapolis police shot over five hundred rounds, while a gun that Madison owned was never fired.

and self-defense".) They also hosted a "Permanent Autonomous Zones" Conference based on the idea of building spaces "liberate[d] ... from capitalist control or from any type of authoritarian control"; members of Chicago's A-Zone, a similar community space linked to Chicago ARA, attended the conference.

Through this type of consistent presence in youth culture, ARA members attempted to make local music and youth scenes more inclusive.

Although punk boasted ARA's strongest connections to youth culture, it wasn't the only relevant culture. Some ARA chapters had strong connections with their local hip-hop scenes. Lansing ARA's Steve is a white dude but has been a prolific hip-hop DJ since the early 1990s; for a time, he, another Lansing ARA member, and another hip-hop DJ co-owned a record store, which Lansing (and later Chicago) member Heather remembers as an important center for community and events, from punk and hip-hop shows and b-boy battles to meetings and political events. In the Twin Cities, Minneapolis ARA had a consistent

HARDCORE PUNK BENEFIT SHOW!

@ Fireside — 2646 W. Fullerton Ave.
Sunday May 30th, 5–9pm, $6

BANDS
1. Reckless Youth
2. Johnny Underdog
3. .xfarcus
4. Excelsior
5. Kungfu Rick
6. Burn it Down

Presented by Chicago Area Anti-Racist Action chapters:
- Chicago ARA: 1573 N. Milwaukee #420, Chicago, IL 60622, 773.252.6019, ara@wwa.com
- N. Side ARA: POB 146601, Chicago, IL 60616-6601, northsideara@hotmail.com
- S. Side ARA: POB 721, Homewood, IL 60430, ara_s_side@hotmail.com

A benefit show for ARA, Chicago, May 1998.

relationship with the Rhymesayers record label and other local hip-hop acts. Minneapolis ARA's connections to hip-hop went as far back as its founding Baldies, when, according to Mic, "many of us would mix our skinhead style with elements of hip-hop and gang culture." On the flip side, Mic also remembers, "When I would dress differently and express myself in ways that were closer to hip-hop than skinhead culture, I would be questioned by some of my comrades," as if deviating from the skinhead uniform somehow meant a lack of dedication.[9]

Toward the end of the 1990s, Chicago ARA became one of ARA's most multiracial chapters thanks in large part to the leadership of young Chicano members Manny and Tito. Like many young Latinos of the era, they were connected both to the city's hip-hop scene and to the local punk scenes—Latine and white. Manny joined ARA after finding a flyer at a hardcore show at the A-Zone and brought Tito out to their first ARA meeting. Manny would go on to be one of Chicago ARA's major connections to the city's punk scene, by organizing benefit shows, among other things. As for hip-hop, "We were all DJs," remembers Manny. Tito recalls that two members in particular, Junior and Eric, first got involved with ARA by DJing a couple of benefit shows:

> I remember that ARA was growing, and our crew was coming in, and we weren't even called the Chicanos, they were calling us the Cicero chapter, which is great, 'cause it makes your group look better, but it was literally four of us. We thought those guys would just come in to spin, but they came to actions too and got their hands dirty, [so] it was a nice surprise, but also humbling, 'cause it was, like, "Now we got a solid crew."

According to Tito, because "we were still connected to our communities, we were still living in those neighborhoods," he, Manny, and the rest of the "Cicero chapter" were able to function as a "bridge" between ARA and their communities. Manny agrees: "To put it, like, more cheesy, we were Latino punks, but we were Latinos first."

Before this, Chicago ARA had not made significant attempts to reach out to or organize solidarity with communities of color or immigrants. As Manny jokes, "If anything, I fuckin' recruited ARA to be in *my* life!" After the arrival of the Cicero members, ARA actively recruited more in the Latine community, in Polish immigrant communities, and alongside Palestinian groups.

Fighting Words

Clearly, many ARA members were the artsy kids. While music was a major cultural arena for ARA members, it wasn't the only one. Written media was crucial to ARA's growth, communication, and politics: all the more important because ARA could not count on, and made little effort to seek out, coverage in mainstream media. There were exceptions to this general rule, like Minneapolis's *City Pages* profile on the Baldies and ARA and the *Chicago Tribune*'s Syndicate profile.[10] The hip-hop and urban culture magazine *Vibe* also covered ARA sympathetically in the summer of 1998,[11] and, in 2001, Columbus ARA member Lady was somewhat surprisingly covered in *Seventeen* magazine.[12] In 1999, the Canadian CBC's *Big Life* produced a television feature on ARA, and Rock Against Racism was featured on *MuchMusic*.[13] In coverage of demonstrations, ARA was often criticized in mainstream media narratives that presaged bad takes on "antifa" today. The *New York Times* ran a piece on ARA's protests against the World Church of the Creator in York, Pennsylvania, in January 2002,

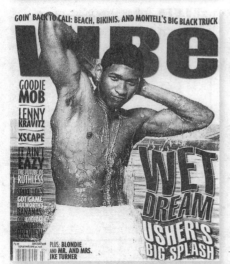

ARA was featured in two high-profile, nationally distributed predominantly youth-oriented magazines: *Vibe* (June–July 1998) and *Seventeen* (April 2001). The *Vibe* story gave a broad overview of ARA, including its opposition to Resistance Records, its direct action against Klans and nazis, its organizing in youth culture, and more. The *Seventeen* story featured a Columbus ARA member and photos of demonstrations she had attended: from left to right, a police brutality protest in Cincinnati, an anti-globalization protest in DC, and an immigrant rights rally in Cincinnati, all in 2000.

In 1999, the Montréal alternative weekly *Hour* ran an in-depth profile on Montréal ARA, one of the higher-profile media looks at ARA during its time, compared to its primarily DIY networks.

which described the WCOTC and ARA together as a "traveling circus of publicity hunters.... Pleased agitators left town saying they would like to return for more free-speech indulgence."[14]

ARA was covered more often and more sympathetically in DIY and youth culture–focused zines—including *Maximum Rocknroll, HeartattaCk* (probably hardcore's biggest zine), and *Profane Existence*, Minneapolis's long-running anarcho-punk zine[15]—and in leftist media. One of the most important publications for ARA was *Love and Rage*, the newspaper put out by the anarchist federation of the same name. As we described in chapter 3, Love and Rage members played an important role in ARA's history. Their newspaper printed a wide variety of coverage and analysis of leftist political issues, where anti-fascism and ARA often featured prominently. According to Chicago ARA member Xtn, who described himself not as a member but as a "fellow traveler" of Love and Rage, the newspaper played a "vital role" in promoting ARA during its publication, from 1989 to 1998.[16]

But the most significant media for ARA's organizing was their own: a huge variety of zines and newsletters. Reflecting the network's decentralized nature, no single written voice of ARA existed; many ARA chapters had publications. Zines were "our social media," as Cincinnati ARA's Eric described it. ARA zines offered members a way to produce their own content with a low barrier to entry, low cost, and no censorship. They're also an obvious tradition in politics, allowing the publisher to self-promote and to convey its message. The format and content of ARA publications ranged from news and political theory through culture- and art-centered works to what we'll politely call "avant-garde." These publications were in conversation with each other, even advertising and selling each other, and consistent ARA members likely read many. Lansing ARA's Steve, for example, who generously provided a great portion of this book's primary materials, wasn't even a particularly avid collector, other than being consistently involved over several years and being organized about keeping publications—his collection included about twenty different publications.

Like ARA's first Rock Against Racism show, ARA's first zine probably came from Chicago. In 1989, when Chicago ARA was still an arm of the skinhead scene, some members published *Colorblind*. It serves as a telling example of an ARA zine format, because it basically has a non-format: issue no. 1 includes "a straight-edge corner," a piece on animal rights, screeds mocking nazis, news clippings (mostly about ARA) with ARA commentary, one man's denunciation of sexism, and more, totaling forty-eight pages.[17]

Just a couple years later, in 1993, Toronto ARA began publishing *On the Prowl*, one of the network's longer-lasting and more influential newsletters. It was quite "professional" in appearance, compared to something like *Colorblind*, but also included a wide variety of content, as did many other ARA zines. A 1996 issue, for example, contained ARA scene reports, ads for ARA merch, a column by an ARA member about infiltrating the fascist scene, fundraising for the Stoney Point Legal Fund, a message of support for US prisoner Khalfani X. Khaldun, and, most heavily, exposés on local fascists.[18] *On the Prowl* published twenty issues from 1993 to 2003.

ARA's two biggest publications were Columbus's *ARA News* and *Turning the Tide* (TTT), published by the ARA affiliate in Los Angles, People Against Racist Terror. *ARA News* was published from 1994 to 1998, with a peak print run of seventy-five thousand copies. (Its quick growth and large distribution reflected the intense pace of ARA's operations,

Dear ARA:
Hello. A friend of mine told me about you. I am very much against racism. I would really appreciate it if you could send me newsletters. I am 14 years old.

—Laura
Gahanna, Ohio

ARA News often printed letters from people who wrote to their office like this one from Ohio, in September 1994. Clearly, ARA was getting the message out and motivating youth.

It's for more than just reading.

Subscribe:
Six full (28-page) issues, nine measly bucks.
(Free to prisoners, PWAs, moms on AFDC, GIs.)

PO Box 7075 • Minneapolis, MN • 55407
P.S. Our full-size issues pack a much bigger wallop.

An advertisement in the anarchist zine *The Blast* (December 1995) exemplifies one vibe in ARA's DIY media milieu.

Claustrophobia no. 12 (Winter–Spring 2001), an anarchist newspaper produced by Baltimore ARA members.

as well as Columbus's logistical strength and financial resources.) Both publications focused on news stories about racism and anti-racism in general, as well as ARA organizing updates; TTT had extensive and influential analysis and opinion pieces. Both had a simple format, run with nearly professional dedication and consistency, and exemplified the essential contributions of older activists to the mostly youth-focused ARA. After accusations of gendered violence within Columbus ARA emerged in 1999 (see chapter 8), Columbus ARA lost the capacity to publish *ARA News*, which PART then agreed to incorporate as a section of *Turning the Tide*.

If these publications represented the more formal and established side of ARA's written culture, the other end of the spectrum would be something like *Don't Fuck with My Cat* (DFWMC). "Winning no awards for layout," as it says on its inside cover, DFWMC opted instead for hand-written stories, including a young man's "I used to be homophobic but

I got educated better and you know what I like kissing boys" stream of consciousness.

Other chapter zines included *Fighting Words* (Minneapolis, MN), *hARAss* (Louisville, KY), *Claustrophobia* (Baltimore, MD), *Breaking the Chains* (Ann Arbor, MI), *Troublemaker* (Lansing, MI), *The Clock Is Ticking* (also Lansing, MI), *Active Transformation* (still Lansing, MI), *The Alarm* (Chicago, IL), *Mob Action* (Columbus, OH), *Expose and Confront* (Kent, OH), *True Colours* (Niagara, Ontario), and many more. Indeed, for Kieran, one measure of a chapter's coherence was its ability to publish some sort of newsletter or zine.

Beyond the words, ARA's zines and publications were filled with visual art, frequently melding the creators' political work and messages with the youth cultures they came from. One common design motif was the use of Calvin and Hobbes characters; in flyers, pamphlets, posters, and manifestos, the cartoon tykes could frequently be spotted smashing swastikas and wearing balaclavas.

Visual media was both a means of connecting ARA members and a key advertising tool. Members distributed and exchanged their publications, stickers, posters, and merchandise at concerts and youth culture events—as well as at political events, anarchist book fairs, or neighborhood festivals. They brought their images to the street with graffiti campaigns, postering, and wheat-pasting (putting up posters with a homemade glue that, if made correctly, is next to impossible to remove). The latter often overlapped with graffiti culture, as both an art style and a political project of claiming public space. This tradition went as far back as the Baldies' initial ARA formation, which first announced itself with flyers declaring a "Nazi-Free Zone." Later on, Columbus's Josh recalled one simple sticker in particular that said "Stop Racism," with the ARA Columbus office's phone number ("614-424-9074, if I remember correctly"). He explains:

> I felt like, in the 1990s, when I hitchhiked across the US, that they were just all over the place. You could go through a toll booth, and there'd be a sticker on it. You could go in the bathroom at a truck stop, or you could go to a punk club, or on a stop sign there'd be a stop racism sticker.... You'd go to a show, you'd pick up a zine, and there'd be an ad for ARA in there, or, like, someone had photocopied the sticker into their zine. Bands, you know, you'd see a band,

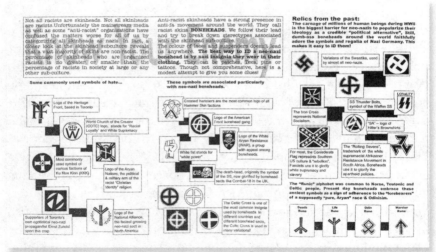

This flyer was printed in Toronto in the 1990s, with space for other chapters to add their contact information, as New Jersey ARA did here.

A spread in *ARA News* (January 1997) advertises anti-racist gear for sale by Attitude, a distributor based in Pennsylvania.

and they'd have a stop racism sticker on their guitar or their drum kit.

All this visual media was a vital element in a dense network of communication and organizing. Altogether, Josh concludes, "It made the world feel smaller. It made it feel like you were more connected."

ARA's unique visual style also made its way onto merchandise worn by supporters to show their allegiance and was used by chapters for fundraising. Toronto ARA's "agitprop crew" actively recruited artists to create images and went on to produce ARA merch at wholesale prices, including stickers, patches, pins, buttons, and T-shirts. Smaller chapters could order merchandise at cost, and then sell that merch at "retail" prices to turn a profit in support of their local work. ARA chapters relied on each other to raise their own funds, with nothing but elbow grease (and sometimes egregious copyright infringement).

Meanwhile, Columbus ARA formed a relationship with a small company called Attitude, which produced large volumes of "ARA-branded" merchandise, alongside products promoting feminist, anti-racist, and other left-wing causes in general. The network's main

Pin produced by Toronto ARA, in the 1990s.

A graffiti design reprinted in ARA's internal bulletin in 1997.

Pins, patches, and T-shirts designed, produced, and distributed by Toronto ARA, in the 1990s.

In the 1990s, these designs were screen-printed on fabric and sold as patches to be sewn or pinned onto clothing. Patches were a great fundraiser for ARA and a creative outlet for those who produced them and those who wore them.

website, maintained by Columbus ARA, linked to Attitude's online store; Columbus ARA invited Attitude to sell at the national conferences, and Attitude represented ARA at some of the music tour dates we describe below. Some disagreement about this came to a head in 1997 in a discussion about an ARA benefit CD planned by Columbus ARA, to be released in partnership with both Attitude and Asian Man Records.[19] A member of Montréal ARA asked how the CD would financially benefit ARA chapters and also complained that Attitude did not offer bulk discounts to ARA chapters, while effectively competing with chapters producing their own goods. In response, a Columbus ARA member defended the initiative:

> First, the project is *primarily* an organizing, movement-building project. Each CD and 100-page accompanying booklet is a piece of propaganda of the highest quality for our movement.... If we didn't make a nickel it would still be a great project to get this CD out....

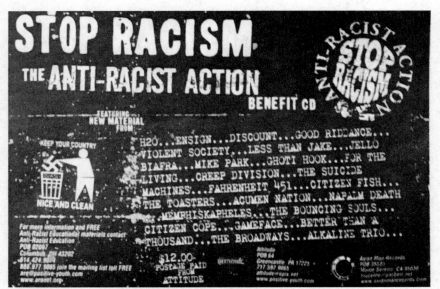

An ad in *Turning the Tide*, in 2000, for an ARA benefit CD put out by Columbus ARA, in partnership with Attitude, a distributor, and Mike Park's Asian Man Records, which also organized the Ska Against Racism tour benefiting ARA and other organizations.

> ARA is a network of autonomous chapters. There has never been
> any organization-wide fundraising of any kind … the people who
> *do the work* of creating the funding opportunity keep the money.
> Period. It's *always* that way in ARA.

Tension around the CD project dissipated through discussion, and it was released the following year. However, discomfort about Attitude's role continued to percolate through 2000, when Montréal ARA proposed that the network establish an ARA online store (managed by chapters in Montréal and Plattsburgh), selling merch, with proceeds directly flowing to active ARA chapters. While some defended Attitude's contribution to the network—"I think it sucks that we make our allies feel like the work they do to help us isn't appreciated," wrote a member from Maryland— Montréal's ARA online store proposal was adopted at the 2000 delegates meeting.

ARA on Tour

ARA's connection to subcultural music scenes, its production of zines and merchandise, and its commitment to mass organizing all came together

ANTI-FEST
COLUMBUS THROWS A PARTY

On May 13, 1995, Columbus Anti-Racist Action put on an all-day outdoor music festival, which we named the "Anti-Festival," right in the heart of the Ohio State University campus. The theme of the event was promoting inter-racial and multi-cultural harmony in our community. Coming, as it did, less than a month after the Oklahoma City tragedy, we held it out as an opportunity for people to take a stand against hate speech. ARA was interested in putting together a fun event for the diverse campus population where local activists could set up tables and introduce themselves and their ideas.

ARA had a couple of tents with a video room that attracted people all day. We also tried to do a little merchandising with Stop Racism buttons and black and white Anti-Festival T-shirts and bumper stickers with the logo of Columbus ARA and the statement "The Anti-Festival--Anti-Racist, Anti-Fascist, Pro-Human Being, Pro-Party" (If you'd like to get any of that stuff, let us know!). It was a success. Thanks to the bands, people who signed petitioners and all who came. See ya next year.

COMFEST 95
In Rain & Shine... a Groovin' Time!
ARA was there, too!

PUNKFEST--DAYTON

New ARA chapters may be starting in Florida and Michigan after hard (but fun!) work by volunteers at Punkfest '95 in Dayton, Ohio, June 23-24. The two-day concert camp-out featured bands from as far away as Belgium and was a benefit for the Leonard Peltier Defense Fund. Attended by almost 500 people, interest in our videos and extensive literature table was wide-spread.

LOS CRUDOS ROCKS THE HOUSE
WITH ARA AT PUNKFEST

LOLLAPALOOZA

130 new people will be receiving ARA News after efforts at Lollapalooza '95, June 14th, in Columbus. Among these are the Mighty Mighty Bosstones, whose singer, Dick Barrett spent time taking pictures of our booth and talking to us. He told us about a concert in Europe where they kicked 20-some nazi skinheads (boneheads) out. The band's policy: "Fuck that shit." Cool.

18

This 1995 *ARA News* page lists three different music festivals that ARA tabled or, in the case of Anti-Fest, organized in a relatively short span of time.

when ARA was invited by bands and promoters to table and speak with touring bands. Spearheaded especially by Columbus, ARA built a massive list of addresses of people interested in ARA and met people all over who became dedicated activists and started ARA chapters of their own. The beginning of ARA's national-level touring was "really just a great stroke of good luck," according to Columbus ARA's Mac, but the touring is perhaps better understood as a payoff from the long-term activist networks to which ARA had access through older members like him:

> Other than local shows in each chapter's town, we hadn't really ever even thought that we would be able to hook up with bands that toured nationally, but I had a friend named John Woods who was a coal miner over in eastern Ohio, who had been active in the anti-Klan work back in the 1970s.... [Since then], he had gotten involved in a movement called Rock Out Censorship, ROC, [which] was set up to oppose and ridicule Tipper Gore and the group that she had that was trying to promote, the idea that you should censor punk rock, and you should censor heavy metal and rap music, 'cause they all made our youth be violent and stuff. And he was very success-ful, and he had a pretty good network. And, uh, the whole music industry really loved what he was doing ... so he had got invited, Rock Out Censorship got invited, to the first Lollapalooza tour.... He invited us to share his table [at] the show ... and so we went out there.

According to *Vibe*, in 1998, "A chance meeting at a 1994 Lollapalooza show hooked ARA up with their plaid sugar daddies,"[20] when the Mighty Mighty Bosstones' "lead man, Dicky Barrett, stopped by an ARA booth at Lollapalooza in Cleveland and chatted up the volunteers. 'These guys told me they had actually been to Klan rallies and fucked them up,' Barrett said.... 'That impressed me. They are the type of people who have the nerve to brawl, but they don't show up to brawl.'" From that meeting in 1994, the Bosstones were consistent supporters of ARA, welcoming ARA tables at their shows, pointing them out "in the back of the club," help-ing them reach supporters and solicit donations, and generally offering publicity to ARA.

After an invitation from Rage Against the Machine to table at their 1996 arena tour, ARA continued to tour across the US and, to a lesser extent, Canada in 1997 and 1998. ARA joined a Bosstones tour in 1997 and tabled at about thirty shows. An in-depth report by Mac reveals what touring looked like and what ARA hoped to achieve with their involvement in youth culture:

> It's my opinion that this kind of work—whether we table shows or street corners or other public events—is one of the best and most useful kinds of work we can possibly do right now. Tabling brings us into contact with large numbers of strangers, most of whom have never heard of ARA...
>
> I believe in the quality of our propaganda. At the shows I set out stacks of *ARA News* and stacks of a short leaflet titled "What is ARA" (with an old *ARA News* cover story "Hate Hits Home" on the back—about PA nazi Mark Thomas and the Freeman boys who killed their parents). I also tear our sheets of "Stop Racism" stickers into individual stickers on a square backing and spread out a pile of 'em around the other literature. The room fills up with dancers with red stickers on.
>
> In all of the 8 cities I worked, I had help at the table. This usually came from local ARA contacts we had been in touch with previously. In 2 cities (Tallahassee and Ft. Lauderdale) I went out into the city earlier in the day and found people who were politically active there and eager to help.
>
> One of my main goals was to build up the *ARA News* mailing list. Our database had gone over 10,000 about a month or two before the tour. In the 8 cities I covered we signed up 949 people. Counting the 3 prior shows Jenni and local folks did, we have increased our mailing list by about 1,300 new people so far...
>
> My second goal was to identify people who are interested in being ARA activists/organizers in their towns. This happened in every city, no exceptions. For example, my first night was at the "Milkbar" club in Jacksonville. Four different people said they wanted to start a chapter there, and I was able to put them in touch with each other. Then, a few nights later, two guys came up to the table in St. Petersburg and said they were from Jacksonville and wanted to start a Jacksonville ARA. I'll be sending them the names, addresses and phone numbers of the others.
>
> In three cities, Orlando, Birmingham and New Orleans, we already had people active. They all came to the shows in their town,

and met new people who offered to help. We have sent follow-up packets (usually 50 zines plus some other articles) to about 35 people—new activists, people who have local bands, book stores, etc., for distribution...

The crowds at these shows were uniformly diverse (by age, "style" or "scene," and somewhat racially mixed) but mostly very young. The vast majority of the crowd is under 20, and at every show there are kids there with their parents.

Our relationship with all 3 bands has grown closer. One great little image—the Pietasters throwing fruit down from a balcony at the 4–5 boneheads outside the club in St. Petersburg.

A couple of months after the Bosstones' 1997 tour, Columbus ARA activists toured with seminal DC hardcore act Avail, as well as the Warped Tour, punk rock's most commercially successful touring festival. They joined the Smokin' Grooves tour, the first ever major hip-hop multi-act tour. In 1998, ARA was one of three anti-racist groups on the forty-date Ska Against Racism tour organized by Mike Park of the ska and punk label Asian Man Records, which later helped put out ARA's benefit compilation. Columbus was the main chapter organizing and attending these tours, but other chapters joined as well when a tour came to their town.

Josh was the Columbus ARA member who toured with Avail, spending about two months traveling across the US and Canada, giving a brief overview of ARA at a table in the back and from onstage in the middle of Avail's set. He describes it as a "public speaking trial by fire," explaining that the tours grew ARA, because he was "talking to people ... and finding out what was going on where they lived and, you know, identifying people who were ripe to be leaders or to start chapters." Josh explains:

All those opportunities to meet people who might be down to organize or get the newsletter into their hand ... basically, everyone who picked up some of our stuff was a conduit to that area. It kind of spread the gospel, so to speak.... We accomplished spreading culture, a cultural idea of anti-racism, and that it has a place in our community.

ARA had gotten a boost outside of its first hometown of Minneapolis, when members of the Baldies followed their friends, the hardcore band Blind Approach, on tour through the Midwest; eight years later, this string of national tours was a major growth push, as ARA grew from 27 listed chapters in September 1996 to 136 in August 1999.

Besides the organizational benefits, and even the money raised, ARA often intended its presence in youth culture and on tours to be an end in itself, making an explicit statement against racism to hopefully impressionable youth. The impact of this sort of "awareness-raising" is difficult to assess, and perhaps open to criticism—which it did receive. During the Ska Against Racism tour, for example, the *Chicago Reader* stated, "Organizer Mike Park conceded that the [partying] had overwhelmed the politics."[21] As the satirical punk rock journalists of the *Hard Times* asked, "Are you proposing … that, somehow, the horn riffs and skank pits that stirred up the emotions of literally hundreds of white teens DIDN'T result in the immediate and permanent end of racism?"[22] Nonetheless, the effect of a consistent assertion that racism was unwelcome in an entire culture can add up—ska and punk have, in general, raised a generation of their fans to fundamentally assume anti-racism. Whether or not the ARA Network had the capacity to mentor and organize with all the people they met on tour is another question, one we'll get into in the next chapter.

NOTES

1   Nigel Copsey, *Anti-Fascism in Britain*, 2nd ed. (Abingdon-on-Thames, UK: Routledge, 2016), 131.

2   Ben Naylor, Chris Mugan, Colin Brown, and Charlotte Cripps, "Rock Against Racism: Remembering That Gig That Started It All," *Independent* (London), April 25, 2008, accessed April 6, 2022, https://tinyurl.com/4yjp5wmu.

3   @boxcutterbrigade, "When we decided to do a fundraiser for Vida Sida, a grassroots HIV/AIDS clinic that focused on the Puerto Rican community in Wicker Park … ," Instagram photo, July 3, 2020, accessed April 13, 2022, https://www.instagram.com/p/CCMHnSfjcZY/?utm_medium=copy_link.

4   @boxcutterbrigade, "Another show. Another venue. This time as a fundraiser for #AntiRacistAction. The Wild Hare was _the_ premier venue for Reggae in the USA at this time … ," Instagram photo, July 13, 2020, accessed April 13, 2022, https://www.instagram.com/p/CCma2e2DUDB/?utm_medium=copy_link.

5   "Anti-Fest: Columbus Throws a Party," *ARA News* (Columbus, OH), August 2, 1995.

6   For a recent reflection on the experience and legacy of *Brat* by its founding editor, see Liz Palmer, "Brat (Almost) 25 Years Later," Taunt, accessed June 2, 2022, https://taunt.me/statusquo/brat-almost-25-years-later.

7   For a historical overview of BRYCC House, as well as *Brat* and other projects linked to Louisville ARA, see "The BRYCC House," Louisville Punk/Hardcore History, accessed June 2, 2022, https://history.louisvillehardcore.com/index.php?title=The_Brycc_House.

8   For more on the 2000 Southern Girls Convention, see "Southern Girls Convention," Wayback Machine, accessed June 2, 2022, https://web.archive.org/web/20141128234541/http://southerngirlsconvention.org/history/sgc2000.

9   Celina Flores, Erin Yanke, and Mic Crenshaw, "Episode Four: The Minneapolis Baldies and Anti Racist Action," *It Did Happen Here* (podcast), December 4, 2020, accessed April 14, 2022, https://itdidhappenherepodcast.com/episode4/index.html.

10   Meleah Maynard, photos by Kara LaLomia, "The Lost Boys," *City Pages*, January 31, 1990, accessed April 6, 2022, http://insurgence.proboards.com/thread/210; Bill Wyman, "Skinheads," *Chicago Reader*, March 23, 1989, accessed April 6, 2022, https://www.chicagoreader.com/chicago/skinheads/Content?oid=873583.

11   Jonathan Franklin, "Power: Skinnin' Heads," *Vibe*, June–July 1998.

12   Laura Schiff, "Fight the Power: Teen Activists Put Their Bodies and Beliefs on the Line," *Seventeen*, April 2001.

13   *Anti-Racist Action Network Bulletin* 2, no. 2 (March 1999).

14   Francis X Clines, "Racial Adversaries Converge on City Trying to Heal," *New York Times*, January 16, 2002.

15   Kieran interview.

16   Xtn, email to author, February 6, 2021.

17   *Colorblind* no. 1 (c. 1999), courtesy of Michael Novick and Malki C. Brown.

18   *On the Prowl* no. 7 (Summer 1996); *On the Prowl* no. 11 (Spring 1998).

19   Advertisement in *Turning the Tide* 11, no. 4 (Winter 1998–1999).

20   Jonathan Franklin, "Skinnin' Heads," 85.

21   J.R. Jones, "Ska's Lost Cause," *Chicago Reader*, July 23, 1998.

22   Dan Kozuh, "How Can Racism Still Exist When It Was Defeated by Ska in 1998?" *Hard Times*, March 18, 2018.

CHAPTER 8

TURNING POINT ARA

The Midwest was an ARA stronghold. To a certain extent, this book replicates that perspective, particularly focusing on places like Minnesota, Ohio, and Michigan, as well as Ontario, across the border. But while many of the network's strongest chapters in the Midwest were active at the start of the 1990s, Anti-Racist Action grew a ton throughout the decade. At its peak, around 1999, the ARA Network had 179 active chapters,[1] spread out across at least six of Canada's ten provinces and thirty-three US states. As we saw in the last chapter, at one time, one ARA sticker or another might be seen at a random bus stop or telephone pole just about anywhere in the US. This expansion showed a meteoric rise from just three years earlier, when ARA had less than thirty chapters listed in its internal bulletin—but just one year after the 1999 high point, only seventeen chapters attended the annual national 2000 conference. To be clear, that was not the end of Anti-Racist Action nor is it the end of our book; our next chapter charts one of ARA's most intense and dynamic anti-fascist campaigns, which, until 2003, mobilized a smaller, perhaps "tighter," contingent of ARA activists, who were organizing effectively within a shrinking network.

This chapter covers some of ARA's activism outside the American Midwest and how ARA was striving to grow. We'll then see how the late 1990s was an inflection point in the history of ARA, the point at which it stopped growing and started shrinking, following three challenges in quick succession in 1998: a concerning escalation of state repression in Michigan, tragic murders in Las Vegas, and internal discord, resulting from accusations of misogyny and violence against women in the midwestern stronghold of Columbus, which affected some of the network's internal infrastructure.

ARA Beyond the Midwest

Michael Novick from People Against Racist Terror (PART) provides an illustrative anecdote about how ARA organizing in Los Angeles looked different than organizing in the Midwest:

> The first week I was in LA, there was a Klan Action.... We heard there was somebody who lived in Sylmar ... who wanted to go with us to confront the Klan in Long Beach. So we drove from Echo Park, which is right near downtown Los Angeles ... up to Sylmar, which is the very far northern end of Los Angeles county, down to Long Beach, which is the southern [end]. Had this demonstration against the Klan ... drove the guy back to Sylmar and came back to Echo Park. So basically we had done something like four hours of driving and never left LA County. I mean, in Chicago, if you drive four hours, you can go to Detroit.

While ARA in the Midwest perhaps had fewer barriers "to get around and to connect and build personal relationships," he says, "the rest of us were more, it was, like, phone calls or correspondence or, later, internet stuff and the occasional meeting up a couple times a year."

Long-distance networks of ARA activists had existed from early on, and after the 1994 MAFNET conference, ARA's *Network Bulletin* served as a communication hub, including event flyers, scene reports, readings, and proposals about ARA's development, all submitted by ARA members. We're going to share a few snapshots of what some of ARA's lesser-known chapters outside of the Midwest got up to.

According to scene reports sent to the *Network Bulletin*, Houston ARA held its first meeting in 1996 and had grown quickly. The chapter was in the process of setting up "extension chapters" in nearby high schools, figuring out ways to reach and educate kids who were younger still, and posing as nazis "to get informed about what they're doing in our area so we can combat it." Austin ARA formed "after the travelling punk rock circus known as AVAIL came through town." It was networking with other radical and direct-action-oriented activist groups in its area, including Accion Zapatista, Earth First!, the Industrial Workers of the World (a radical union), and Food Not Bombs. It was involved with "the Austin Police Brutality Hotline (which may at a later time grow into a fully fledged Copwatch)," it was distributing literature, and it was prepared

Albuquerque ARA Scene Report

Hey we're the new kids on the scene checkin' in from the southwest. We've been representing the 'Burque since November of '97 and are off to a solid start. In February we helped plan and organize a rally for indigenous rights addressing the twenty-second year of Leonard Peltier's imprisonment, the struggle at big mountain, the ongoing fight of the Zapatistas, and the protection of Albuquerque's National Petroglyph Monument. There were speakers from a wide array of local groups in support of these causes. The local petroglyph struggle is in support of indigenous spiritual rights in opposition to a proposed six lane road being paved through the park. We've also been working on an ARA benefit show for March twenty-eighth (props to Minneapolis ARA for setting us up with tons of goodies.) A couple of projects we're working on now are searching out political prisoners in New Mexico to support them and coordinating with local group Migra Watch (a sub-group of Immigrants Rights Coalition) and other local political groups.

Until next time...

ABQ ARA

by juju and monny

Milwakee Report

Dearest Cool Cats of ARA

How's everybody in ARA-land hopefu.ly doin good and feelin fly. Since the last time you heard from us we attended our statewide ARA meeting which was held in Madison, WI It was small- but lots of love was there along with good discussion and possible upcoming projects. Thanks to Madison for hookin' it up.

Our ship came in and we landed a free of charge office space which will no doubt serve as the launch pad for the revolution here in Milwaukee. We even have a filing cabinet. Two of us recently came back from a Mexican excursion which included couple weeks in a peace camp in the state of Chiapas. Look to a repeort on that in the next bulletin.

Take Care and God Bless

Mo & Trent

Two 1998 scene reports printed in the *ARA Network Bulletin*.

STOP ARYAN NATIONS

On Saturday, July 10th, in Coeur d'Alene in North Idaho, the Aryan Nations, a Nazi group which has carried out many bombings, shootings, and other acts of terroristic violence is scheduled to march through downtown Coeur d'Alene to publicize their objective of establishing a "white homeland" throughout the Northwest U.S. and driving out all those who don't fit in. Many Nazi supporters come to this event, 7 1/2 miles from the Aryan Nations Compound in Hayden Lake.

If you oppose violent racists and bigots, then join with people from all over the continent who are coming to Coeur D'Alene to confront these genocidal fanatics.

We Go Where They Go !
No Nazis Anywhere !
July 10, 1999
Coeur d'Alene, Idaho

If you're interested in going to Idaho, or if you need more info, please contact:

Moscow, Idaho, Anti-Racist Action
PO Box 8968
Moscow, ID 83843
(208) 882-9755

Anti-Racist Action Bay Area
P.O. Box 3103
Oakland, CA. 94609
(510) 433-9995

or your local contact

ARA organizing was largely in its own backyard, in Moscow, Idaho, in 1999, but the listing of Bay Area ARA is an example of ARA's attempts to organize on a wider regional basis.

to "be there when the Klan protest on MLK Day ... [and] whenever and wherever they show their stupid mugs."

Austin ARA reported: "we have also forged a relationship with Houston ARA and hope to work in the future with them," but didn't mention Tyler or Pasadena ARA, also listed as Texas chapters. However, despite being relatively geographically isolated, it was playing out a lot of the same trends that defined Anti-Racist Action as a whole: roots in an underground, countercultural scene, opposition to radical white supremacists, and a generally radical, direct-action political orientation. This report also reminds us of the sometimes transient nature of ARA chapters. The chapter writing to the network mentions that it was trying to connect with another chapter that had formed to protest the Klan just a year before and had successfully connected with an Austin ARA chapter from 1989. Obviously, earlier iterations of ARA organizing had not lasted.

From the East Coast of the US, New Jersey ARA, based in Cranford, wrote in a 1997 scene report:

> ARA NJ doesn't do as much on-the-street action as other ARA groups for various reasons (lack of money, transportation, local participation, & other resources and since there's not as much open bigotry where we are to name a few). We currently do more "educational" type things (for lack of a better term) like the anarchist/radicalist/anti-[authoritarian] distro center. This will change in the future though, as we get more money, people to help out, & connections.

New Jersey ARA was at least successful enough at distributing literature that its material had recently been "banned from local high schools for being 'controversial.'" It was working on a newsletter but struggling to find "material for it and help." Finally, however, it's interesting to note that it seemed dissatisfied to only be doing "'educational' type things." Other chapters engaged in education, but New Jersey ARA, at least in its own perception, was somewhat unusual, because it wasn't very directly countering racist activism on the street. Two years later, in 1999, there were at least three New Jersey chapters (North Western New Jersey, South Jersey, and Trenton). New York state had eleven chapters, behind only Ohio and Ontario in terms of chapters per state/province,[2] reflecting an increase in fascist activity in the region, which continued beyond the time period that is the focus of this book.

Based in the American Northwest, Moscow ARA may have been one of the more isolated ARA chapters, working out of Kootenai County, Idaho, near Coeur d'Alene and the rural compound/organizational headquarters of the Aryan Nations. It sent a few news clippings to the *Network Bulletin*, including one in 1999, stating "officials from the Moscow chapter of the Anti-Racist Action group ... announced [Kootenai] county will award [two] protesters $80,000 in damages" and admit the county made wrongful arrests. The two ARA activists had been arrested for obstruction "after they refused to allow police to search their backpacks at the Aryan Nations parade in Coeur d'Alene."[3] In July 1999, Moscow ARA and Bay Area ARA together joined a thousand-strong counter-demonstration against the Aryan Nations' annual parade; ARA specifically held a sit-in in the middle of the parade route, a success, because it "generally stymied the cops and totally flummoxed [Aryan Nations head Richard]

Butler and his cohorts." Moscow ARA, thus, exemplified a common ARA theme by organizing in direct opposition to a nearby and prominent fascist group.

ARA activists attempted to organize, forge connections, and support one another across chapters. Columbus ARA, a common first point of contact for newly interested people, followed a semiformal process when people first got in touch. According to Gerry, writing in a March 1999 email later printed in the *Network Bulletin*, Columbus ARA sent packets "with zines, flyers for upcoming events, a few sheets on how to start an ARA chapter," stickers, and catalogs to anyone who expressed interest in ARA. Only some of these were seen as having the potential to "be an organizer for us (as opposed to stores and bands who just want free stuff)." Columbus would then alert already existing ARA chapters to the existence of these new prospective organizers and encourage them to establish ongoing contact.

At the time, Kris from Toronto ARA asked Gerry what would help grow the network more sustainably. Gerry emphasized inter-chapter mutual support:

1) Stronger or "established" chapters taking a conscious role of building up younger chapters near them. Go to their demos. Help them organize. Go to shows. Hang out. Party with them. Be young, have fun. You know, be their friends. People in ARA know how to make friends right?

2) More regional gatherings that focus on skills building and short-term campaign planning. Not long-term stuff or structure questions or political workshops. Just business of the immediate kind.

3) Travelling organizers. Full time people who go from town to town, spending a week or two doing intensive training and education to build local chapters. Spending an hour or two with everybody in the group and getting to know them. And then moving on to the next chapter. Introducing people in different young chapters to each other and teaching them to work together.

Some ARA activists attempted to formalize these ideas, particularly by organizing regional gatherings. In January 1997, for example, California chapters had several network events, including a southern California regional ARA gathering ... that drew over 100 folks from around the region and restarted San Diego and jump-started Riverside. For the future, we want to have more on-going contact in the huge southern California region to keep relatively isolated anti-racists connected and sustain each other in our work.[4]

Later that same year, Minneapolis ARA co-hosted a hip-hop/punk show fundraiser to support a new ARA chapter in Rochester, Minnesota, gathered with Fargo ARA "to do the mini-conference thing" in mutual support of both chapters, and, finally, organized a regional conference. Likewise, a 1998 Milwaukee ARA scene report mentioned, "We attended our statewide ARA meeting which was held in Madison, WI. It was small—but lots of love was there along with good discussion and possible upcoming projects." In Ontario, ARA organized weekend campouts involving between fifty and a hundred members from Ontario and sometimes Québec and Michigan. Chicago ARA formally proposed a regional structure for the network in 1999 and, by 2001, ARA was publicly listing "regional contacts." These rotated over time, but in 2001, for example, were Chicago, Columbus, Louisville, Maryland, Montréal, LA, Toronto, and Model City, New York.

Many other proposals were made to develop a more successful organizing infrastructure for the network. There was discussion about setting up a national office at the network's 1998 national conference—but not much was done, because there were no concrete proposals. The idea morphed into doing a network-wide publication, which was then discussed at the ARA delegates' conference six months later. In the notes, one person's response is paraphrased: "initial reaction is that it would take a lot of very firm organization—we are not ready for this type of thing, and the last thing we want to be is another political organization that sells papers." The proposal for a national publication was withdrawn.[5] At the same 1999 meeting, delegates voted in favor of splitting ARA's delegate conferences into east and west meetings, to allow for easier travel, and of setting up a "Network Fund" to support ARA organizers and chapters in emergencies. (Canadian chapters had already established a Canadian "Warchest" with a similar mandate the year before.)[6]

Despite multiple efforts, the network was not a tightly organized formation. A member of Toronto ARA wrote a cautionary note in 1998:

We put together the Network flyer with almost no support from other chapters. After ONE YEAR, there were 35 submissions to the flyer out of supposedly over 100 chapters, even after two snail mailings about it and countless emails. We also got no financial help with printing. This has made me very skeptical about Network-wide projects. We need to be realistic about how much support we can expect from other chapters.

Between 1994 and 1999, ARA tried its best to grow, develop infrastructure to support new chapters, and generally be as effective a movement as possible. It faced challenges, some of which it never overcame; ARA veterans to this day often agree that the network's infrastructure and internal organization were insufficient. Before we turn, in the next chapter, to the successful ARA organizing continuing into the twenty-first century, we're going to examine three challenges faced by ARA in 1998.

Michigan Anti-Klan Arrests

By this point, parts of the ARA Network had nearly a decade of experience in organizing against various Ku Klux Klans, building up such a consistent movement and tactics that even police tactics evolved in direct response to their anti-fascist demonstrations. Early on, in 1990, Oxford, Ohio's overwhelmed police department had simply released arrestees when their anti-racist comrades surrounded the station.[7] Over time, the police moved to setting up one fenced-in pen for Klan events, then having two pens to keep fascists and anti-fascists separate.[8] But on May 9, 1998, an anti-Klan demo in Ann Arbor, Michigan, evolved quickly from a rally to a riot, and the state responded—two months later—with new tactics of repression.

The Ann Arbor demonstration was massive. Heather, a member of Lansing ARA, remembers, "It was probably the biggest, most unruly thing that I had been to, by far, at that point.... There were hundreds of people there. [There was] tear gas deployed, masses of people running through the streets, you know—lines of riot police." But in addition to being so large, it was what founding ARA member Kieran called a "merging of ARA militancy with local community/youth militancy," an example of truly "popular" anti-fascism. Xtn, a member of Chicago ARA, agrees:

It wasn't just ARA or communist groups. The surrounding communities of Ann Arbor actually were pretty multiracial, pretty working-class or lower middle-class, pretty liberal, and had actually had a history of anti-nazi activity. There had been over, oh—two decades?—several, violent, anti-Klan rallies. Like, the Klan, they had come to Ann Arbor several times and people fought them in the streets. I mean wild stuff, like beating the nazis up and stealing their banners and their helmets, and then a mass parade marching down the streets of Ann Arbor, with a spear, you know, holding up a ... captured nazi's helmet.

Heather agrees that while most of her anti-fascist experience up to this point had been "fighting nazis at punk shows," as well as some doxxing, Ann Arbor "was much more of a mass community response." ARA and local community members fought side by side in the streets against the Klan. The police responded and pushed anti-fascists away from the Klan and the demonstration area into nearby streets; Heather remembers that when tear gas was deployed, locals opened their homes to let anti-fascists shelter inside. Altogether, the anti-fascists saw Ann Arbor as a big success—but it did get ARA, in Xtn's words, "once again on the radar of the police."

Two months later, on June 27, ARA and other anti-fascists attended another Klan rally in Kalamazoo, Michigan, but in this case they were greeted by a massively militarized police response. Xtn remembers that he'd seen police decked out with "crash helmets and billy clubs" before, but he "had never seen police in snatch squads, dressed in riot outfits" like he did in Kalamazoo. Although federal law enforcement had almost certainly attended ARA events before, this Kalamazoo rally also had officers from the Bureau of Alcohol, Tobacco, Firearms and Explosives present *in uniform*, which was uncommon. While this was the police presence that Xtn saw at the rally, Heather doesn't think she even made it that far.

When Heather's group arrived, they "parked on the far side of kind of like this public green in the public downtown space" and started walking across the green toward the rally. They had barely started when a police van suddenly rolled up, kettled the entire group, and arrested one of Heather's fellow Lansing ARA members. In the short time they'd been walking, police had identified that ARA member based on photos taken two months earlier at Ann Arbor; they were waiting. At Ann Arbor, Heather explains, some ARA members had been "black bloc'd

Emergency Meeting of Midwest ARA Chapters

this meeting is a short notice response to a crisis. it is not a delegates meeting. it is not an opportunity for making network decisions. we will further our understanding of the issues we now face. we
can develop proposals to present to the network. we can make consentual agreements among the
groups present.
chicago ARA is confident of our ability to provide resources for approximately 50 people to meet and
work for these two days. Please assist by being prepared. If there is a problem with the logistics
and content outlined below, it can be modified. this is your meeting.

An August 1, 1998, document from an emergency inter-chapter meeting organized by Chicago. Its
language exemplifies the attempt to balance organizing a non-hierarchical and anti-authoritarian
network with organizing a strong, coordinated network-wide response to an emergency.

ARA SECURITY CONCERNS

A direct action movement like ours needs to prepare itself against state repression and right-wing attacks. In the last
year alone, ARA has seen its members openly and covertly surveilled (Fargo, Louisville, Toronto to name a few) and
targeted for arrest by the state (Kalamazoo/Ann Arbor). Racists have also targeted us with fake web pages,
biohazard mail threats (Louisville), surveillance (www.whitepower.com), attacks (Montreal) and assassination (Las
Vegas). Other movements have been targeted as well: Earth First has received mailbombs and abortion clinics,
doctors and staff have been under increased fire.
       The Bulletin Crew would like to see some input on how we can better prepare and defend against these
attacks, and how best to cope with them. Send in yer thoughts!

A 1999 request from the editors of the internal bulletin to submit writings on the many security
threats that placed increasing pressure on ARA during the late 1990s.

up and all that sort of thing," but at one point her friend "doubled back
to throw a rock, and exposed a little hint of a tribal tattoo on his neck."
Police in Kalamazoo had now identified this ARA member two months
later, "based on that little bit of a tattoo ... exposed on his neck ... [in]
one photo." Law enforcement had issued thirty-six arrest warrants for
anti-fascists based on photos taken at the Ann Arbor demo and had
prepared in advance to make arrests at Kalamazoo. In the end, they
arrested sixteen anti-fascists that summer, including two members of
Lansing ARA, in Kalamazoo.[9]

The police response in Michigan felt to ARA like a major step up in
state repression. It now goes without saying that one could be arrested
at some point based on surveillance photos taken months previously, but
according to Heather, "Back then, in the nineties, [it] was, like, phenom-
enal technology." Fellow Lansing member Steve agrees, "At the time, that
was really unheard of"; Kalamazoo "felt like a trap."

It wasn't the first time ARA members faced arrest, but the numbers,
the deliberate nature, and the new level of surveillance all reverberated
throughout the network. First and foremost, it affected ARA members'
morale. Xtn remembers, "People were facing felonies—people were
facing serious jail time. And these are twenty-year-olds, you know? ...

People were scared." Beyond the immediate consequences for the specific arrestees, some saw it as a signal of deeper trends that could continue: a raising of the stakes for ARA and a general worsening of potential legal consequences. One Lansing ARA member said the charges were "political—when I was arrested, they immediately asked if I was in ARA. They said that I was speaking on the steps, saying that I was in ARA. The cops are definitely going after ARA and NWROC."[10]

The charges were significant enough to affect some ARA organizing. As Heather explained, chapters she was involved in became "a lot more security conscious.... And that sort of changed some of our organizing too ... from more attack mode to kind of some political defense, as well as the [other] organizing that we were doing." Another member, paraphrased in some meeting notes, explained:

> The tendency is to look at Ann Arbor [and Kalamazoo] as an isolated or new tactic; I think that's wrong. The police have been very effective in disrupting ARA in Michigan. The Ann Arbor police apparently have complete photo files, which probably came from the FBI. Therefore, we need to be worried about this on a federal level in addition to the local level. We need more security-conscious practices.

Then, while ARA was reeling from these events in the summer of 1998, they were hit by tragedy.

Las Vegas

In the early morning of July 4, 1998, Daniel Shersty's body was found in the Nevada desert outside Las Vegas. The body of his friend Lin "Spit" Newborn was found nearby two days later. On July 3, two young women had come into the piercing studio where Spit worked and invited him to a party, to which he invited his friend Dan. Lured to the desert under this pretense, the two were executed by white supremacists.[11] Well-known figures in Las Vegas's anti-racist counterculture and members of the anti-racist Unity Skins and Las Vegas ARA, they were targeted because of their anti-racism.

In 1998, Las Vegas was a hub for white supremacists. Law enforcement officials quoted in the media saw it as a checkpoint between white supremacists in southern Utah and southern California.[12] As one ARA member explained in a 2001 documentary:

Being such a transit town, it's really easy for boneheads to recruit in Vegas. Here you have this new kid come to town who doesn't know anybody, and everyone around them is friendly to them, and so you have this big tough guy saying, "Hey, we'll be your friend, and you'll have a family. Just wear these boots, and we'll just warp your mind a little bit to be racist."[13]

But the nazis didn't have a monopoly on the Las Vegas punk scene. Punks and skinheads of all affiliations held their shows in the desert outside of the city, gathered around bonfires at a few well-known spots under the stars; as a Las Vegas punk named Brandon put it, they would "drag a generator up there … house lamps, whatever we can get our hands on." Taking place in such close proximity, rival scenes commonly had conflict, which Brandon saw firsthand.

He was a close friend of Spit's and bandmates with him in a punk band called Life of Lies. The first time Brandon remembers a real run-in with the nazis, Life of Lies was playing a show, and the boneheads "showed up with guns to kill us." They were looking mainly for Spit, who was outspoken in his anti-racism; he often performed a poem, for example, called "Boot Boy," about his anger at nazi skinheads. That show, says Brandon, was "when we knew we were on their radar."

Originally from Florida, Dan Shersty had joined the Air Force to pay for college and was based at Nellis Air Force Base. Drawn into town by the local punk scene, he met Spit, and the two quickly became friends. Dan had been a popular kid at his Florida high school, playing in the school band,[14] and Spit was a major figure in Las Vegas's punk scene. According to Las Vegas ARA member John Toddy, Spit was a "very key figure in the anti-racist movement here."[15] According to Brandon, "We couldn't go anywhere without someone coming up to Spit." He was outgoing and lovable (and "mean, if he needed to be").

In March 1998, Spit asked Dan to help him start a Las Vegas chapter of ARA. They got flyers and a sign-up sheet of members, on which "smiley faces crowned names of teen-age members who defected from fascist skinheads," according to a media profile.[16] They were making headway in their organizing—but only a few months after they formed their chapter, they were murdered.

ARA members from across the network responded to condemn the murders and support the fledgling Las Vegas chapter. Rath Skallion

On August 29, 1998, anti-racists from the western United States joined ARA members from many chapters for a memorial march for Dan Shersty and Lin "Spit" Newborn. Courtesy of Toronto ARA Archive.

and Gerry Bello jumped on the Greyhound bus from Columbus to offer support. Rath remembers that the surviving ARA members were "all, like, nineteen years old," and needed a "crash course" in dealing with this crisis. Elsewhere, Chicago hosted a small emergency meeting on August 1, at which a few chapters discussed the murders (as well as the arrests in Kalamazoo) and ARA's response.

With support from Columbus, the Las Vegas chapter organized a national memorial march on the Strip on August 29, with endorsements from the National Organization for Women, the NAACP, and the AFL-CIO. "ARA was a lot about getting the word out and using media as a tool to our advantage," says Rath. As Michael Novick remembers it, "There was a challenge to the left and to the 'human relations' types to see it as a political assassination of anti-racist activists, similar to those that took place during the civil rights era." According to the January 2001 *ARA Bulletin*: "About 250 attended. ARA people from Toronto, Columbus, Yellow Springs, Detroit, Berkeley/East Bay, Chico, and Vegas were there." Rath was among the speakers.

> I shouldn't have been the one doing that press conference. I didn't live in Vegas. But none of them felt comfortable, and I had less to

lose; I was going to leave. They didn't want to be a target, so that makes sense. In retrospect, we could have done a better job in kind of encouraging them to take more of the leadership in these things, but as with so many of the newer chapters, they want to establish themselves and have the visibility, but they didn't always know how.

Beyond ARA's memorial march and press conference, uncertainty arose about how to respond. The second ARA point of unity was to "not rely on the cops or courts." Yet as a Chicago emergency meeting attendee said, "ARA is very DIY ... but we don't have a DIY way of solving the murders." According to an ARA member from another city, Las Vegas ARA was "not thrilled about working with cops, but they want to see the bone[head]s arrested." When police only arrested one man, even though at least two other people (the women who lured Dan and Spit to the desert) were already known to be involved, the Las Vegas chapter explicitly called for a stronger police response;[17] they had backing from Columbus ARA, which began a postcard campaign, and the network as a whole, which agreed (by majority vote) to take out an ad in a Las Vegas newspaper a year later.[18] Was ARA, then, "relying on cops and courts"?[19]

The traumatic violence of the murders, compounded by difficult questions about how to respond, dealt a severe blow to ARA's members and the network's culture of action. Kieran recalled, "We were, like, physically beating the fascists in lots of places and lots of times, and I think it gave us a sort of overconfidence.... [Then,] besides it being this really emotional tragedy, really traumatic experience, to have two people killed and killed in the way they were, we also were unsure how to respond." Charles, from Detroit ARA, agrees "that was a level of violence that wasn't present. I mean, you fight—somebody might be stabbed, somebody might get beat up, but for them to kill them, and then it was very obviously a pre-planned action," was shocking. According to Walter, from Edmonton, "It was terrifying, because that could've been any of us."

While many ARA members felt that "any" of them might have been vulnerable to the sort of attack that killed Dan and Spit, one key fact didn't escape notice: of all the people to be targeted by nazis, Spit was one of very few Black skinheads in ARA at this time. Charles, a Black punk in Detroit ARA, remembers the impact he felt:

My friend, who I lived with and hung out with, and who was in Detroit ARA ... he was white, and I was Black, and we were two of the main organizers in Detroit. And then what happens? A Black guy and a white guy got killed in Las Vegas. I definitely had some feelings about that.... It was quite a blow to me, personally, being a Black organizer in Detroit ARA.

Reeling from back-to-back experiences of repression and violence, ARA spent the fall of 1998 dealing with yet another major challenge.

Gender Violence and Conflict in Columbus

As we've seen, despite ARA's informal horizontal structure, the Columbus chapter played a key role in the network: distributing the *ARA News*, maintaining a mailing list of supporters and ARA chapters, making arrangements with commercial music tours, and providing practical support to chapters in crisis, like Las Vegas. Columbus was able to do this largely because of financial resources, as well as the dedication of a core group of younger activists (including Gerry, Josh, and Rath, who we've interviewed). However, the informal structure that allowed a certain dynamism, as well as ARA's united front politics, meant that the network did not have a clear way to respond when a conflict arose within the Columbus chapter.

Sometime in 1998, a few people around Columbus ARA formed another chapter called Central Ohio ARA (COARA) and attempted to advocate against internal sexism that they believed was hampering the network. According to COARA, "While some of us have openly challenged and criticized sexism within Columbus ARA for years, the breaking point for all of us was seeing Columbus ARA members function as [counsel], witness, and support for an accused batterer in a local courtroom against a woman who was seeking a protective order." Columbus ARA, for its part, claimed that COARA was essentially only engaged in untrue sectarian attacks against Columbus, and that "their local work revolves around undermining us politically." The conflict spilled into the network at the national conference in 1998.

At the October conference in Columbus ... a group of people, some of whom had been part of ARA Columbus before and some who had not, raised several criticisms of ARA Columbus. They called themselves "Central Ohio ARA," Columbus ARA disputed that this group was in fact a chapter, and accused the group of using the name "Central Ohio ARA" to get into our internal meeting and to give their criticisms of Columbus more weight. However, the meeting facilitators were not comfortable banning this group from the meeting, and accepted them as a chapter at that point.[20]

An ARA member from Louisville volunteered to mediate between the two groups, but that mediation didn't come to any resolution. The next year, Columbus even proposed a motion to expel Central Ohio from the network, which got enough support to come to a vote, but not enough to be adopted.

With some of COARA's criticisms centered on people close to him, Mac left ARA in 1999 to establish a new group, Anti-Racist Education (ARE). Although he didn't cut all ties, he no longer devoted the same time and resources to *ARA News*, and the network's overall outreach strategy substantially declined. Meanwhile, the conflict was a wake-up call for Rath, who up to that point "had been very active in ARA, in the office, going to the conferences, the regional conferences, being a delegate often, and very much being a loud voice in protests." Although she knew the COARA members as "all very complicated people," she says, "They weren't wrong." Feeling she'd been "complacent" about sexism in and around the chapter for too long, she left Columbus ARA; Rath says, "It was time for me personally to take a stand."

Other members stayed in Columbus ARA. Gerry says the chapter actually grew after the conflict, because less time was spent on administrative tasks relating to the national network and more time was devoted to local organizing. Lady agrees; she joined Columbus soon after the crisis in 1998, after the key figures in the conflict were gone and internal conflict was minimal.

For the network as a whole, however, the events raised concerns both about gendered oppression and about how a decentralized network could institute mechanisms of accountability or conflict mediation.[21]

Furthermore, Columbus ARA was by no means the only chapter where women challenged men on sexism, sexual violence, or harassment. Jane recalled how Toronto ARA contended with "multiple" sexual assaults in and around Toronto, beginning in 1999. Two men were expelled from ARA, and the group resolved to appoint members to stay sober at shows,

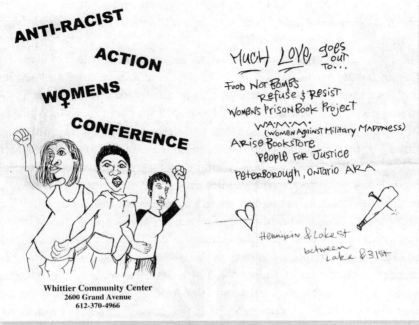

The program cover from a 2000 women's conference hosted by Minneapolis ARA.

to better watch out for sexual violence and other dangerous behaviors, and through discussion suggested older members should refrain from hitting on new recruits. It was a draining but necessary reckoning, according to Jane:

> It diverted so much of our resources. Just dealing with this internal clusterfuck. I had nothing left for organizing. And I'm not at all saying that it wasn't important work. It was incredibly important work. And I feel like the work we did around that was in some ways just as important as the external-facing work. But we had no choice; we had to do it. We can't just let that shit go.

Gendered violence is a societal problem and not an issue exclusive to ARA or to the left, but given ARA's ideological commitment to fighting sexism and abuse of power overall, many members found it devastating to witness or learn about gendered violence perpetrated within their groups. Beyond that, it was frustrating and, for some, enraging that ARA's accountability processes were sometimes inadequate to address incidents when they were exposed. There were instances when the "process" in an individual chapter was to expel the perpetrating member, but there was not necessarily a mechanism to follow through with a network-wide cohesive, consistent resolution.

The significance of the Ann Arbor arrests, the murders of Dan and Spit in Las Vegas, and the conflict in the Columbus chapter and gender violence more broadly is difficult to quantify for the network. ARA members like Kieran and Walter look back on them as serious blows, beginning a gradual decline in size and activity. It would be simplistic, however, to argue that they had a single, resounding, negative effect. ARA was able to mobilize large numbers of activists in response to the tragedy in Las Vegas. Accountability processes and women's organizing within the network, including women's caucuses and a separate email list, and even an ARA "Wimmin's Conference" in Minneapolis in May 2000, got a shot in the arm after the Columbus conflict. We are not seeking to erase the very real trauma that these events caused for the people closest to them, but rather to acknowledge that some of Anti-Racist Action's responses were positive and dynamic, and organizing continued. Our next chapter will cover some of ARA's most effective organizing, which took place after these three challenges. This wave of organizing was against two new fascist threats: the World Church of the Creator and the National Alliance.

NOTES

1   Gerry interview. The most ever listed in ARA's internal bulletin was 138, in August–September 1999, but as Mac was paraphrased as saying in *Bulletin* no. 9 (c. 1997), "ARA is much bigger than the list implies, due to the fact that many don't have secure mailing addresses."

2   "ARA Chapter Listing," *ARA Bulletin* 2, no. 4 (August–September 1999).

3   Associated Press, "County Settles Lawsuit with Aryan Nations Protesters," *Times-News* (Twin Falls, ID), March 24, 1999.

4   Anti-Racist Action, "Introducing the ARA Network," Fall 1998.

5   *Anti-Racist Action Network Bulletin* 2 (no. 3, May 1999): 19.

6   Anti-Racist Action Montréal, "The ARA Anti-Racist Defense Fund," c. 2000, accessed April 14, 2022, https://web.archive.org/web/20010309222515/http://www.antiracistaction.ca/defensefund.html.

7   John Dougherty, "Hate vs. Hate in Oxford," *Dayton Daily News*, April 8, 1990.

8   Gerry interview; Matt interview.

9   From the meeting notes of the "ARA Emergency Midwest Meeting, 8/1/98," *Anti-Racist Action Bulletin* no. 11 (c. August 1998).

10   NWROC, the National Women's Rights Organizing Coalition, was a Michigan-based anti-fascist group affiliated with the Revolutionary Workers League.

11   For details, see Shawn Gaynor, "Murder Trial of John 'Polar Bear' Butler," *Asheville Global Report*, January 2, 2001; Don Terry, "Skinhead Split on Racism Is Seen in Killing of 2 Friends," *New York Times*, August 29, 1998; Lynda Edwards, "Death in the Desert," *Orlando Weekly*, June 17, 1999. Rest in Power, Dan and Spit. Some memorial details are provided by the Torch Antifa Network; "Remember Dan and Spit!" April 26, 2018, accessed April 11, 2022, https://torchantifa.org/remember-dan-spit.

12   Terry, "Skinhead Split."

13   Beverly Peterson, dir., *Invisible Revolution: A Youth Subculture of Hate* (New York: Filmakers Library, 2001), accessed April 4, 2022, https://vimeo.com/131350523.

14   Terry, "Skinhead Split."

15   Jonathan Franklin, "Nevada Man Is Gripped with Sorrow as Skinheads Celebrate Son's Slaying," *Boston Globe*, July 5, 1999.

16   Edwards, "Death in the Desert."

17   Joe Schoenmann, "Marchers Urge More Arrests in Slayings," *Las Vegas Review-Journal*, August 30, 1999.

18   "ARA, Other Anti-Fascists, the Nazis, and the Cops: What's Happened After the Murders"; reprinted in *Anti-Racist Action Bulletin* (January 2001).

19   John Butler was convicted of both murders in 2000 and ultimately sentenced to two life terms. In 2014, he admitted his guilt and testified against Ross Hack and Leland Jones, who were also charged with the murders. (A fourth man named by Butler, Daniel Hartung, died in a motor vehicle collision in 2012.) Also testifying against Hack and Jones were Melissa Hack and Mandie Abels, who admitted to luring Dan and Spit to their deaths and were sentenced to prison time for conspiracy to commit murder. However, with no physical evidence connecting them to the crime, Ross Hack and Leland Jones were acquitted of all charges in 2014; Carri Geer Thevenot, "Former White Supremacist Testifies at Murder Trial," *Las Vegas Review Journal*, August 21, 2014; Southern Poverty Law Center, "Pair Acquitted in Infamous Double Murder of Anti-Racist Skins," *Intelligence Report*, November 2014.

20   "Statement from Toronto," *Anti-Racist Action Network Bulletin* 2, no. 3 (May 1999).

21   *ARA Bulletin* 2, no. 4 (August–September 1999): 11.

CHAPTER 9

END OF AN ERA: FIGHTING THE RIGHT AT THE DAWN OF THE MILLENNIUM

Coming through the difficult transitional experiences described in chapter 8, after 1998, members of Anti-Racist Action looked to reclaim the vibrancy and collective power of ARA. Meanwhile, a handful of already established but newly dynamic and increasingly dangerous fascist organizations compelled a response, particularly the World Church of the Creator (WCOTC) and the National Alliance (NA). This phase of ARA's anti-fascism combined elements of both the early turf wars against nazi punks and its public activism against the Klans in the Midwest and Canada, while developing new strategies and political analyses. Physical confrontation, including outright street fighting, took on some new prominence, raising questions of tactics and efficacy and requiring a balancing act of public-facing activism with potentially illegal activities that necessitated internal security. Many ARA chapters also attempted to be "sharper," developing deeper and more explicit political analyses of fascism and the specific fascists they were facing.

This period also saw thousands of protesters shut down the streets of Seattle on November 30, 1999, hobbling the work of the World Trade Organization (WTO) and initiating days of anti-capitalist street fighting, with at least a few ARA members in the mix. By the time the summit-hopping anti-globalization movement arrived in Québec City to oppose the Summit of the Americas in the spring of 2001, many larger ARA chapters were out in the streets in full force. And when protests broke out across the US and the world against imperialist responses to the terrorist attacks of September 11, 2001, ARA crafted a powerful anti-war statement and backed up their words with yet more street actions. At first glance, these major shifts in geopolitics and the consequent growth in mass protest movements might have been expected to lead to substantial growth in ARA membership and activity. Instead, the years after 9/11 marked the end of an era for ARA and a passing of the torch to a new and more security-minded set of anti-fascists, whose history this book does not cover in detail. This chapter will chart the culmination of the ARA era, at the end of one millennium and the beginning of the next, looking at its organizing against the World Church of the Creator and the National Alliance and the impact of the anti-globalization movement and 9/11 and will seek to explain how and why Anti-Racist Action was unable to adapt and thrive in the twenty-first century.

Going Where They Go: A Brief History of Chicago ARA

While ARA remained a decentralized movement at the end of the nineties, Chicago ARA took on new prominence because of its work opposing the Illinois-based World Church of the Creator (WCOTC). When the National Alliance began teaming up with and later superseding the WCOTC, events in Pennsylvania, DC, and Maine would shift ARA's center of gravity closer to the East Coast. We will return here to the early days of Chicago ARA to chart its path.

As discussed in chapter 2, Chicago anti-racist skins had played a major role in establishing both the Syndicate and the earliest version of ARA, but, by 1992 or so, this crew had largely dissipated, leaving a void of local anti-fascist organizing. Despite ongoing organizing efforts by young anarchists like Sprite, ARA Chicago didn't really come together again until a Klan rally was scheduled in the nearby suburb of Cicero in the spring of 1998. This timing also coincided with Kieran, a founding member of Minneapolis ARA, moving from Detroit to Chicago, and with the renewed participation of Tricia, a veteran of Chicago's early skinhead-oriented ARA group. Initially, beyond opposing the Cicero Klan rally, the newly energized chapter focused a lot of effort on reproductive rights and combating the religious right.

Gremlin, who joined around this time, remembers, "One of the things that I always kind of loved about ARA [was] that we would not just be reactive, but we would try to be proactive and actively go to the places where these things would be happening, before they happened." Chicago ARA often collaborated with other local groups, including the Emergency Clinic Defense Coalition (ECDC) and the Lesbian Avengers, taking a stance of direct confrontation that would define their strategic orientation over the next several years. Sprite credits Toronto ARA's campaign against the Heritage Front for inspiring a spirited demonstration at the Chicago home of Joe Scheidler, founder of the Pro-Life Action League and the most prominent local anti-abortion figure.[1] Counterintelligence was also a crucial piece of this work, including taking photographs of those attending anti-abortion events and cross-checking them with Chicago ARA's growing files on local and regional fascists.

Ben Smith

In the fall of 1998, Bloomington, Indiana, ARA produced a leaflet outing Ben "August" Smith, then a student at Indiana University, as "a local organizer for a fascist white-power group called the World Church of the Creator," the person responsible for "distributing 12,000 anti-Semitic propaganda pamphlets" around the university campus.[2] Smith was born and raised in the wealthy Chicago suburb of Wilmette and, in the early summer of 1999, with Smith now back home with his parents, Chicago ARA began to track his efforts to distribute WCOTC literature at New Trier High School, which he had attended.

Smith's emergence led Chicago ARA to research the local operations of the WCOTC. Founded in 1973 as a white supremacist organization, self-styled as a religion, WCOTC believes "the White Race is the finest and noblest creation of Nature" and "the originator and Creator of all worthwhile Culture and Civilization."[3] Its adherents oppose "evil forces," namely people of color allegedly led by Jewish people.[4] The WCOTC experienced some turmoil around 1993, when its founder committed suicide and members faced charges for a racist murder, a firebombing of an NAACP office, and a plot to bomb a Black Los Angeles church and assassinate Rodney King. In 1995, however, the group was given new direction and energy after being taken over by Matthew Hale. From his bedroom in his dad's house in Peoria, Illinois, the then-twenty-four-year-old Hale printed literature, ran a website, and had some success in expanding the World Church.[5]

To learn more about the group and its plans, Chicago ARA members "joined" the WCOTC, using fake identities, and began receiving regular missives from Hale. Still, according to long-time member Xtn, Chicago ARA initially concluded "the WCOTC did not seem like a very 'serious' nazi group to us." It was, he says, "more just part of the mix rather than a standout" fascist grouping—worth compiling intelligence on, but not

PUBLIC SERVICE MESSAGE
TO THE COMMUNITY OF BLOOMINGTON

Fascism, in all its various forms, such as Nazism and white nationalism, is a political strategy of dividing racial unity through favoritism of white men, acts of violence and terrorism against Jews, blacks, and against non-white immigrants for the purpose of establishing a totalitarian dictatorship.

So what does this have to do with Bloomington? Benjamin August Smith, a Chicago native, is a law student at Indiana University. He is also a local organizer for a fascist white power group called the World Church of the Creator (also known as the Creativity Movement). August has spent the last two months disrupting his teachers that he disagrees with as well as the IU campus group UNITE!. He has also put tremendous effort into distributing 12,000 anti-Semitic propaganda pamphlets entitled "FACTS that the Government and Media Don't Want You to Know".

Isn't everyone entitled to his or her own opinion?

Everyone definitely has a right to their own opinion and their right to print and publicize. Their OPINION is protected by the First Amendment. But was it the freedom of speech of Ray Leon, a friend of August Smith and member of the World Church of the Creator, to put a gun to the head of a clerical worker at an adult video store in Chicago at 9:30 October 20, 1998 demanding money?[1] Was it the freedom of speech of John Edward Butler, a neo-nazi in Las Vegas, Nevada, to kidnap Anti-Racist Action member's, Dan Shersty and Lin Newborn, and take them to a remote part of the desert to shoot them execution style over this year's Fourth of July weekend?

[1] Robbing Pornography Stores is heavily used by the white power terrorists, "The Order", back in 1984. They robbed over 6 million dollars from Pornography stores and armored bank cars that was filtered into the fascist movement.

It is necessary for you, as a member of this community, to realize that August Smith's propaganda campaign is for the sole purpose of establishing a fascist organization in Bloomington.

It does not take censorship laws and endorsement of state censorship to eliminate a fascist. All it takes is for us to unite in community self-defense through demonstrations by using our constitutional laws such as free public assembly and free speech (like this public service message) along with other creative ideas to make terrorists not only leave, but realize that their ideas of a totalitarian white government is a hopeless pursuit.

To get involved in the struggle against fascism, contact

ANTI-RACIST ACTION BLOOMINGTON:

arabloomington@hotmail.com   ***P.O. Box 1052***

Bloomington, IN 47402

August Smith:

For more information about the World Church of the Creator, contact August Smith: 420 E. 19th Street, Apt.7 (phone # 812-339-9375). We are positive that he is looking for interested people.

A 1998 flyer alerting the Bloomington, Indiana, community about the activities of a young and then largely unknown white supremacist named Ben Smith, who at the time was a student at Indiana University.

NEVER AGAIN!

RALLY AND SPEAKOUT AGAINST THE RISE OF RACIST AND RIGHT-WING VIOLENCE

Ricky Byrdsong, slain by white supremacist Benjamin Smith

Won Joon Yoon, slain by white supremacist Benjamin Smith

Matthew Shepard, killed by homophobic bigots

Dr. Barnett Slepian, murdered by an anti-choice sniper

Daniel Shersty, anti-racist activist assassinated by a neo-nazi

Lin "Spit" Newborn, anti-racist activist assassinated by a neo-nazi

Benjamin Smith, an avowed white supremacist with ties to the racist World Church of the Creator, killed two people and wounded nine others in a shooting spree throughout Illinois and Indiana this past weekend. Smith's actions are but the latest in a string of right wing terror attacks which must be countered and stopped! Join us in voicing your opposition—We will fight back!

SATURDAY—JULY 10TH—6PM
Halsted and Roscoe (the Matthew Shepard memorial)

Sponsored By: Chicago Anti-Racist Action
ara@wwa.com, 312.409.1432

A 1999 flyer advertising a memorial honoring those killed by WCOTC member Ben Smith, linking their murders to those of other victims of hate crimes and far-right violence, including Spit and Dan. The memorial marked the beginning of a campaign by Chicago ARA to disrupt the WCOTC that lasted for several years.

a major immediate threat in the eyes of Chicago ARA. That low-key approach changed the weekend of July 4, 1999, when Smith turned to racial terrorism. Beginning in Chicago's heavily Jewish Rogers Park neighborhood, he went on a two-day, multistate shooting spree. He shot at over twenty people, wounded nine, and killed two. All of Smith's victims were racial or religious minorities. Once the police caught up, he fatally shot himself.[6]

Within ARA, the reaction to Smith's rampage was palpable. Sheila, who had moved from Bloomington to Chicago earlier that summer, remembers:

> My Bloomington ARA friends there were terrified. They did not have a network of well-trained, prepared people. They were college students, and they were rightfully fearful that they would be targeted and shot, because those kids in ... a relatively small liberal oasis in the middle of a racist sea of small towns in Indiana had doxxed Ben Smith when he was a student at IU and had organized against his organizing.

Meanwhile, Chicago ARA members assessed the spree in relative safety, compared to their Bloomington comrades. As events unfolded, they felt confident the perpetrator was a fascist, and soon found out that the shooter was "sure enough ... one of the very people we were gathering information on."[7] The horrific murders carried out by Smith made it painfully clear that the WCOTC was a threat ARA needed to take seriously.

After some debate, Chicago ARA decided to dedicate themselves to a campaign against the WCOTC. As an initial action, they organized a public rally, which they announced as a memorial for Smith's victims. Holding banners and speaking to a modest crowd, including reporters, ARA members called out Hale and the WCOTC as fully responsible for Smith's murderous spree. Gremlin recalls, "The memorial was our chance to make a statement publicly, specifically to the World Church of the Creator, saying 'We see you, we know you, we know you are behind this, and we're sick of these killings.'" ARA held the memorial in a largely gay neighborhood called Boys Town to link the Smith killings to the infamous murder of Matthew Shepard, a gay student in Wyoming, the previous October. For the small but growing Chicago ARA crew, the memorial was a powerful public statement and a sign of things to come.

The World Church of the Creator (WCOTC)

Once the memorial was over, ARA escalated its anti-WCOTC campaign, as the World Church attempted to capitalize on its newfound notoriety. After Smith's killings raised the group's profile, the WCOTC distinguished itself from the alphabet soup of nazi organizations by taking a dual approach to organizing. They built an elitist "cadre" organization with a slick image. Hale had earned a law degree in 1999 (though he was denied a license due to his neo-nazi beliefs)[8] and invariably appeared in public in a suit and tie. According to a 2001 article in the *ARA Research Bulletin*, WCOTC doctrine called for "only eating raw, natural foods." At the same time, under Hale's leadership, the WCOTC cultivated a militant street presence and actively recruited among nazi skinheads and in prisons, invoking violent revolutionary rhetoric, using slogans like "RAHOWA" (racial holy war), and decrying the "Jewish Occupation Government." As Chicago ARA noted in the *Network Bulletin* that same year, "Hale publicly presents his organization as a political group committed to a 'non-violent' strategy of issue raising, yet the attraction for many members of the WCOTC is the organization's calls for violent race war and genocide." "Hale attempts to walk the line between kicking ass and working within the system," according to the *Research Bulletin*. (For what it's worth, the contemporary alt-right uses a very similar model; as coauthor Mike puts it, "No one who was around for the WCOTC campaigns could watch Richard Spencer without thinking of Matt Hale.")

Shortly after Ben Smith's murders, the WCOTC began a strong push to promote itself and its ideology. On November 21, 1999, it held a rally in Decatur, Illinois, about three hours south of Chicago, a city in the media spotlight after seven Black high school students were expelled for fighting; critics said the punishment was overly harsh and motivated by racism, and the Rev. Jesse Jackson entered the fray to advocate for the students' reinstatement.[9] Around the same time, Hale was dismissed from his role as violinist in Decatur's local orchestra.[10] Hale decided to exploit the town's tension and media spotlight (as well as perhaps avenge his slight) with a WCOTC rally "to show white people we're here for them."[11]

Chicago Anti-Racist Action showed up that day, implementing a key strategy in their campaign against the WCOTC: to "go where they go." Arriving after the WCOTC but before most police, about twenty anti-racists confronted about a dozen World Church fascists, heckling and "trading taunts." More cops showed up, protecting Hale and

NOT WANTED!

These pictures depict a group of neo-nazi skinheads who have been active in this neighborhood. If you see any of these nazis or signs of racist activity, please report it IMMEDIATELY to Anti-Racist Action at 312.409.1432.

An example of "outing" local neo-nazis, Chicago, 1990s.

BANDA NEO-NAZISTÓW

w polonijnym środowisku.
Są już ofiary ich przemocy wśród Polaków.
Jeszcze jest czas aby powstrzymać tą agresję!

Jeżeli zobaczysz te twarze:
* Bądź ostrożny * Obserwuj ich każdy krok * Powiadom:

Chicago **Anti-Racist Action**
1573 N. Milwaukee Ave., #420
Chicago, IL 60622
(312) 409-1432

Another "outing" flyer targeting local neo-nazis, in Chicago, in the 1990s. The text is in Polish and translates as: "A neo-nazi gang. In the Polish diaspora community, there are already victims of their violence. There is still time to stop this aggression. If you see these faces: be careful; watch their every step; contact ARA."

his followers, who had hidden in a park bathroom, while targeting the anti-fascists with violent arrests, including the use of pepper spray. Four members of Chicago ARA and one other anti-fascist were arrested for allegedly attempting to physically confront the fascists.[12] This included Sheila, who was targeted for holding the bullhorn, and almost certainly because she was one of the few people of color present. Gremlin remembers, "They were pepper spraying [Sheila], and I ... shout at the cops, 'She has asthma, you fuckers!'" Due to her family dynamics and class status, Sheila remembers feeling "isolated and scared in a way that others I knew were not.... For me ARA was both a feeling of family and a serious and dangerous existential risk I was taking." Gremlin stayed in Decatur for an extra day to help bail out those arrested, using money donated on an emergency basis by ARA chapters across the country. Decatur wasn't Chicago ARA's largest demo, and it wasn't completely successful, but it was the first example of the group counter-protesting and confronting the WCOTC's public events. It would not be the last.

Alongside counter-protests, ARA developed another, more proactive approach to fighting the WCOTC. This involved "outing," a real-world version of what's now more commonly called "doxxing." Chicago ARA members gathered information about WCOTC activists and other neo-nazis, distributing it through public demonstrations and "unwanted" posters in their neighborhoods to raise the fascists' day-to-day cost of doing their organizing. An early poster targeted fascists in Chicago's large Polish immigrant community; as Sprite recalls, "We'd been chasing down some of the Polish nazis, after some Polish punks came to us to tell us about problems they'd had with them in the scene." Xtn remembers when the focus turned to the World Church:

> We started making flyers that had pictures of all the [WCOTC] people on it, and the flyers would say something like "unwanted ... if you have more information, contact ARA," and then we would just make flyers with photos of all these people, and what information we did have, and we'd put them in clubs, or we'd put them in record stores, or even supermarkets or on light poles. And we actually got people that would call us and give us information, that helped us fill out our profiles of who these nazis were.

On three occasions in the fall of 1999, Chicago ARA members knocked on the doors of neighbors of known WCOTC members and other fascists, handing out the flyers and encouraging these neighbors to join them in a protest at a chosen nazi's home. As Gremlin recalls, "To have a successful outing, you have to have a *lot* of people. For safety purposes, to actively canvass, it can't just be, like, five people. So a lot of what happened beforehand was doing the work to convince people that this was important work to do." She remembers recruiting activists, including a number of dedicated local animal rights militants who happily took on the fascists. But she also approached her own semi-political friends: "It's pretty easy to be, like, 'Nazis are bad, right?' That's a good talking point, but then to actually get people to care enough or to recognize that this is actually worth going and doing something was sometimes the challenge for me." In addition, she continues, each action was preceded by anxiety: "I definitely remember the feeling of the tension building up as we'd get into the cars to go out to these neighborhoods where we don't know anybody."

At an outing, the flyer was the key tool, and the language choices mattered. The Richard Mayers flyer title, for instance, was "Your Neighbor is a Racist Organizer!" It included Mayers's photo, home address, phone number, and a basic rundown of his work with the WCOTC. Readers were encouraged to take action:

> Perhaps you know, have met or will meet Richard Mayers. Take some time to let him know you will not tolerate his racist views. Let him know that you will not stand aside while racists like him organize and commit acts of violence. Do you know his friends or his family? Ask them why they associate with a man who's [sic] goal in life is to instigate a race war.

Mayers lived in the diverse working-class suburb of Berwyn, and Sprite remembers that "the neighborhood was kind of engaged with what we were doing." After door-knocking, Xtn recalls:

> We'd converge in front of the nazis' houses ... with banners and megaphones; we'd basically alert the neighbors that this is who lives here. "They're a member of a neo-nazi organization that's murdered people. Do you want this person [as] your neighbor? It's your responsibility, this is your community, how do you want to respond?" ... [Outings] got pretty wild at times. Sometimes the nazis would hide indoors. One nazi [Mayers] had his mother come

out on the front porch and tell us to, like, "Shoo," go away, and then she actually said, "My son's not a nazi. I don't know what you're talking about."

[Another time], we had a pretty violent encounter with nazis. Two nazi brothers attempted to drive their car into a crowd of ARA and anti-fascists. We showed up at their house, you know, punch-ups, people wielding baseball bats, guy tried to let his Doberman Pinscher loose on us and, sadly, … somebody punched a Doberman Pinscher in the face, and the Doberman Pinscher ran away.… And then the neighbor across the street runs out with a pistol and basically aims it at an ARA person. Actually, there's a picture of the gun aimed at my head. And he's screaming at us to go away.

Gremlin remembers that day as "feeling like I was in this slow-moving dream," but she also recalls more favorable responses at other outings:

I remember a lot of times we'd give people the information, and they'd take it, but they'd look at us, like, "Who the hell are you, you weirdo freaks on my doorstep?" But the ones that surprised me the most were the ones who said, "Oh, I know who he is, and we've been keeping an eye on him too" or "Yeah, that guy's a piece of shit."

Chicago ARA was exerting a steady and highly unwelcome pressure on the WCOTC.

When Portland ARA was doxxing fascists as early as the late 1980s, according to a Portland activist named Tom, the idea was to raise "the cost of doing business … more than just getting beat up or getting in a fight. It's, like, you aren't gonna be able to rent a place or be employed here if you're a white supremacist." Chicago had similar ideas in 1999 and 2000. According to Xtn, these outings "led to an intensification of the campaign.… We never said we'd be nonviolent—we were always militant, we were always determined—but there weren't a lot of fights at the beginning of the campaign. After the outings, after the pressure we were putting on their local cadre, that all intensified our work." While the biggest clashes with the WCOTC and allied groups like the National Alliance were still to come, a major transformation in ARA's political organizing context came not from the right but from the left.

Globalization and Its Discontents

ARA had blazed a trail of militant, direct-action-oriented activism, primarily consisting of youth from countercultural backgrounds and heavily influenced by anarchist and anti-authoritarian politics. Because ARA had been uniquely active and successful during the 1990s, it benefited for a long time from being the obvious movement for young people (often white) interested in getting involved in militant politics. This was especially true in smaller communities where activists needed to seek out geographically far-away comrades. When the anti-globalization movement arose, ARA—in some ways, for the first time in its history—faced competition for members and investment.

The anti-globalization movement was largely left-wing and is not to be confused with today's far-right opposition to "globalism," a new link in a long tradition of xenophobia and anti-Semitic conspiracy theories. But the anti-globalization movement of the late 1990s was heterogeneous, and far-right and white nationalist forces did sometimes attempt to insert themselves, drawing predictable opposition from ARA and other anti-racists. Especially at its most radical, the anti-globalization movement was sometimes also called "anti-capitalist," an attempt to capture opposition to the Global North's strategy of neoliberal economic globalization. This movement's profile surged in North America after the "Battle of Seattle."

On and after November 30, 1999, sometimes referred to as N30, thousands of militant activists protested the World Trade Organization (WTO) conference happening in Seattle with an intense level of direct action in the streets, raising the profile of the dreaded black bloc in mainstream consciousness. It was a moment of radical, anarchist-influenced activism that was perceived to be, as Walter says, "wildly successful for leftist circles." Steve and Jason, ARA members in Lansing who were on the streets in Seattle, wrote weeks later, "Not in the past 20 years has an action by the left in the US had such an impact," which "changed the terms of debate of what is possible and what is desirable in our fight against global capitalism."[13] The Battle of Seattle exemplified and contributed to the growth of North America's anti-globalization movement. However, the success of this new, radical and confrontational movement ironically undermined its older sibling: ARA.

"ARA had been growing, growing, growing, growing, and then all of a sudden it stopped growing and started shrinking," according to Kieran.

"If you were a young militant who was willing to take some risks, all of a sudden the anti-globalization movement became sort of the center stuff." According to a 2001 letter in ARA's internal bulletin, "many young people who might have previously joined the Anti-Fascist Movement are instead orienting to the 'Spirit of Seattle'—the growing Anti-Globalization movement."[14] This was especially true for smaller communities, where often only a handful of young activists struggled to decide where to focus their limited energies. In the second half of the 1990s, that was often ARA, as evidenced by the dozens of small-town chapters involved in the network. Post-Seattle, however, "summit-hopping," as it was sometimes called, provided an attractive alternative for small collectives of young radicals who struggled to organize in their local communities but could easily travel to the next big protest.

At least partly as a response, a trend quickly developed within the network promoting anti-globalization as an anti-racist issue,[15] initially capitalizing on the dynamic anti-globalization energy. Kieran believed that energy that might have previously fed ARA had shifted to the anti-globalization movement—but "ARA joined that movement, became a part of that movement ... even though we weren't the ones leading that movement or defining it." Indeed, ARA chapters and individual members mobilized for every major international trade meeting in North America between Seattle in 1999 and the 2003 Summit of the Americas in Miami, sometimes, but not always, as part of a black bloc.[16] They continued, in fact, to make significant contributions and sacrifices: Jordan Feder, a member of New Jersey ARA, contracted spinal meningitis at the Miami Summit of the Americas and died five days after helping treat the many victims of police chemical weapons at the protests.[17]

At the 2001 Québec City Summit of the Americas, a substantial percentage of active ARA members were on the ground, including three of the coauthors of this book. Prior to the summit, Toronto ARA collaborated with BIPOC-led radical activist groups on a forum to develop an anti-racist response. They coordinated design and production of the trilingual Carnival Against Capitalism poster that was distributed across Canada and advocated for "diversity of tactics" at the planning meetings in Montréal and Québec City. True to the concept, the actions in Québec City ranged from permitted mass marches to hours of pitched street battles between cops and militants, as police fired thousands of teargas canisters in futile attempts to disperse protesters. Afterward, ARA

Poster for the Carnival Against Capitalism, in Québec City, in 2001, hosted by Montréal's Convergence des luttes anticapitalistes (CLAC). Poster illustrations by Rocky Dobey, layout and production by Kristin Schwartz, Toronto ARA.

Columbus ARA's bloc protesting against the Trans-Atlantic
Business Dialogue, Cincinnati, November 16, 2001.

groups in Toronto, Chicago, and elsewhere organized anti-repression
demonstrations in support of those arrested during the protests.

Still, in retrospect, many veterans agree that the shifting focus
stretched ARA's time and resources too thin. Even though he felt energized at the time, coauthor Mike agrees that the anti-globalization
movement probably undermined ARA's momentum, believing that some
ARA members were overenthusiastic in orienting toward anti-globalization and naive in assessing ARA's ability, as a small movement rooted
in direct action, to affect globalization. Globalization was an anti-racist issue, but ARA had struggled for years to mobilize against forms of
institutional and systemic racism at the local and national level; by its
very nature, globalization amplified this problem to a scale light-years
beyond ARA's capacity. Thus, as the radical left shifted much of its focus
and attention away from ARA's wheelhouse, the remaining core ARA
chapters proved unable to shift with it, and many who had leaned hard
into anti-globalization work were demoralized when that movement itself
declined after 9/11. But the days of ARA's fighting the fash were not over
yet. Major confrontations at the beginning of the new millennium were
still in store.

Trying New Things: The WCOTC in Peoria

In 2000, the World Church was frequently in the news: in January,
for attempting to get a student chapter recognized at Northwestern
University outside Chicago; in April, for a demo in Mattoon, Illinois;
and in July, Hale announced a Decatur memorial for Ben Smith a year
after his shooting spree.[18] According to the Chicago-based Center for

New Community (CNC, a nonprofit tracking extremists, with whom Chicago ARA had an on-again, off-again relationship), Matt Hale had steadily exploited media coverage of Ben Smith's shooting for further growth. By the CNC's estimate, the WCOTC had jumped from forty-one to seventy-six chapters in one year. It was still a small group but had unquestionably grown—fast.[19]

Just as ARA was experimenting with new tactics, Matt Hale also took a new approach: free and widely advertised speaking events at public libraries.[20] A significant shift in WCOTC organizing style, it posed a new challenge to ARA activists. Until then, Hale had held just a few outdoor, public, KKK-style rallies. By hosting indoor events, the WCOTC hoped to spread their message and actively recruit curious members of the public who might not have been bold enough to go to an outdoor rally, which implied more allegiance. Xtn suggests that the library events "seemed to be about creating a public but intimate way to organize and recruit." They remained a clear case of "we go where they go" but felt, in the moment, qualitatively different than the much more familiar outdoor KKK rallies.

Responding to the new paradigm, ARA members carried out an initial reconnaissance mission to see what actually happened at the library events, and then, alongside allied forces, attempted to shut down or at least disrupt them. Initially, being loud was often enough. Some strategies were more creative; at one of the library events in the fall of 2000, local college students staged a same-sex kiss-in to disrupt the World Church in Bloomington, Illinois, while Chicago ARA members shouted Hale down and took photos of his entourage for their growing files on the group's members. Gremlin remembers that ARA attempted to avoid violence in the libraries, out of concern for staff and regular library users. Nonetheless, fights sometimes broke out before, after, or even during the day's events, which were indoors and open to the public. Unlike at Klan rallies, there were no protest pens or fencing to separate rival sides.

At the fourth WCOTC library event in Illinois, in Peoria, on March 24, 2001, ARA took disruption to another level. It was a much smaller demo than, for example, ARA's earlier anti-Klan demonstrations but was marked by a militant approach and tactical flexibility by ARA counter-demonstrators. Arriving to find the fascists outnumbered, unprotected by police, and largely oblivious, ARA's original plan of blocking the library entrance by waving a banner somehow didn't happen.

Stills from video footage of a 2001 confrontation between anti-fascists and WCOTC supporters in the basement of the Peoria Public Library, in Illinois, where Matt Hale was scheduled to speak. Note the airborne chairs. The event was canceled just as it was about to begin.

"There was a decision made on the spot to basically engage the nazis," Xtn recalls. Matt Hale took two hits to the head from a 2 x 4 used to hold up an ARA banner, while Sprite suffered a broken hand when a World Church supporter hit him with a metal WCOTC flagpole. After the two sides separated briefly, the fascists went inside the library to set up for their event, with many of the counter-protesters joining them. The few security guards inside didn't seem to know what had happened outside and made no attempt to separate the two groups. Just as Hale was about to speak, a "chair-throwing melee" erupted.[21] The WCOTC flag was soon "confiscated" by anti-racists.[22] Pepper spray was used, though by whom has always remained unclear, and the event had to be completely canceled.

It's important to note that physical confrontation was not ARA's ultimate goal. Xtn stresses that, sure, ARA "wanted to smash the nazis, we wanted to defeat the nazis," but "we didn't see a physical defeat

Members of Muncie and Chicago ARA with WCOTC flag captured during the 2001 Peoria Public Library brawl.

of the nazis as necessarily being *the* victory." In other words, physical confrontation was not a goal but *could* be a useful aspect of their struggle. According to Xtn:

> When you have a bunch of what seems [to nazis] like ragtag degener-ates—we weren't degenerates—but when you have a bunch of people who don't fit your bill of some kind of superhuman basically fucking up your shit constantly, well, then it creates real internal questions within the organization, and it created real internal questions about Matt Hale's leadership. They were not able to defeat us, and that all just created a real atmosphere of tension, questioning, splits, and—so that fits into our strategy of crippling a group, you know.

Shortly after Peoria, Hale sent an internal email soliciting appli-cations for the WCOTC's security legions, the White Berets and the White Rangers, as their current set-up was evidently not cutting it.[23] The WCOTC wanted to do public rallies and maintain a street presence, but Hale was being forced to speak only when accompanied by police escorts, which undercut his invectives against the cops as part of the "Jewish Occupation Government." Therefore, anti-fascists saw Peoria as a success—in Xtn's eyes, even a "turning point"—but the WCOTC certainly wasn't finished.

Hale spoke in Schaumburg, Illinois, five months after the Peoria conflict, in August 2001. Hale had sued the Schaumburg library after it initially barred him from speaking. According to local media, "the library board cited a policy that says meeting rooms may not be reserved for activities that could disrupt regular library functions" and noted the breakout of violence that had recently occurred in Peoria, as well at a WCOTC event in Wallingford, Connecticut, though to a lesser extent.[24] When a judge refused to dismiss Hale's lawsuit in June, the library decided to drop the legal defense and let Hale speak.[25] Chicago ARA believed that Hale had likely anticipated the possibility of such legal obstacles; fighting them allowed him to seem like a champion of free speech.

The Schaumburg speech and counter-demonstration, while large, were less confrontational and riotous than some previous WCOTC events; about 250 police attempted to maintain control by separating over 100 protesters from about 100 audience members.[26] ARA members attempted to "attend" the speech but were ejected after Hale recognized them and pointed them out to police. There were sporadic punch-ups throughout the afternoon and evening; WCOTC members' car windows were smashed by local anti-nazi youth.

Schaumburg mainly sticks out because it was probably the last event Hale hosted alone. Soon after, the WCOTC began working in a coalition with other fascist groups. Schaumburg was also ARA's last large confrontation with neo-nazis before the events of 9/11 changed the global political landscape forever.

September 11 and After

Anti-Racist Action held its annual network conference in Canada for the first time in 2001, perhaps an overdue reflection of Canada's nearly decade-long strong presence. Giving a boost to the conference plans, host Montréal ARA started a sister chapter in the form of a student group at McGill University, opening access to institutional funds. Of course, when the conference was planned, no one knew that the attacks of September 11 would result in a suddenly fraught international border crossing for most conference attendees less than a month later.

While it took some time for the full ramifications to become clear, ARA was deeply affected by 9/11's dramatic reconfiguring of North American (and, indeed, global) politics. ARA had been an unusual bright spot of political activity within the sometimes inactive left during the

ARA Against The War

CNN tried to censor content of town meeting

The Dispatch published a large photo of me (Feb. 19) being forcibly ejected from St. John Arena during the recent CNN town meeting. What was not reported is that I was first in line at one of the three microphones after the question period was announced, and that I was forcibly removed because my remarks were to be critical of CNN and the event. When it became obvious that the disturbance was CNN's fault, I was allowed back in.

At that time, a CNN producer promised me that if I would cooperate by letting things cool down first, I would be given an opportunity at the mike. I agreed and patiently waited for about an hour. When CNN moderator Judy Woodruff announced that no more questions would be taken, it was obvious I had been lied to. So, I stepped forward and demanded that CNN keep its promise. Again, I was in the right. CNN capitulated, allowing me to point out the fatal flaws in both the event's format and in the policy of bombing Iraq.

I have heard it said that the constant disruptions at the event put Columbus in a bad light. On the contrary, Columbus now forever has shed its image as a backward cowtown. The Clinton administration and CNN thought that they could bring a biased presentation to Columbus and pass it off as an open forum. But vigilant Columbusites made sure a diversity of opinion was expressed. It was a proud day for our city and for our democracy.

Rick Theis
Columbus

Associated Press/CNN

Defense Secretary William S. Cohen, Secretary of State Madeleine K. Albright and Samuel R. Berger, the national security adviser, at Ohio State University yesterday.

Reuters/CNN

Protesters stood and shouted as Madeleine Albright tried to speak yesterday. There were some 200 protesters, scattered in groups around the university's St. John Arena.

Coverage of the February 18, 1998, Columbus, Ohio, Town Hall meeting held by then secretary of state Madeleine Albright, meant to build support for a US military strike against Iraq. Anti-war protesters, including Columbus ARA members, loudly heckled and disrupted the meeting, making national news. Courtesy of Toronto ARA archive.

1990s, but its outlook also made sense in context. With the end of the Cold War, the US was looking inward during the 1990s, and ARA was likewise focused on domestic politics, dedicated to opposing locally and regionally active fascist groups with concrete activity within the borders of the US and Canada. One memorable exception to this rule was what was described in the *Network Bulletin* as "fucking up the town hall meeting" hosted by Secretary of State Madeleine Albright, at Ohio State University, on February 18, 1998, heckling and challenging her adminis-tration's aggression against Iraq, all caught live on CNN.[27] Nonetheless, ARA was focused on domestic fascist organizing and racism.

With the rise of anti-globalization, and especially after 9/11, American politics shifted outward and toward issues that ARA had less experience with. But ARA was not instantly rendered a hapless observer. At the 2001 Montréal conference, ARA departed from its usual practice and issued a political statement on the so-called war on terror, the US invasion of Afghanistan, and solidarity with the Afghan people, as well as with people facing racist backlash and government repression in the US, also drawing connections to struggles against capitalist globalization.

True to form, ARA strove to follow up on words with action. On December 10, 2001, ARA chapters in Columbus, Montréal, New Jersey, Philadelphia, Phoenix, and Toronto protested at immigration detention centers in solidarity with those inside. "Some prisoners saw and heard our demonstration, and waved to us excitedly from behind the walls. As we chanted 'No Borders, No Nations, Stop Deportations,' we were glad to make a bright spot in their day," reported Toronto's *On the Prowl*.[28] In Los Angeles, ARA worked with the Revolutionary Association of the Women of Afghanistan (RAWA) to mount a demonstration that same day in support of human rights. Across the continent, members and support-ers were suddenly in reading groups about the Taliban and RAWA and attempting to support RAWA and other grassroots groups they perceived as allies around the world.[29]

September 11, 2001, seemed, at least at first, to give new energy to fascism in some unexpected ways. National Alliance organizer Billy Roper infamously argued:

> The enemy of our enemy is, for now at least, our friends. We may
> not want them marrying our daughters, just as they would not want
> us marrying theirs.... But anyone who is willing to drive a plane

into a building to kill jews [*sic*] is alright by me. I wish our members had half as much testicular fortitude.

Organizationally, the NA positioned itself as anti-war, blaming 9/11 on US support for Israel, while other fascists tried to ride the swell of xenophobia and racism in the US. But the far right as a whole struggled to stake out political space in the post-9/11 era. Changes in fascist organizing tactics were coming, but not before several other important clashes.

The Battle of York

On January 12, 2002, a library speech in York, Pennsylvania, was "jointly sponsored by the World Church of the Creator and National Alliance and supported by Aryan Nations, Eastern Hammerskins, WAR, the National Socialist Movement and others."[30] The fascists once again attempted to capitalize on preexisting tension over racism, as two trials in York for the homicides of a black woman and a white police officer killed in race riots in 1989 were fast approaching. One defendant was the city's former mayor, who admitted that, as a police officer during the riots, he had "shouted 'white power' and supplied ammunition" to racist rioters.[31] Instead of the fell swoop for the master race that they were hoping for, what the fascists actually got was the "Battle of York." According to local media, "Anti-racist anarchists … roamed the streets," brawling broke out, and anti-racists threw objects at passing trucks with National Alliance stickers; one truck, in turn, ran through a crowd and carried one anti-racist, who was luckily not seriously injured, about twenty feet. Intense street fighting occurred throughout the day.[32] In the end, twenty-five people were arrested, including both anti-racists and fascists; eight were locals and seventeen were from out of town.[33]

The anti-fascist response, not just of experienced activists but of locals, sets York apart. On the one hand, narratives of "out of town radicals" are often overblown and weaponized by fascist sympathizers to suggest anti-racist protest is somehow illegitimate. Radical activists and locals make up a spectrum, not a binary, dating back to ARA's anti-Klan organizing and the Syndicate's battles with nazi boneheads. On the other hand, ARA activism was undeniably heavily based on widespread travel— going where fascists go. The *New York Times* classified York as the work of outside "agitators" but, according to ARA members present that day, the level of physical anti-fascist participation by local youth was significant.

Anti-fascists, neo-nazis, and the police engage in street fighting, York, Pennsylvania, January 12, 2002.

On January 12, 2002, in York, Pennsylvania, anti-fascists (left) attack neo-nazi boneheads driving a pickup truck, during a confrontation between the two groups. The melee began when boneheads in another pickup truck drove through the crowd, striking an anarchist. Photo by Steve Mellon, *Pittsburgh Post-Gazette*.

Business card from Aurora ARA, featuring a scene from York, Pennsylvania, 2002.

"It wasn't 'antifa,'" Xtn recalls, "it was much more of a popular response from the working-class communities and people of color of York. You basically had ... Black, Puerto Rican, youth of color, and white kids joining with black bloc'ers to fight the nazis." He continues:

> I think that's a significant thing in thinking about where anti-fascism kind of ended up many years later, and in the most recent past. Whereas a lot of antifa [today], they're their own cell, their own entity, we were always hoping and trying to build for popular mobilization and popular resistance against fascists. And I think York was important, because 9/11 had happened. There was this atmosphere of fear. Bush was building up the repressive aspects of the state ... and yet people en masse came out to fight the nazis.

Sprite argues:

> The problem with a lot of anti-fascist work is that it is quasi- or extralegal. So how do you go about that work but then still try to publicly organize and build an actual movement and get people out in the streets that are willing to be militant? We had discussions about that, and we were interested in building up a militant movement in that sense.

Beside the merging of ARA and locals' militancy, the other important thing to come out of York was a decline in Matthew Hale's importance in the fascist movement. While Hale was the featured speaker, the event was sponsored and supported by a varied coalition of fascists. After York, the WCOTC largely took a backseat to the National Alliance, in terms of prominence and danger.

National Alliance (NA)

Having carefully built itself up for two decades, the NA now practiced a highly centralized and hierarchical style of white supremacy (the Führer principle). As discussed in chapter 1, founder and leader William Pierce authored *The Turner Diaries*, a 1978 novel depicting a white supremacist insurgency, a blueprint for the fascist terrorist network called The Order and inspiration for Timothy McVeigh's 1996 Oklahoma City bombing. In the eyes of the Southern Poverty Law Center (SPLC), "the National Alliance (NA) was for decades the most dangerous and best organized neo-Nazi formation in America." They had largely eschewed street-level activism but in 1999 they acquired the nazi music label Resistance Records (discussed in chapter 4), founded by Church of the Creator member George Burdi. Resistance offered the NA a serious new income stream and recruiting power among nazi boneheads. By 2002, the National Alliance "had 1,400 carefully vetted, dues-paying members"; from this relatively well-established position, they were willing to consider branching out.[34]

The National Alliance began a foray into the sort of street-level activism that appealed to boneheads and other militants, and their mobilization at York was a prime example. This new organizing was led by Billy Roper, seen by both Xtn and Sprite as someone with Hale's tactical smarts, but with more credibility on the street-fighting side—that is, potentially very dangerous. But in the NA, Roper was actually a sort of second-tier leader, the deputy membership coordinator. According to the SPLC, "there was no membership coordinator ... his 'deputy' title reflected [the NA leadership's] lack of complete trust in him." In Xtn's analysis, the National Alliance was focused on being an elitist vanguard group, but the first-tier leadership was interested in seeing how Roper's street-level organizing would play out.

By 2002, the NA was already on ARA's radar. That spring, for example, Roper had led a demo at the German consulate, protesting Germany's prosecution of a neo-nazi and ban on Nazi symbols, where he took a tire iron to the face.[35] However, new alarms went off after one event in particular. On May 12, 2002, the National Alliance staged a march on the Israeli embassy in Washington, DC.[36] The march was to promote their nominally anti-war stance, in which, driven by anti-Semitism, the NA blamed 9/11 on US support for Israel and said the correct response was to renounce Israel, not to invade the Middle East. It was, as very, very few fascist events are, basically an unqualified success.

Perhaps four hundred neo-nazis marched essentially unopposed. Chicago ARA member Tito searched for the words to describe it: "It was, no joke ... like, a fucking ... parade; a parade of white nationalists. And it would not end.... I never seen so many fascists. I started waving at the motherfuckers after a while, it was so many!" Tito and Xtn said anti-fascists only numbered somewhere between fifteen to thirty—in Xtn's words, "nobody. That's a nobody group of ARA." The show of fascist strength was a "wide-eyed glare, [a] look, into something we weren't ready for. We weren't ready for a semi–mass nazi movement." So "for the next couple of months, we got ourselves ready."

The National Alliance was building toward a weekend-long mobilization in August 2002, advertising a march on August 24 as a historic show of force, followed by a concert hosted by Resistance Records. Xtn explains, "They were attempting to build and draw out a mass united march of all the racialist, fascist, nazi, white supremacist groupings." After the shocking May demo, ARA immediately began organizing to oppose the August fascist mobilization. When NA leader William Pierce died in July, the possible significance of the August events heightened further; how the weekend played out could have an impact on the leadership transition.

A fairly extensive network of ARA people and chapters were involved at this point. Through the consistent successful anti-WCOTC campaign from 1999 to 2002, Chicago ARA had about quintupled its count of committed core activists. Alongside Chicago were old stalwart chapters like Columbus, Lansing, and Toronto, lesser known Midwest chapters like Indianapolis and Muncie, Indiana, and active East Coast chapters from Baltimore, New York City, South Jersey, and others. Various chapters sent activists to DC before the nazi mobilization to work alongside local anti-racists and anti-nazi coalitions: local anarchists, the Northeast anti-fascists (of the Northeastern Federation of Anarcho-Communists [NEFAC]), and sections of the Palestinian movement that explicitly rejected so-called solidarity from anti-Semitic white supremacists. ARA and other anti-fascists gathered intelligence, networked, and were well-prepared and well-organized by August. The weekend warrants some level of detailed examination as a standout case study of anti-fascists physically confronting fascists.

It began with a vouched-in meeting on Friday night, at which anti-fascists discussed strategy for the weekend—in particular for the nazis' main march the following day. Anti-fascists had received intelligence that some fascists would rendezvous the following morning at a travel plaza outside Baltimore. They decided to oppose the fascists at this site. Xtn recalls the events:

> Now, remember, I said there's, like, one hundred, maybe a little bit more, people at [the Friday night] meeting. [Saturday] morning [the anti-fascists] had about seventy-five people show up. So they had the bare minimum of what they'd asked for. And they were, like, fuck, but, this is it.
>
> They departed that morning en route to intercept the nazis who were at a travel plaza. They had some scouts there already. [The nazis] had … you know, those big fuckin' tour buses—four buses full of nazis hangin' out at the travel plaza waiting for their other folks to get there. This is where shit broke down…
>
> People did not anticipate the stop lights, the stop signs, other traffic.… People were getting caught and lost in traffic. So by the time that the anti-fascist caravan reached the travel plaza, that seventy-five was down to, like, forty…
>
> But they were there. And what happened was the nazis had no idea that the anti-fascists had arrived, and the next thing you know, forty or fifty anti-fascists just descend on the nazis with baseball bats, chains, smoke bombs, mace, who knows what else.… Several of the nazis were beat up really bad. Smoke bombs or tear gas canisters were thrown into some of the buses. One bus's tires were punctured, so it totally resulted in bus 4 unable to do any traveling. And the bus drivers were, like, "We're not driving! Fuck this; this is crazy shit!" Uh, that's what I heard later. But anyway, one bus, bus 4, was totally demobilized, fascists were left lying in the street, some unconscious, some bleeding, some fucked up. The anti-fascists made a hasty retreat. This all happened in ten minutes. This was like a blitz. It was quick, in and out. All the anti-fascists left.

While one of the four buses that had converged in Baltimore couldn't continue to DC—some anti-fascists chanted "Where's bus 4?" later that day—three of them did. In total, about a thousand fascists still marched on DC, according to the *Washington Post*, faced by about a thousand counter-demonstrators of various stripes and protected by about a thousand police.[37] Anti-fascists never learned the time or place of the white-power music concert planned to cap the weekend, so it took place unopposed (although, Tito later heard secondhand that it had much

This photo distributed by neo-nazis shows damage done to the bus in the travel plaza outside of Baltimore on August 24, 2002, the morning of the DC rally. This bus was unable to make the trip.

Anti-fascists block a car being driven by a neo-nazi attempting to attend a National Alliance rally, Washington, DC, August 24, 2002.

poorer-than-expected turnout). The National Alliance tried to make a show of strength and, in some ways, succeeded—but, in others, definitely didn't. In particular, their defeat at the travel plaza destroyed any remaining internal confidence in Roper's strategy to build a street-fighting NA force; he left the group the following month.

ARA faced consequences as well. The anti-fascists left the travel plaza immediately after the brawl and then, according to Xtn:

> A number of anti-fascists, some who had not been at the previous night's discussion about what to do, showed up late to the travel plaza with banners. There had been some kind of communication breakdown, don't know how ... [but] somehow, one group of anti-fascists who weren't present in any of these conversations ended up showing up with a banner or banners after all these nazis had got physically assaulted—a tour bus, like, incapacitated. And the cops swooped down on them and arrested the anti-fascists, all twenty-eight of them, and they were being charged with, like, felonious assault.

Notably, FBI records indicate at least three FBI agents "were conducting video surveillance at the Travel Plaza" and watched the entire conflict without intervening.[38] They also appear to have failed to notify local police and prosecutors that the twenty-eight arrested had arrived later and were not participants in the fight itself. Although eventually cleared, people were charged with felonies at the time. The cost of bailing out the group totaled about $26,000, which ARA raised in three days. Some were worried about reprisals by fascists, because their arrests and addresses were a matter of public record. The same evening, police also raided a local anarchist organizing center in Baltimore, though no one was arrested. The aftermath of the weekend had its costs, Xtn believes, as it "undermined the local organizing, of ... an anti-racist network [that] had emerged with a lot of good, interesting people, and work, and communication. And then, all these arrests, and then the paranoia and the suspicion and the frustration and anger and trauma of it all ... really kind of undermined that anti-racist organizing as well."

Last Gasp

Just five months after their allegedly "historic" DC mobilization, the fascist phase of the early 2000s was at its last gasp. The World Church

ARA banner at the rally to oppose a WCOTC public event in the increasingly diverse working-class city of Lewiston, in southern Maine, held on January 11, 2003, just days after Hale's arrest on charges of soliciting the murder of a federal judge. Courtesy of Hamzeh Mystique Films.

of the Creator sponsored a talk in Lewiston, Maine, on January 13, 2003, once again seeking to exploit a preexisting controversy. In the least diverse state in the union, Lewiston had a burgeoning Somali refugee community, and its mayor sparked controversy when he wrote a letter "asking Somali immigrants thinking of moving there to find somewhere else to live."[39]

Lewiston is a solid example of how ARA anti-fascists were working behind the scenes and in the streets at this point and how they understood themselves. Activists came into town before the event to meet with local organizers and set up lines of communication between cities. They created literature to distribute before and during the event, including via door-knocking and conversations with residents. Many residents were frustrated about genuine issues of economic disempowerment, which the controversy about Somali refugees had brought to the fore: poor housing options, lack of welfare, and general economic precarity. However, anti-fascists made the case that the refugees were not the ones to blame for such problems.

On the day, ARA and NEFAC members marched through the streets in a black bloc. Police had directed local protesters to two parking lots far from the World Church talk, and when the bloc came marching through those areas, many locals decided to join them. Some members of the bloc were able to engage in productive conversations with other nearby locals, reiterating the points made while canvassing earlier in the week. Between them, the unity rally held across town and the anti-fascist march attracted several thousand participants, whereas the fascists were only able to draw a few dozen racists. Matt Hale did not end up speaking, because he had been arrested on January 9 for directing a subordinate—an FBI informant—to kill a federal judge. Xtn called Lewiston the ending "whimper" of the early 2000s fascist phase; police declared it "a nonevent."[40] The World Church's Lewiston mobilization is mostly memorable because it was its last.

Coauthor Lady was among the ARA members who joined NEFAC. She remembers how Lewiston's mobilization exemplified several key organizing trends:

> With the good news that Hale got disappeared and the NA was lookin' kicked, perhaps we were free to *practice* our tactics during Lewiston. At this stage in our lives, some of us were able to self-critique: constructively criticize our actions and report back to larger networks in an attempt to fine tune what we could. The opportunity for political growth was starting to be seen as something to capitalize on. Many of us were transitioning from ARA to organizations like NEFAC. It felt natural to shift *some* of my reactive efforts to founding or joining other groups that had heightened structure, a deeper analysis, and a plan to proactively combat oppression. The collaborative effort in Lewiston—from all of these morphed groupings converging with the same goal—is what we would keep practicing for years to come.

Aftermath

After Lewiston, the declines of the World Church of the Creator and the National Alliance rapidly accelerated. To what degree can that fall be attributed to ARA's counterorganizing? Had ARA "won"? Militant anti-fascist action, including but not limited to the work of ARA, certainly had consequences. Physical confrontation was an integral ARA tactic during this period and was successful in undermining the image of and, thereby, rank-and-file faith and investment in fascist groups. Chicago ARA argued in the *Network Bulletin* in 2001 that "the constant pressure and challenge applied by ARA and other anti-racist activists has forced

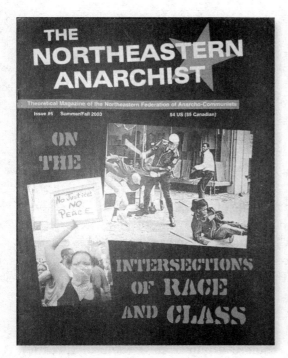

The Northeastern Anarchist no. 6 (Summer–Fall 2003). This issue included the feature article "Claim No Easy Victories: An Anarchist Analysis of ARA and Its Contributions to the Building of a Radical Anti-Racist Movement," by Rory McGowan. To our knowledge, this article stood for about twenty years as the only in-depth and overarching history of ARA.

the WCOTC rank and file up against a wall where they can no longer obey Hale's [public] pleas and strategy [of nonviolence]." By forcing Hale to rely on police protection, ARA visibly undercut his revolutionary anti-state rhetoric. (Although, more accurately, ARA forced Hale to require physical protection in general—he may not have relied on the police had his own security forces been stronger.)

According to an *ARA Research Bulletin* piece, York was "one of [the fascists'] largest mobilizations in years and many had to flee in humiliation. Some fascist leaders claimed a victory based on turnout and media attention alone, though even they must understand that it hurts their organizing to lose confrontations."[41] Daryle Lamont Jenkins of the One People's Project compares York to the 2017 "Unite the Right" rally in Charlottesville, Virginia, pointing out, "The [fascist] groups that put everything together in York started falling apart from then on … just like what you saw in Charlottesville." Xtn has a similar analysis with regard to the Travel Plaza incident:

> They were humiliated. A bunch of scrawny, gay, Black, freaky, anti-fascist humanists rocked their shit. When you're the master

race, and you've come together under the leadership of the preem-
inent nazi organization, and this happens to you—man, how
humiliating. *It was a political as well as physical defeat of the fascists*
[emphasis added].

Overall, ARA can't be credited with singlehandedly bringing down
the World Church of the Creator or the National Alliance. ARA's dogged
opposition, including physical confrontation, caused pressure and tension
in far-right organizing, but the fascists also faced internal conflicts and
law enforcement. The WCOTC had two internal conflicts in late 2001:
first, two women who ran their "Women's Frontier" and "Sisterhood,"
dedicated to recruiting and involving women, left, and, second, two
members of the WCOTC's "Guardians of the Faith Committee" secretly
asked the National Alliance to take control of the church. The National
Alliance chose to forward their letter to Hale,[42] who stayed in control.

Subsequently, in 2003, Chicago ARA was outside the local federal
courthouse when Hale and several core supporters showed up for a
contempt of court hearing in the civil trademark lawsuit filed by the
Church of the Creator, a religious group from Oregon, in operation
since the 1970s, which combined a range of views antithetical to the
WCOTC, advocating for a "synthesis of New Age thought, Christianity,
and Jewish mystical ideas, such as kabbalah and [gematria]."[43] After some
fairly routine shouting back and forth, the WCOTC forces went through
the metal detectors and into the elevators. ARA members didn't follow,
and only later did they learn Hale had been arrested inside the building,
charged with directing his head of security, who turned out to be an FBI
informant, to assassinate Joan Lefkow, the judge in the case, because he
believed she was part of a Jewish conspiracy against him. The feds had
waited for Hale and his men to go through the metal detectors—unarmed—
before arresting him, since they knew through the informant that several
of them were otherwise routinely armed.[44]

Obviously, ARA was not responsible for Hale's solicitation of murder
or for his indictment, conviction, or imprisonment. Still, like with the
Heritage Front discussed in chapter 4, ARA made it almost impossible for
the remaining WCOTC members to pick up the pieces and move forward
with any possibility of recovery.

So there were many reasons, ARA among them, for the crumbling
of the World Church of the Creator and the National Alliance. By the

time of Hale's arrest, Xtn believes he had already become irrelevant to the broader white-power movement. Hale and the WCOTC were playing second fiddle to the National Alliance, thanks to both the Battle of York and what Xtn calls Hale's "ineptness, his own egocentrism, and his own inability to actually develop any kind of serious organization, let alone movement." After DC, in August 2002, NA second-tier leader Billy Roper's attempt to move into street organizing had largely failed, and he left in the fall of 2002. Despite the early danger he appeared to pose, Roper has had little subsequent impact on white-power organizing. After William Pierce's death, the National Alliance was never able to coalesce under new leadership and quickly collapsed due to internal conflict.

Beyond the new contours of the anti-fascist struggle, ARA struggled to adjust to other post-9/11 changes. Many ARA groups did their best to oppose the sharp rise in anti-Arab racism and Islamophobia. Coauthor Mike remembers a telling example: Chicago is home to a large Arab population, including the largest Palestinian community in the US, and at the time two members of Chicago ARA were Palestinian. So when xenophobic and intimidating rallies took place outside a Chicago area mosque in the days immediately after September 11, Chicago ARA went to offer support to the Muslim community. Mike remembers the chapter arriving; they were about a dozen people, and about half of them were people of color. Looking out at a sea of literally thousands of angry white faces, Mike realized, having come to protect a mosque, they couldn't even protect themselves. The crew reconvened a few blocks away and then drove home demoralized, even scared in a way that Mike, at least, hadn't experienced before.

ARA's world and its worldview had been rocked. Political conditions outside the group changed. These factors coalesced such that shortly after the turn of the century ARA was on shakier ground. In the end, it wasn't in a position to pivot when, on top of everything else, the forms of racism it had always fought both declined and changed. By 2003, the United States and Canada would be involved in two different theaters of war, Afghanistan and Iraq, despite the efforts of mass movements in North America and across the globe.[45] While the fight persisted, the failure to stop the attack on Iraq in the spring of 2003 was undeniably demoralizing. Combined with the escalation of government surveillance of radical organizing on both the left and the right, it became harder to build the kind of mass direct-action mobilizations that had been the bread and butter of ARA's activism in the preceding era.

The attacks of September 11 led to a rise in Islamophobic and xenophobic racism, as well as to the normalization of a massively escalated level of government surveillance and repression, and ARA struggled to keep up. Finally, the street-level fascist organizing that ARA was best at opposing declined, shifting in part to new arenas like the internet, and the prior century's far-right movement was partially undercut and co-opted by the ultraconservative presidency of George W. Bush. ARA had notable successes even during these transformations, but it was unmistakably in decline.

The network did not disappear, though it certainly faded in public left consciousness. Several chapters persist even to this day, with others both coming and going. The online ARA store was still selling merchandise until at least 2006, and ARA tabled the Warped Tour that summer. It's hard to date precisely the end of the ARA era as we have described it in this book, but one small marker is the moment in 2007 when, as a security precaution, the ARA remaining core initiated a process to "re-vouch" participants on the email list, meaning that people who were not personally known to other members, or who were no longer active, were removed. Several formerly active members lost complete touch with the functioning of the network at that point, including coauthor Kristin. Annual network conferences continued, often closed to the public, until 2013, when the remnants of ARA officially reconstituted into the anti-fascist TORCH Network.[46] By then, most of the anti-fascist fighters identified in this book had long since ceased to work with or through ARA, even though many of them remain active and committed to this day.

NOTES

1   For more on Joe Scheidler, who finally kicked the bucket in 2021, see Robin Marty, "Meet Joe Scheidler, Patriarch of the Anti-Abortion Movement," *Public Eye* (Winter 2015), accessed April 11, 2022, https://www.politicalresearch.org/2015/01/23/meet-joe-scheidler-patriarch-anti-abortion-movement.

2   Anti-Racist Action, "Public Service Message to the Community of Bloomington," c. Fall/Winter 1998.

3   This quote came from a website affiliated with the Creativity Movement, which we choose not to direct traffic to. Happily neither the WCOTC or Matt Hale have made the news since 2016, when Hale was sent to a lower-security prison; see "Matt Hale

Is Out of Supermax," Idavox, 2016, accessed June 2, 2022, https://idavox.com/index.php/2016/06/05/matt-hale-is-out-of-the-supermax.

4   Ben Klassen, "A Call to Action," quoted in Southern Poverty Law Center, "Creativity Movement," accessed September 4, 2021, https://www.splcenter.org/fighting-hate/extremist-files/group/creativity-movement-0.

5   Ibid.

6   Edward Walsh, "Racial Slayer Killed Himself in Struggle," *Washington Post*, July 6, 1999; Xtn interview.

7   Xtn interview.

8   Christi Parsons, "Separatist Leader Is Denied Law License," *Chicago Tribune*, February 9, 1999; Associated Press, "State Court Rejects Hale's Law License Appeal," *Herald and Review* (Decatur, IL), November 13, 1999.

9   Keisha I. Patrick, "Students React to Expulsion Decision," *Herald and Review* (Decatur, IL), October 9, 1999; Brad Mudd, "Arrests Follow Anti-Racists' Clash with Decatur Police," *Herald and Review* (Decatur, IL), November 21, 1999.

10 Brad Mudd, "Not in Our Town Speaks Out," *Herald and Review* (Decatur, IL), October 9, 1999.

11 Mudd, "Arrests Follow Anti-Racists' Clash with Decatur Police."

12 Ibid. This was the first time that Chicago ARA took arrests, at least in many years. It wasn't the last. Accumulating arrests meant time—and money!—needed to be spent in court, on lawyers, and so forth.

13 Jason and Steve, "The Battle for Our Lives," *Arsenal* no. 1 (Spring 2000): 23.

14 Chicago ARA, "Our Take on the State of the Network," *Anti-Racist Action Bulletin* (January 2001).

15 Walter interview.

16 See Columbus ARA and Green Mountain Anarchist Collective, *A Communiqué on Tactics and Organization to the Black Bloc, from within the Black Bloc*, 2nd amended ed. (July 2001); David, X, Mike A., Melissa, and Lady, "The Black Bloc Papers: An Anthology of Primary Texts from the North American Anarchist Black Bloc 1999–2001," 1st ed. (2002).

17 R.I.P. Jordan; see Anti-Racist Action New Jersey, "Jordan Matthew Feder—PRESENTE!—Habituary," *A-Infos News Service*, January 7, 2004, accessed April 11, 2022, http://jordanfeder.com.

18 Associated Press, "NU Weighing Whether to Ignore or Stand Up to White Supremacist," *Daily Herald* (Chicago, IL), January 23, 2000; Valerie Wells and Debbie Pierce, "Hale Support Sparse in Mattoon," *Herald and Review* (Decatur, IL), April 23, 2000; Arvin Donley, "Hale Pledges July 4 'Memorial,'" *Herald and Review* (Decatur, IL), July 1, 2000.

19 Associated Press, "Rampage Coverage Swells Hale's Church Numbers," *Daily Herald* (Chicago, IL), July 2, 2000.

20 This strategy mirrored that of Paul Fromm and other "suit-and-tie" fascist organizers in Canada; see chapter 4.

21 "Anti-Racist Action vs. Matt Hale" (video), travellerjonesprod, January 9, 2008, accessed April 11, 2022, https://youtu.be/kQvsq-qHuQA.

22 "Peoria, News from the Front Lines," *ARA Research Bulletin* no. 1 (May 2001): 17.

23 Matt Hale, "Join the White Berets!" (email), April 7, 2001; reproduced in *ARA Research Bulletin* no. 1 (May 2001): 13.

24 Mickey Clokajlo and Matthew Walberg, "Hale Sues Library, Says Rights Violated," *Chicago Tribune*, March 30, 2001.

25   "White Supremacist Stirs Protests, but No Violence," *Chicago Tribune*, August 26, 2001.

26   Ibid.

27   "US Policy in Iraq Draws Fire in Ohio," CNN, February 18, 1998, accessed April 11, 2022, http://www.cnn.com/WORLD/9802/18/town.meeting.folo; audio of the disruption can be found at this site.

28   "Stand Up for Human Rights: Defending Immigrants and Refugees," *On the Prowl* no. 18 (Winter 2002): 5.

29   Michael Novick interview.

30   Editorial, "Notes on the Battle of York," *ARA Research Bulletin* no. 3 (Winter–Spring 2002): 4.

31   Francis X. Clines, "Racial Adversaries Converge on City Trying to Heal," *New York Times*, January 16, 2002; as the "both sides" title implies, this is an exceptionally annoying and shitty article.

32   Dennis B. Roddy, "York Street Fighting Between Neo-Nazis, Anti-Racists Leads to 25 Arrests," *Pittsburgh Post Gazette*, January 13, 2002.

33   Ibid.

34   "National Alliance," Southern Poverty Law Center, accessed April 11, 2022, https://www.splcenter.org/fighting-hate/extremist-files/group/national-alliance.

35   Daryle Lamont Jenkins interview.

36   Allan Lengel, "Neo-Nazis, Foes Clash at Israeli Embassy," *Washington Post*, May 12, 2002, https://tinyurl.com/7s243dpw.

37   "White Supremacists March in Washington," *Washington Post/Los Angeles Times*, August 25, 2002, newspapers.com.

38   FBI Files: Q82338_R357889_D2508499.

39   Tom Groening, "'Not in Our House,'" *Bangor Daily News* (ME), January 13, 2003.

40   Ibid.

41   "Notes on the Battle of York."

42   Sprite, "Fascist Dirty Laundry," *ARA Research Bulletin* no. 3 (Winter–Spring 2002): 10.

43   George D. Chryssides, *Historical Dictionary of New Religious Movements* (Lanham, MD: Scarecrow Press: 2012), 91.

44   For more on Hale's arrest, see "Race Extremist Jailed in Plot to Kill Judge," CNN, January 9, 2003, accessed April 11, 2022, https://www.cnn.com/2003/US/Midwest/01/08/white.supremacist/index.html.

45   Canada did not join the US in the invasion of Iraq, reflecting strong popular anti-war opposition, but did offer political support for the invasion and tactical assistance; see Greg Weston, "Canada Offered to Aid Iraq Invasion: WikiLeaks," CBC News, May 15, 2011, accessed April 11, 2022, https://www.cbc.ca/news/politics/weston-canada-offered-to-aid-iraq-invasion-wikileaks-1.1062501.

46   Heather interview; TORCH Network, "History," accessed April 11, 2022, https://torchantifa.org/history.

CHAPTER 10

LEGACY

After 9/11, the ARA Network did not have the political vision or institutional fortitude to adapt to changes in the way necessary to maintain a mass popular movement, which is both a lesson and a warning for North American anti-fascists. At the same time, it is important to remember and celebrate ARA's victories—because nobody will do it for us. The powers that be, as well as opponents of how ARA fought for their beliefs, are loath to acknowledge the impact or significance of a militant direct-action strategy. With this book, we have shared these stories not to glorify our past but to recognize the part played by (mostly) youth in defending their communities from organized racism. In this closing chapter, speaking for ourselves as coauthors, we offer a brief recap of ARA's achievements and our thoughts on lessons for today and tomorrow.

Through the 1980s and the early 1990s, the far-right marriage of nazis and Klan, advanced most conspicuously by Tom Metzger in the United States and Wolfgang Droege in Canada, brought new energy into the far-right movement. Nazi boneheads were regularly featured on TV, while white-power bands distributed by labels like Resistance Records were further fanning the flames. ARA and ARA-like groups came together across the US and Canada to defend youth cultures from being taken over by far-right goon squads. They used a mixture of education, persuasion, subcultural fun/positive role modeling, and straight-up violence. This worked.

Anti-racist punks and skins took back the streets from organized racism, largely under the banner of ARA. Former white-power skinhead turned anti-racist activist Frank Meeink, from Philadelphia, remembers that racists "weren't worried about the FBI"; it was ARA, and other anti-racist street kids, who gave them pause: "We knew, it was their *job* to fuck with us." ARA "stopped us from being able to recruit ... like, 'No way, I'm not gonna do this, 'cause what happens when you're not around and those ARA guys show up?'" ARA "knew all of our names, and they knew our participations, and they knew our ranks, and they knew who our leaders were." The fascists knew: try anything on the street, and "there might be retribution coming." Besides shutting down fascists, ARA made major, positive contributions to anti-racist and liberatory youth culture. They hosted shows, tabled tours, ran venues, proliferated literature and propaganda, and more, by being, as Columbus ARA member Josh put it, "omnipresent" in punk and hardcore and other youth cultures.

ARA organizers in the US Midwest and even toward the South (Louisville) worked hard to deny a platform to KKK groups seeking to build a base in smaller cities and towns through regular rallies. As Columbus ARA member Gerry put it, ARA might get one car each from ten different chapters, "put that together, and make it work." ARA both worked alongside and very often were the locals showing up in the streets. But whatever the details, one thing was for sure: anywhere the Klan was, ARA was there to oppose them. Quite simply, says Gerry, "we ground them down." Faced with relentless opposition on the ground, no Klan leader or group could develop momentum. While direct causation is difficult to establish, we want to come close: Anti-Racist Action was ferocious in undermining Klan organizing; Klan groups faced with this opposition fractured repeatedly and their membership declined through the 1990s.[1]

During the same decade, in Canada, ARA saw dramatic victories against far-right organizations, playing a key role in the collapse of the Heritage Front. Through rallies and demonstrations, some clandestine confrontations, and vibrant popular education campaigns (flyers, postering, graffiti), ARA denied HF space to organize. ARA members assisted up-and-coming fascist HF leader Elisa Hategan to defect and testify against the HF leadership. George Burdi of Resistance Records was also pulled into this downward vortex by street-level resistance. ARA turned up the heat on Toronto resident Ernst Zündel, the internationally known and locally active nazi propagandist, at a time when legal strategies to challenge him were at a standstill. And ARA defied geography to build a grassroots anti-fascist network capable of disrupting fascist and far-right events across the country.

ARA groups in Chicago, Baltimore, and cities and towns in Ohio and New Jersey used militant direct-action tactics against the fascist World Church of the Creator, contributing to its demise. ARA constantly harassed WCOTC activists, disrupting events, and inexorably undermining the credibility of their so-called Pontifex Maximus, Matthew Hale, helping to stop a coalition between the WCOTC and the National Alliance before it began. As for the latter, one of the best-funded and most coherent fascist organizations in the US at the time, the National Alliance, was majorly fucked-up by ARA's "travel plaza attack," prior to their 2002 march in Washington, DC, and collapsed in infighting within a year.

While ARA's style can be criticized for *re*acting to fascist organizing, groups within the ARA Network always encouraged each other to adjust to the ebb and flow of anti-fascist activities by taking on other struggles when possible. ARA chapters sought to connect with organizing against police brutality, Indigenous struggles for land and self-determination, and other campaigns against systemic racism. ARA's anti-fascism was informed not only by European traditions but also by the centuries-old struggles against racist terror among Black and Brown communities of the Americas.

ARA also fought for abortion rights and reproductive freedom, offering tangible support to health care providers and women seeking their services, while striving to politically isolate Christian far-right organizations by interfering with their public events. ARA's successes here were a testament to its on-the-ground orientation, beating many anti-racist institutions to the punch in understanding the significance of the racist right's ties with the Christian right. According to anti-fascist researcher and writer Matthew Lyons:

> When I look at the different kind of upsurges in far-right activism, they tend to come out of different ideological streams converging, whether it's Klan and nazi in the 1980s or nazis and Christian right in the 1990s. That was one of the things that was striking to me, that it was something that ARA addressed. That was an important connection to make. One of the things that I continue to push against is the tendency for people to not even talk about the Christian right when they talk about the far right.... It's not just about race and about one ideology.

By the early 2000s, according to Walter, "neo-nazis," at least the public-facing fascists that ARA knew best, "were very scarce in the US and Canada," and in both countries this decline was associated with fewer reported hate crimes throughout the 1990s and into the 2000s, with a brief jump right after 9/11.[2] It mattered that racist and fascist organizing was shut down, disrupted, or at least driven underground by ARA's brand of anti-fascist organizing. But despite ARA's efforts to broaden and deepen, the decline of organized fascist groups with a street presence also contributed to the end of ARA as a mass movement. Anti-fascists who remained connected to ARA by and large moved to tighter, less public organizing styles, more focused on online counterintelligence and intervention.

While some anti-fascists took note of the far right's pivot to online organizing, others missed the signs and were caught off guard. During the early Obama years, when he was no longer involved in ARA, Kieran remembers thinking:

> Okay, here's the US: still a recession, still two foreign wars, Black president. Why weren't the fascists growing? But in my head I was thinking of the fascists as the same organizations we were used to dealing with—so the National Alliance, the Ku Klux Klan, the World Church of the Creator, the National Socialist Movement.... I was still thinking in terms of old organizational frameworks for what growth of movements looked like, and I wasn't tapped into, like, 4chan and all the ways in which fascists were growing, but they were growing in this different way. They weren't filling out membership cards anymore. They were just joining threads and subreddits.

Matthew Lyons observes that the far right's new online strategies brought in new allies and tactics, new to ARA and key to today.

> On the one hand, you had a kind of race-based politics but also the whole manosphere, which started out very distinct from the alt-right. Then they brought all these guys into the alt-right—and not just numbers, but this whole misogynistic ideology ... [and] ways of doing political action. The Gamergate campaign pioneered the strategy of coordinated massive harassment and threats. Then the alt-right said, "Hey, we can do this in the presidential campaign." And it continued to have a strongly misogynistic edge.

The lack of broad-based direct-action organizations resisting the fash during the Obama years had consequences; an anti-fascist movement built around small-scale structures couldn't raise the alarm against the alt-right until it was too late.

Themes and Lessons

Our world is experiencing a massive resurgence of hate groups and action. Grassroots fascist organizing is successful both for specific groups and in terms of societal acceptance. In North America, the constellation of far-right forces confronting an anti-fascist left today includes at least seven elements: organized street violence; fascist use of the internet, including rampant dissemination of conspiracy theories; lone wolf mass shootings; far-right involvement in the electoral process; infiltration of law enforcement and the military; anti-choice organizing; and mass public events.

On the streets, particularly in the US, fascists have improved their tactical capabilities over the past decade. They gather *en masse* and inflict casualties in a methodical, tactical manner. In public settings, groups like the Proud Boys move in riot squad formations, employing batons, pepper spray, and body armor; they attack "easy targets" and the rear ends of marches, picking off individuals (either anti-fascists or anyone they despise). After demonstrations, they regularly move as roving thug squads looking for people to attack, most often people of color, queer folks, women, and anyone who shouts back at them. The rise of at least nominally multiethnic fascist organizations (i.e., Proud Boys, 211 Boot Boys, Patriot Prayer Movement) has aided in the widespread acceptance of nazi ideas, even as racist militias have also staged a comeback. Bonehead crews also openly walk our streets again. They form record labels, hold shows, attack social justice demonstrators, commit hate crimes, and otherwise unleash campaigns of terror on those who oppose them.

At the same time, an array of internet forums has created and been created by real-world hate groups that have shown themselves to be a major part of the new fascist threat. Social media has given the far right an enormous platform, through promotion of their pages or posts. Nazi podcasts broadcast their messages of racial superiority and hate daily. Conspiracy theories and tired old works of nazi fiction like *The Turner Diaries* have inspired misogynistic, anti-Semitic and xenophobic mass shootings in both the US and Canada. Even once-fringe race war accelerationists are gaining committed followers who carry out solo terror attacks. Some of the original Nazi propaganda concepts have been reinvented—"fake news" instead of "Lügenpresse" or lying press—with such widespread acceptance that they are now household terms.

Right-wing populism is enjoying widespread success around the globe, as racist conspiracy theories have found homes on mainstream news networks and with major parties and politicians. The mainstreaming of openly racist ideas by a US president with ties to organized hate groups boosted fascist movements around the world. Donald Trump became yet another in a long line of reactionary white supremacists who have held the office of president of the United States. His support for hate groups is in line with Woodrow Wilson's fondness for the KKK. During the Trump years, extremist organizations exerted influence over the Republican Party to levels not seen since the 1960s Civil Rights Movement, while other sectors of the far right continued to operate outside of and in some cases against the party apparatus. The impact of Trump's support of white supremacy and hate groups is almost immeasurable. Predictably, the Canadian political sphere has found its own champion in reactionary far-right politics in the new People's Party, which grew its share of the popular vote to 5 percent in the 2021 national elections, up from 1.6 percent two years before.[3]

Both before and after Trump, nazis have increasingly adopted the tactic of joining law enforcement and the military in order to infiltrate, recruit, and gain training and combat experience.[4] At the same time, the development of sophisticated surveillance technology has exploded in the last two decades, used in a widespread fashion by both government agencies and private actors. Blatant cooperation between law enforcement and the extreme right magnifies the dangers of both.

Tragically, far-right and theocratic groups and individuals are operating on terrain conditioned by the campaign of terror waged by the anti-choice movement over the past four decades. This movement has utilized a full range of tactics from ballots to bombs and is supported by heavily funded mass marketing/propaganda and grassroots organizing that includes youth indoctrination marches and camps in which tens of thousands of young people participate. In the US, anti-choice zealots have won a huge victory with the Supreme Court's 2022 ruling to overturn *Roe v. Wade*. While abortion remains legal in some states and in all of Canada and Mexico, we can anticipate ongoing intimidation and pressure on medical clinic workers and patients, criminal charges against doctors, bans on interstate travel to receive an abortion, and intensified assaults on sex education, access to birth control, the right *not* to be sterilized against your will, and the right to give birth in a safe and affordable environment.

Many of these elements of far-right upsurge have come together in a series of high-profile events, including the Unite the Right mobilization in Charlottesville, Virginia, in 2017, the January 6, 2021, attack on the Capitol Building in Washington, DC, and the so-called "Freedom Convoy" occupation of Ottawa in 2022. In short, the North American far-right has become larger, more organized, much more violent, and, thus, much more dangerous than it was a decade ago.

Still, the fascists have had their own problems. Many of the celebrity far-right leaders of the last five years have imploded from some combination of personal failings, anti-fascist resistance, and state repression, including Richard Spencer, Matthew Heimbach, and Jeff Shoupe (though they're still attempting to organize and should not be completely discounted). We feel it would be a grave mistake, however, to expect that self-destruction or the government will stop the new generation of nazis; independent anti-fascist organizing continues to be essential.

For anti-fascists, our current landscape looks very different from the one that ARA operated on in an earlier era. The repressive apparatus of the state, at both the national and local levels, is far stronger than it was in the 1980s and 1990s, in significant part due to the aftermath of the terror attacks on September 11, 2001, and the emergence of the domestic front in the United States' endless "war on terror." Meanwhile, liberal versions of multiculturalism and concerns for "diversity, equity, and inclusion"—which bear only a superficial resemblance to the radical anti-racist commitments that animated ARA—have been fully incorporated into mainstream politics, particularly since the rise of Barack Obama a few years after our narrative concludes, followed by Justin Trudeau in Canada. This incorporation lent itself to more mainstream coverage and criticism of police brutality over the past several years, even as uprisings predominantly led by the Black Lives Matter movement continue to face deadly state and far-right repression.

Indeed, the emergence of the broad-based grassroots struggles against police violence and white supremacy have been a source of inspiration in the depressing political landscape of the past several years. Rebellions have followed police murders in Ferguson, Missouri, in 2014 (Michael Brown), Baltimore in 2015 (Freddie Gray), Milwaukee in 2016 (Sylville Smith), and Louisville in 2020 (Breonna Taylor), to name a few. When George Floyd was killed by Minneapolis police officer Derek Chauvin in 2020, uprisings exploded across the US, led by a generation of young militants whose actions captivated the world. Together these events call to mind the 1992 LA Rebellion that inspired so many members of ARA. Furthermore, following decades of determined effort, Indigenous people have been able to tell stories of, in particular, abuse they suffered at residential schools and have begun unearthing mass and unmarked graves of thousands of Indigenous children on the grounds of schools they were forced to attend. The resurgence of Indigenous arts, culture, and political participation at all levels has kickstarted an anti-racist reckoning with the genocidal record of Europeans in the Americas.

While the fascists are emboldened by the events of the past several years, so too are the anti-fascists. We assembled this book because we believe that today's organizers can gain valuable insights from looking back on both ARA's achievements and its shortcomings. Contemporary anti-fascism walks on the paths that ARA paved over parts of three different decades, connecting anti-fascism to youth culture and broader anti-racist struggle and deploying tactics of mass, physical, and militant confrontation, alongside careful counterintelligence/doxxing. In short, the institutional, cultural, and tactical through lines to modern-day "antifa" in North America come from ARA.

To close this book, we will humbly offer some considered suggestions regarding ARA's lasting legacy, revisiting each of ARA's four Points of Unity (as amended in 1998)[5] and considering their implications for today and the foreseeable future.

1. **We go where they go.** Whenever the fascists are organizing or active in public, we're there. We don't believe in ignoring them or staying away from them. Never let the nazis have the street!

ARA was, first and foremost, a defensive movement. We aimed to *stop* a small but growing fascist movement by defending ourselves, our scenes, our schools, and our communities from fascist organizing and violence. This strategic orientation led to many of the movement's greatest successes, though not without costs, and left an enduring legacy for today's militant anti-fascists. While the last twenty years have seen the rise of internet activism, doxxing wars, and keyboard commandos, various lessons can be learned from ARA's method and tactics: "old-school," boots-on-the-ground activism. Whether it be operating within a public group, utilizing a phone tree, real-time surveillance and reconnaissance, sitting in courtrooms, hanging informative flyers, talking to your neighbors and co-workers, or showing up in large numbers to call out a nazi by name, these tried-and-true methods will help us to once again undermine the far right.

ARA's mass orientation—its general tendency to face the public and attempt to mobilize *significant* numbers of people—is an essential part of its successes. Whether shutting down the Heritage Front in 1993 Toronto, preventing Bound for Glory's St. Paul show in 1995 or anti-Klan rallies in Ann Arbor and Pittsburgh in 1998, or waging the Battle of York in 2002, ARA was prepared for militant confrontation but, most importantly, directly mobilized and worked alongside great numbers of people, especially locals, standing up against racism. Anti-Klan rallies, according to ARA founding member Kieran, were frequently "about the merging of ARA militancy with local community/youth militancy." As Chicago ARA's Xtn put it, "Whereas a lot of antifa [today] kind of, they're their own cell, their own entity, we were always hoping and trying to build for popular mobilization and popular resistance against fascists," and York was important, because ARA joined in the streets with local people, who, "en masse, came out to fight the nazis."

Although "never let the nazis have the streets" was a recipe for confrontation, actual violence was often avoided because of both ARA's numbers and reputation. Judith of Toronto ARA reckons that ARA had enough "mystique" to "scare [fascists] and probably inhibit them from organizing" even without huge numbers, but this mystique, while powerful, worked because it had the genuine possibility of mass action to back it up. Today's anti-fascists should certainly aim to develop and/or maintain a comparable public perception of our collective capacity to disrupt the far right based on popular mobilization.

ARA was not an organization of pacifists, and members viewed violence as a strategic rather than a moral question. In ARA's early skinhead scenes, according to Eric of Cincinnati ARA, it was sometimes a question of survival:

There was no, ever, ever, talk about, like, "Oh, is it okay to hurt somebody? Is violence the solution?" You—it's just not even... it was not an intellectual thought. It wasn't, like, "What's the best way to overcome racism in my community?" No, it wasn't that; it was "How can I survive when these fucking fascist scum are fucking beating the shit out of all my friends when we fucking walk out the door?"

For many, ARA's openness to violence was directly related to the movement's heavily working-class and punk identity. Says Judith:

It is privilege to not have to engage in a physical altercation with a nazi or a racist or a cop. I think there is a class dimension to the organizing and the analysis. Punks and working-class people are just more familiar with physicality as part of their politics. There's just not a big distinction to be made with "do you raise your fists or not?" It's just more part of people's sense of being in the world and being politically engaged—that it's part of the risk.

I think that what we achieved internally was a remarkable balance between physical confrontation and being willing to be physically confrontational and also organizing in an aboveground, acceptable kind of way. I guess what we achieved was that we pushed the needle a bit on people's understanding of what it means to organize against racism and white supremacy. Yes, there is a component that takes place in the street.

As Kitchener-Waterloo ARA member Julian Ichim put it:

There was always a split between the different organizers, whether you were at a university organizing or whether you were based within the street, and one of the issues was violence versus non-violence. We said that this wasn't an issue. The issue is: "Who sets the agenda? Is it the people or the state?"

While the history of ARA demonstrates that mass anti-fascist mobilizations can actually *limit* violence, the risks remain real. The brutal assassinations of Dan Shersty and Lin "Spit" Newborn are the most obvious examples. Today, open carried firearms have become a much more common sight at political demonstrations in the US than they were in ARA's heyday, and organizations like the National Rifle Association are broadcasting threats of violence against anti-racist activists under the guise of self- and family defense. Meanwhile, US lawmakers are making speeches and passing laws to legalize vehicular assault on left-wing protesters.[6] The widespread distribution of memes celebrating the murders of anti-racist demonstrators in Kenosha, Wisconsin, seek to normalize this violence and inspire future attacks.[7]

As many ARA veterans can attest, trauma and its aftermath are never far from the experience of violent confrontation. As Xtn put it, when "you try to go home, and there's a bunch of boneheads sitting in front of [your] apartment at 3:00 in the morning—you know, to live like that for years, you get to a point where you need a break." Many ARA organizers dedicated years, even decades, of their life and essentially worked full time as anti-fascists, often quitting high school or putting paid jobs on the backburner. While this need not, and should not, be seen as a prerequisite of anti-fascist organizing, for some, the costs were—and still are—very real.

Some ARA members, perhaps especially the skinheads who fought protracted turf wars, speak of PTSD. As Cincinnati ARA's Eric put it:

> To be involved in that [level of violence], especially as a young person, stays with you the rest of your life. I have nightmares—I have the same one over and over. That's being chased by nazis through abandoned buildings, and when they catch me I can't throw a punch or speak. It takes a toll.
>
> And I will say this: it's not the violence that was perpetrated on me, which was very serious. It's the violence that I did to others. That's what keeps me up at night. The thing is these are fellow human beings that are an existential threat to you, but they are human beings, right? And sometimes we use all this language to remove their humanity.

For people who choose to have a family, a real threat of intergenerational trauma exists. A number of comrades from past and current struggles have taken their own lives. Others have fallen into destructive patterns, such as addiction, social isolation, or unchecked violent responses. Those who are currently involved in anti-fascist struggles would do well to place an emphasis on community care that addresses trauma associated with violent physical confrontations, death at these events, or just living under the constant stress that this type of organizing brings.

A political commitment to freedom and equality is how anti-fascists avoid replicating violence for violence's sake, which could be a struggle in ARA. As Judith remembers, "because it was confrontational, and people focused on the issue of violence to the exclusion of the more political issues, it could have gone the other way too, where some people could be just drawn to either side because of the violence, because of the opportunity to fight." Anti-fascism today must stay vigilant on this issue.

There were other downsides to the emphasis on direct confrontation. First, it was always easier to shut down individual events than to win extended wars; it was easier to shut down a single white-power concert than to develop a long-term international campaign to shut down a white-power label like Resistance Records. ARA was usually a bit better at specific events than ongoing campaigns; anti-fascists in the post-Trump era should aim to improve on this record. Moreover, employing a confrontational strategy without the ability to assess the situation can leave anti-fascists vulnerable to traps set by fascists, who may "leak" information about upcoming events for their own purposes. ARA veterans can attest to incidents where fascists attempted to lure anti-fascists into dangerous situations or to provoke a fight in the presence of police or unsympathetic witnesses. Developing reliable intelligence about fascist opponents and their tactics is essential to guard against this.

Information-gathering about fascists was also critical to ARA's efforts to expose fascists to community pressure, and to interfere with fascist recruitment. As fascist organizing began to move online in the early 2000s, ARA developed a number of effective strategies in counter-intelligence and doxxing, from photographing and running license plate searches on fascists' vehicles to the sort of hacking efforts that later, when directed against intelligence firm Stratfor, resulted in the seven-and-a-half-year imprisonment of Chicago ARA affiliate Jeremy Hammond.

Research and communications are all the more important when fascists are seeking to grow among people who have grievances that the far right addresses, but who may not identify with a full fascist program. Anti-racist and anti-fascist resistance to the 2022 "Freedom Convoy" in Canada, for example, included many strategies and tactics discussed in these pages: determined research and exposure of the fascist ties of some Convoy organizers; the hacking of the fundraising portal GiveSendGo; interference in web-based communications among Convoy participants; and physical interference in the Convoy itself.[8]

Based on ARA's experience and more recent examples like these, we recommend that online research and exposure campaigns be combined with direct mass-based confrontation when the fascists do emerge from behind their keyboards seeking to take over public space.

2. **We don't rely on the cops or the courts to do our work for us.** This doesn't mean we never go to court. But we must rely on ourselves to protect ourselves and stop the fascists.

The second point of unity is both a political point, partially born from understanding that the police are a major institution of white supremacy, and a straightforward strategy for a sort of DIY anti-fascism: taking the fight directly to the nazis rather than petitioning the government to stop the fascists. In some cases, contemporary anti-fascists are entirely willing to work with, or even depend upon, varying levels of government. This collaboration with the state will unfortunately grow as the Biden administration seeks to contain the various far-right tendencies unleashed during and after the Trump administration. As we write this, the US government is actively hunting a large number of far-right activists for their participation in the January 6, 2021, Capitol Hill riot. The FBI is claiming that this is their largest-ever domestic operation, involving field offices in all fifty states. The US government has been identifying organizational command structures of militia and fascist groups. Members of hate organizations are being identified, arrested, and charged. Public records of all arrest warrants and people of interest in these investigations are being archived by anti-fascist groups and terrorism studies departments at major US universities for online public access. Investigative journalists are publishing uncomfortable truths about hate group leaders, such as Henry "Enrique" Tarrio's history of being a willing police collaborator and informant before he became leader of the Proud Boys, a group placed on the Canadian government's list of designated terrorist organizations in 2021. In 2022, the Trudeau government invoked the Emergencies Act for the first time ever to break the far-right "Freedom Convoy" occupation of Canada's capital city.[9] Under the authority of the act, the government froze bank accounts of protest participants, drawing criticism from whistleblower Edward Snowden.[10]

There are dangers to endorsing the state's repressive apparatus. The police can use action against fascists as window dressing to seem anti-racist, but history, from COINTELPRO to the Animal Enterprise Terrorism Act, has shown that state political repression has always been predominantly used against the left. For this reason, we should resist attempts to expand the state's political repression; the "domestic terrorism" bill some liberals are calling for, post–January 6, for example, is a bad idea, even if its pretext is to "fight white nationalism."

Moreover, state action is no substitute for community action and the deeper transformation anti-fascists strive for. As the *It Did Happen Here* podcast hosts, former ARA member Mic Crenshaw and Celina Flores, put it, "While imprisoning boneheads [or other fascists] may result in a temporary grace period, in the brotherhood of prison, racist skinheads have access to recruitment of new members comfortable with criminality and violence." Although "jail time kept fascists off the streets ... most understood it as a temporary fix to systemic problems." While prisons can hold individual fascists, they cannot end the systemic problems of white supremacy, patriarchy, queerphobia, and capitalism that are so fertile for fascism.

While we encourage today's anti-fascists to rediscover ARA's style of public-facing mass organizing, internal security undeniably poses challenges. Especially in the 2000s, ARA attempted to balance its public orientation with increasing internal security culture, from early adoption of (more) secure modes of digital communication to later vouching systems and partially public, partially closed conferences. Acknowledging that internal security may be harder now than in ARA's heyday, Detroit's Charles describes his time in the late 1990s as "in a way, more anonymous, even though we [usually] didn't mask up"; under today's mass surveillance, when "everybody has a damn camera in their pocket ... now, people could take [your] picture ... figure out who you are, where you work, live." At a public annual conference, police infiltration would now be a near certainty (if it wasn't already back then; the FBI did halfheartedly infiltrate the Washington, DC, ARA chapter around 2006, for example).

Nonetheless, we believe it is important to balance security culture with the sort of mass public organizing that made ARA capable of *not* relying on the cops and the courts. We hope that we have offered educational examples of how ARA attempted and often succeeded in doing so, planning with trusted comrades, while mobilizing larger numbers of people. ARA's public conferences, for example, hosted broad discussion and networking among hundreds of people, not announcements that individuals would like to do something illegal. Meanwhile, sustained efforts to build an anti-racist youth culture gave ARA the opportunity to organize with people in their own familiar spaces and to connect with networks of friends, enhancing ARA's capacity to act independently of the state.

We encourage contemporary anti-fascist comrades to maintain the focus on collective grassroots action against fascists, apart and away from the government.

3. Non-sectarian defense of other anti-fascists. In ARA, we have lots of different groups and individuals. We don't agree about everything and we have a right to differ openly. But in this movement an attack on one is an attack on us all. We stand behind each other.

Two elements here deserve attention from contemporary anti-fascists. First, the Anti-Racist Action Network was proudly and successfully non-sectarian. It was consistently a space open to varying tendencies of the left, conditioned only upon the embrace of the four Points of Unity. While anarchism was the strongest political tendency, ARA was never an anarchist group, and the network always featured prominent members who were Trotskyists, independent Marxists, or social democrats, as well as those who came out of women's liberation and Indigenous traditions, among others. There was political discussion and division, but an alliance among us to maximize friends and minimize enemies was undeniably ARA's modus operandi. Avoiding sectarianism was directly linked to building mass opposition to fascism. For example, some ARA members recall purging party builders: they were welcome as individuals but were expressly forbidden from creating any kind of internal bloc, one action among many to try and prioritize a horizontal structure in the network. This structure was successful at fostering the participation of many people, without fear of being politically dominated by others within the network.

Second, ARA recognized the importance of collective defense, including but absolutely not limited to legal support for members and supporters arrested at actions. The summer of outrage against racism and police brutality in 2020 highlighted the continuing need for legal defense, as thousands of anti-racist protesters were arrested and, in many cases, faced very serious charges. In Chicago, these protesters were supported monetarily by the Chicago Community Bond Fund (CCBF), which provides bail money for anyone arrested at anti-racist protests in or around Chicago.[11] CCBF can trace its history, in part, to ARA: after several members and supporters of Chicago ARA were arrested in the campaign against the World Church of the Creator, people in and close to ARA founded the Chicago Anarchist Defense Fund (CADF). Years after CADF ceased operations, former members donated the last remaining funds to help establish CCBF. Similarly, the International Anti-Fascist Defense Fund explicitly credits the ARA Warchest, first founded after a decision by Canadian caucus participants at the 1998 ARA Network conference, as its inspiration.[12] "The Warchest was ... one of the more enduring and cohesive factors, related to implementing non-sectarian defense of anti-fascists, and, despite not relying on courts, recognized that we had to defend people against charges in court politically and financially," says Michael Novick of People Against Racist Terror/Los Angeles ARA. "There was a consciousness about both fighting repression and supporting political prisoners, including from our own movement, but also COINTELPRO and Green Scare prisoners."

Non-sectarianism remains an important strategy for anti-fascists of today. Remaining focused on a shared commitment to opposing fascism allows us to build a broad, diverse, and strong movement capable of defeating fascism.

4. **We support abortion rights and reproductive freedom.** ARA intends to do the hard work necessary to build a broad, strong movement against racism, sexism, anti-Semitism, homophobia, discrimination against the disabled, the oldest, the youngest and the most oppressed people. WE INTEND TO WIN!

This was the most basic, overarching statement of ARA's overall political perspective. Early organizers hoped most of all to create an environment where people new to politics could see themselves, feel included and respected, and commit to taking action. As Columbus ARA's Josh put it, ARA was "cultural, and much more approachable to someone who was not deep into Marx. I think the significant thing was that it was easily accessible anti-racism that could get you to the next level and get you on the continuum toward more radical or more militant anti-racism and anti-fascism."

An image mailed to supporters of ARA member Kieran's non-sectarian defense against felony charges, in January 1996, in celebration of his acquittal. Original art by Ivan Daniels.

Says Steve of Lansing ARA:

> It wasn't, like, a cadre organization. It was meant to be a broad tent anti-fascist thing, so that kids who were just getting into anti-fascist stuff in high school at age fourteen could come, and there could be communists who've been doing stuff for, you know, forty years, and all in the same room, all learning from each other, and all getting an experience that's meaningful to them that helps propel them to do some good stuff.

ARA strove to be open to the same disaffected white youth who were targeted for fascist recruitment, which also had an impact on our strategies and messages. As Matt says:

> To do that requires a discussion that goes beyond white privilege: that recognizes white privilege but says there's far more to be gained from being a traitor to your race and loyal to your class.... ARA was interested in building majorities. I think the left doesn't even know what that means anymore, much less how to do it.

While ARA strove to build a big tent, some ARA organizers expressed their frustration at ARA's lack of position, as a network, on how the state and capitalism create and foster systemic oppression. This gap led to many hours of debates, which ultimately yielded little in the way of tangible decisions. Michael Novick compares the John Brown Anti-Klan Committee (JBAKC), an organization built around a "very high level of political unity," with ARA, which "kind of came from the other end.... JBAKC had to go through a big struggle to try to open up and broaden its political base, whereas ARA kind of had the opposite struggle of trying to tighten up and develop its political depth and understanding." The adoption of the pro-choice amendment as part of the points of unity was the only formal resolution of a political debate on the network level. Clearly, it's a perennial balancing act, but anti-fascists today may wish to be more deliberate and upfront about founding statements than ARA was. Who are our main audiences? Who are the people we most want to organize with? Who are the community allies we want to connect with? What image do we want to project to our fascist enemies?

On the ground, most ARA groups with any longevity took part in a wide array of anti-racist, anti-capitalist, feminist, and pro-queer campaigns and struggles. Their paths to get there varied. In a few cities, ARA chapters were the main activist option for young people, especially young white people, and members brought a variety of interests to the group. In other cities or towns, when there wasn't enough fascist activity to keep ARA members engaged, but they wanted to keep working together, they sought out new outlets for their political energy. And the determination by women and allies in ARA to deploy anti-fascist strategies against the Christian right and the anti-abortion movement refined ARA's politics and attracted new allies. Rather than draining energy from anti-fascist work, involvement in broader campaigns (pro-choice, anti–police brutality, economic justice) can be a vital sustaining force over a longer term. We urge anti-fascists today to embrace that lesson.

Finally, ARA manifested both the enthusiasm and creativity of the youth cultures it came out of—and the shitty behaviors endemic to North American culture in general. At its best, ARA created a positive and nurturing community for young people. For example, Emmy joined Toronto ARA in order to find a caring community within the punk scene:

> Definitely I had some trauma around racism, and I wanted to address it. [ARA] was really punk rock; it appealed to me the way it was being addressed. And there was a community that felt more respectful, because it was political—instead of this thoughtless or careless scene where everyone is drunk or high all the time, and

so much abuse happening.... I still wanted to be connected to a community, but a righteous one, one that would care about me. So that's why I joined ARA.

Many ARA members we spoke with similarly highlighted the opportunities they had to learn and grow within ARA. Yet there were failures too. Sexual assault within chapters eroded trust in those chapters and in the national network that struggled to respond to them, and ARA members could and did act out homophobia, sexism, and racism. Regarding racism, for example, Chicago ARA's Tito remembers that "ARA was really good at physically holding fascists accountable, and not good at holding themselves accountable.... I'm not saying pay my fucking rent, just, come on, be an ally." Chicago ARA's Manny agrees. In trying to counter a racist statement, for example, he says:

You bring it up and people think you're, like, crying wolf ... like, "Oh, why does everything have to be about being Mexican?" And I'm, like, "No, how do you not see how this is a problem?"... To add the layer of dismissiveness about it gets infuriating, and you don't want to spend time on it. Like, again, going around today, that it's not my job to educate you on this stuff. Educate yourself. I can't be out here being the "angry Mexican."

Others speak of the challenge of putting into practice the cooperative, democratic, and anti-oppressive values that ARA espoused. As Xtn put it:

It's not easy to be up front and democratic and transparent and honest all the time. But, if you're not trying, then—then, fuck, you know. You can quote me! "Then, fuck."

It's hard. People aren't trained to do this. We're trained in this society to be dishonest, to be manipulative, to get one up over other people, to be competitive in an egotistical, pro-capitalist kind of way. We're not taught the skills and the psychology and the intellectual kind of ways to... to have a participatory alternative.

Columbus ARA's Mac agrees:

Cooperative interaction is an art, you know; it really is an art. Not caring who gets the credit. Not caring, you know—putting your ego at the door, and just coming in to get as much as you can done toward the prize that you're going for.... Criticism, self-criticism.... Being able to be criticized, you know—"you had this idea, and you convinced us all to do it, and we did it, and it was a total failure, bust, nothing we expected to get from it we got from it." And instead of being defensive, you go, "Yep, that's exactly right. My mistake. How can we do it better?" where—an accurate criticism is actually a gift to you.

Cooperative, democratic, and liberatory interaction, let alone organization-building, is not easy, but ARA members kept at it over many years—refining tactics and politics, adopting new in-person and online organizing tools, challenging themselves and each other to do better. The closing statement of the points of unity—"WE INTEND TO WIN!"—motivated people. An anti-fascist movement can have clear-cut victories. A white-power show can be shut down. The Klan can be surrounded and drowned out at a rally and sent home packing. A racist band's albums can be removed from online sales and brick-and-mortar record stores. A nazi gang can be banned from a neighborhood bar. Michelle, one of the skinheads of Chicago and later Minneapolis, reflects:

> Keeping our city nazi-free—that makes me proud. To know that no citizens of Chicago were harassed by nazi skinheads, if there was anything we could do about it. Considering that we were a ragtag group of, you know, a lot of us didn't graduate high school. You know, we were the original antifa ... and if we kept those guys from organizing, I'd do it again in a heartbeat.

The sense of danger and urgency that loomed over the tasks that ARA members had set for themselves could and sometimes did foster impatience with the careful work needed to embody the ideals stated, however imperfectly, in the fourth point of unity. Yet danger and urgency can also fuel solidarity, loyalty, and determination to get the job done.

We intend to win!

A Call to Action

A tremendous opportunity has presented itself. The need for a broad-based anti-fascist movement has never been clearer. The ARA model of public organizing provides a unique way of dealing with these threats. A

Minneapolis, 1990s. Courtesy of Anna Stitt.

An anti-fascist mural in memory of Dan and Spit. Courtesy of Antifa International and Sydney Anti-Fascist Action, Australia, July 2018.

network binding its chapters and members together through points of unity allows many different types of people to participate. A network of chapters allows for more trusted information sharing between cities and regions. Conferences where these chapters regularly come together to tackle agenda items, deal with differences, support each other, and report on challenges and successes help to build and strengthen a larger anti-fascist movement. Bail funds or war chests to support our prisoners in this struggle are vital to mutual support. The wave of right-wing populism that is enabling and assisting the growth of this new wave of fascists can be countered by tapping into the large pool of everyday people who reject racism in principle and are willing to take action. For everyday people to plug into a militant anti-racist public organization, one must exist.

As we come together to oppose today's rising fascist movements, we each bring our individual experiences, interests, political assessments, and skill sets. Nurturing these differences makes us stronger. Not everyone will want to directly confront violent fascists in the streets, and there will be different ideas of what that confrontation could and should look like. There are an infinite number of roles to be filled. Many of us are still active today, in indirect and direct ways. You can take on this work as well. You are ARA's legacy.

NOTES

1   Also a factor in the Klan's decline were court lawsuits brought by the Southern Poverty Law Center on behalf of victims of specific attacks: against the United Klans of America, in Mobile, Alabama, the Invisible Empire, Knights of the Ku Klux Klan, in Forsythe County, Georgia, in 1987, and against the Christian Knights of the KKK, in South Carolina, in 1996. Similarly, the SPLC sued Tom Metzger and White Aryan Resistance in Portland following the murder of Mulugeta Seraw in 1990. These lawsuits put fascist groups on the defensive, and when successful depleted their financial resources.

2   See FBI, *Hate Crime Statistics*, Uniform Crime Reporting; annual reports beginning 1996 are available at https://ucr.fbi.gov/hate-crime.

3   Todd Gordon, "Fascism Is as Canadian as the Maple Leaf," February 2, 2022, Midnight Sun, accessed April 11, 2022, https://www.midnightsunmag.ca/fascism-is-as-canadian-as-the-maple-leaf.

4   See House Committee on Oversight and Reform, "Experts Warn Oversight Subcommittee that White Supremacist Infiltration of Law Enforcement Poses a Threat to Cops, Communities," September 29, 2020, https://tinyurl.com/yxdjejvb.

5   This is the wording used in ARA Chicago's *ARA Research Bulletin* no. 1, May 2001.

6   See Nitish, Pahwa, "Why Republicans Are Passing Laws Protecting Drivers Who Hit Protesters," Slate, April 25, 2021, accessed April 11, 2022, https://slate.com/business/2021/04/drivers-hit-protesters-laws-florida-oklahoma-republicans.html.

7   See Neil Augenstein, "Judge: Car Crash Meme Admissible in Charlottesville Murder Trial," WTOP News, accessed April 11, 2022, https://wtop.com/virginia/2018/11/judge-car-crash-meme-admissible-in-charlottesville-murder-trial; Alex Ward, "People Are Running Over George Floyd Protesters. Are Far-Right Memes to Blame?" June 1, 2020, accessed April 11, 2022, https://www.vox.com/2020/6/1/21276941/george-floyd-protests-truck-police-attack.

8   Brian McDougall, "Building on the Battle of Billings Bridge," Midnight Sun, February 24, 2022, accessed April 11, 2022, https://www.midnightsunmag.ca/building-on-the-battle-of-billings-bridge.

9   The Emergencies Act was passed in 1988 to replace the previous War Measures Act, used twice in Québec in recent decades, during the so-called FLQ October Crisis of 1970 and against Mohawks during the so-called Oka Crisis, in 1990.

10   Edward Snowden, "Governments claiming the authority to *freeze people's bank accounts*..." Twitter, accessed April 11, 2022, https://twitter.com/snowden/status/1495460828270714880.

11   Chicago Community Bond Fund, accessed April 11, 2022, https://chicagobond.org.

12   International Anti-Fascist Defense Fund, accessed April 11, 2022, https://intlantifadefence.wordpress.com.

GLOSSARY OF TERMS

Disclaimer: Our glossary is meant to be brief, not definitive. It relies heavily on Devin Burghart's *Soundtracks to the White Revolution: White Supremacist Assaults on Youth Music Subcultures* (as denoted by entries marked with an asterisk*).[1]

Anarchism: Rejects all involuntary coercive forms of hierarchy, including the state and capitalism; usually described, alongside libertarian Marxism, as part of the libertarian wing of the socialist movement. While many ARA members may not have held strong, overarching political ideologies, anarchism was the strongest influence among those who did. For more on the most organized anarchist tendency in ARA, see "Love and Rage" entry below.

Anti-Racist Action (ARA): Read this book.

Anti-Semitism*: Hatred, prejudice, discrimination, or persecution directed against people of Jewish descent or faith. Typically considered by white supremacists to be the ultimate enemy engaged in a conspiracy to destroy the white race, Jews are often accused by fascists of manipulating or directing people of color.

Aryan Nations: Neo-nazi organization founded in the 1970s, in Idaho; a major hub for white supremacist networking and training, both at their Idaho compound and in other cities they traveled to. In 1992, Floyd Cochran, a high-ranking official in the group, renounced his beliefs and founded the Education and Vigilance Network, an anti-racist information and resource center based in Pennsylvania.

Bonehead: Used especially by anti-racist skinheads to describe a racist skinhead.

Communism: An ideology seeking a socioeconomic order with common ownership of the means of production and the absence of hierarchy and the state. Broad schools of thought include anarcho-communism (which sees the state as an impediment) and Marxism (which seeks state control to build communism).

Often used by fascists and the far right as a choice insult for their opponents, with a malleable definition. Some Marxists were involved and influential in ARA's history; see "Trotskyist League/US" entry below.

Direct action: Direct use of power by people to reach certain goals, rather than petitioning existing powers (like a government) to solve a problem. Direct action might target people, groups, or property using nonviolence (sit-ins, strikes, mutual aid) or violence (politically motivated assault, arson, property destruction). ARA members used the term "direct action" from the movement's beginning, with anti-racist skinheads usually using the term to mean violence against nazi skinheads.

Fascism: Political system promoting the complete dominance of one group over others in a society, often referring to mythical past greatness. Fascists reject liberal democracy, rely on charismatic leadership and popular enthusiasm, and embrace violence as a redemptive and purifying force. More concerned with exercising power than intellectual consistency, fascists may advance starkly different economic programs and may be small activist formations, may be rooted in mass political parties, or may be in a position to rule society. The Ku Klux Klan, which brutally suppressed Black political power after the US Civil War, in the late 1860s, epitomized many strategies embraced by the Italian and German fascist parties in the twentieth century. Organizers and thinkers from the Global South like Aimé Césaire have long observed that the methods of European fascists (genocide, denial of civil liberties, slave labor) have always been part of colonialism. While Michael Novick, among others, promoted this analysis within ARA, the network had no single definition of fascism.

Heritage Front: Canadian neo-nazi white supremacist organization founded in 1989 and disbanded around 2005. The Heritage Front formed an alliance with the Church of the Creator and its Canadian leader George Burdi. Other prominent Canadian far-right figures (Paul Fromm, Ernst Zündel) worked with but did not join the organization.

John Brown Anti-Klan Committee (JBAKC): Anti-racist, anti-Klan organization formed in the late 1970s. A white organization predicated on solidarity with the Black liberation/New Afrikan struggle. For more, see James Tracy and Hilary Moore, *No Fascist USA! The John Brown Anti-Klan Committee and Lessons for Today's Movements* (San Francisco: City Lights Books, 2020).

Ku Klux Klan (KKK)*: White supremacist organization emerging after the US Civil War to violently oppose Reconstruction, reborn in the early twentieth century. ARA combatted numerous KKK factions, including the Knights of the Ku Klux Klan, the American Knights, and the Christian American Knights.

Love and Rage: Anarchist organization, active from 1989 to 1998. It began as a newspaper and renamed itself the Love and Rage Revolutionary Anarchist Federation in 1993. Having a strong influence on the development of ARA's national network and ARA chapters (Minneapolis, Detroit, Lansing, Flint, Harlem), it was a highly organized "ideological" anarchist organization, compared to the "anarchism by default" often claimed by less ideological people in the punk scene (and, by extension, ARA).

Maximum Rocknroll (MRR): San Francisco–based punk zine, published in print from 1982 to 2019 and then online, primarily featuring punk and hardcore artist interviews and music reviews but also "scene reports" of punk events in various cities (including nazi problems). These scene reports, as well as classified ads and coverage of ARA, helped ARA expand beyond its Minneapolis beginnings.

Midwest Anti-Fascist Network (MAFNet): Its 1994 Columbus, Ohio, conference, held on October 15–16, first formalized the network, renamed the Anti-Racist Action Network in 1995.

National Alliance (NA): White supremacist and neo-nazi political organization active from 1974 to the early 2000s, based in Hillsboro, West Virginia. Founded by William Luther Pierce, author of the white supremacist novels *The Turner Diaries* and *Hunter*. At its height, in 2002, around the time ARA organized against it, membership was estimated at 2,500, with an annual income of $1 million. A boycott of the NA's Resistance Records label resulted in a steep drop-off in generated funds. Pierce died in July 2002, and internal power struggles severely weakened the NA.

National Socialism*: Subset of fascism, a political philosophy most notorious for being Adolf Hitler's National Socialist German Workers' Party (Nazi) ideology, combining an appeal to workers and the middle classes and an ambivalent anti-capitalism with political opportunism, anti-Marxist agitation and violence, and fierce ethnic nationalism, anti-Semitism, and racism. National Socialism claims to resolve the contradictions between capital and labor, often through a "third way."

Neo-nazi*: Individuals and organizations coming after the Nazi regime collapse, whose ideology directly resembles or attempts to resemble that of the German Nazi Party or one of its factions.

Northeastern Federation of Anarcho-Communists (NEFAC): Bilingual (French and English) organization of revolutionaries from northeastern North America identifying with the communist tradition within anarchism. Active from 2000 to 2011, the federation was organized around the principles of theoretical coherence, tactical unity, collective responsibility, and federalism, and activities included study and theoretical development, anarchist agitation and propaganda, and intervention within the class struggle, including the York and Lewiston conflicts described in this book.

Oi!*: Musical form arising from punk music in the late 1970s, adopted by skinhead subculture. Cockney for "Hey," it is not a racist term.

One People's Project (OPP): Founded in 2000 by Daryle Lamont Jenkins. Monitors and publishes information about racist and far-right groups and individuals, mostly in the US. It is probably the best-known militant anti-fascist formation in the US. Idavox.com, launched in 2015, is the OPP news line. Daryle lived in Ohio in 1995 and worked with ARA on pro-choice campaigns.

Operation Rescue/Operation Save America (OSA): Militant anti-abortion group founded by Randall Terry in 1986. Known as the Operation Rescue Network (ORN), in 1990, it began using the name Operation Rescue/Operation Save America. It remains active.

Pro-Am: Short for "pro-American" (based on a personal definition of American values and way of life). Label for some skinheads. Less prominent over time, pro-Am skinheads were significant in early ARA and the Syndicate.

Punk*: Both a musical style and a subculture, punk music is characterized by loud, chord-based guitars and faster drums but has diversified into many subgenres. The subculture can be very ideologically diverse but is generally anti-conformist and anti-establishment and encourages a do-it-yourself ethos that also informed ARA, whose chapters, especially early on, were often concerned with booting fascists out of their punk scenes. Punk culture remained central to ARA recruitment and fundraising.

Racist*: An individual, group, institution, or action disliking, hating, and/or oppressing person(s) unlike oneself, grounded in perceived or actual racial or ethnic differences. More precise than *prejudice* or *discrimination*.

RAHOWA: Abbreviation of "racial holy war," it is a term associated with the World Church of the Creator; see "World Church of the Creator" entry below.

Red: Term, symbol, or flag representing socialism, communism, Marxism, and other left-wing, working-class-centric politics. A redskin is a left-wing skinhead, usually Marxist communist, sometimes anarchist, and is militantly anti-fascist and pro–working class.

Red and Anarchist Skinheads (RASH): Left-wing, anti-racist, anti-fascist skinhead network originally founded in January 1993 in New York City as RASH NYC by anarchist members of the MAYDAY Skinhead Crew. With small chapters worldwide (Canada, Italy, South America, Mexico, Spain, the US), RASH has never officially disbanded. RASH was formed by circulating a call for unity among skinheads via snail mail, calling for the winning back of skinhead subculture that had been all but stolen by boneheads, which was going to take a fight. RASH NYC were in ARA chapter listings from 1996 to 1999.

Resistance Records (RR): Neo-nazi music label founded by Church of the Creator member George Burdi in 1993. Owned and run by Canadians but based in Detroit, RR was a major player in the white-power punk scene, and ARA chapters like Toronto and Detroit waged specific campaigns, encouraging record stores to boycott the label, for example. In 1999, the National Alliance bought RR, thus securing a major new income stream, but that declined steeply in the 2000s.

Skinbyrd/skinhead: Member of a subculture with few consistent, well-defined markers besides working-class roots and distinctive fashion: simple work pants or mini-skirts; suspenders; button-up shirts; bomber or similar jackets; high-laced Doc Martens; and a shaved head or a Chelsea cut (mostly shaved head with a front fringe/bangs, mostly worn by femmes).

Skinheads Against Racial Prejudice (SHARP): Founded in New York City in the mid-1980s. A decentralized network that emerged as a leading contributor to the same anti-racist skinhead movement that produced the Baldies and the Syndicate. Early ARA members in Cincinnati, Portland, and elsewhere were also active SHARP skins. It persists today.

Syndicate: Network of anti-racist skinheads in the late 1980s, mainly in the midwestern US. Syndicate skinheads were either closely related to or synonymous with ARA. It wound down by about 1990, while ARA lived on.

Trotskyist League/US: Small group of Trotskyists (communists aligned with the ideas of Leon Trotsky, an early Soviet communist later ousted by Joseph Stalin) that formed in the US Great Lakes region in 1990. Members included long-time Cincinnati and Michigan ARA activists.

Warchest: Treasury fund established by a group, allocating all money deposited to costs associated with working toward the cause of said group (e.g., bail funds, legal fees, medical and relocation costs). Allocations typically require group members' consent, usually by vote.

Wheatpasting: Method of poster application, mixing wheat flour and water into a glue that, when made correctly, can be nearly impossible to remove. Tried-and-true propaganda method among youth in the 1980s, 1990s, and early 2000s.

World Church of the Creator/The Creativity Movement (WCOTC): White supremacist organization founded in the 1970s, revitalized by Matthew Hale in the 1990s, and reaching new prominence after a multistate killing spree by a member in 1999. ARA chapters, including Chicago, waged an intense and successful campaign to confront the WCOTC. In 2005, Hale was sentenced to forty years in prison for soliciting an FBI informant to kill a federal judge.

Zine*: Abbreviation for *magazine*. Publication of a do-it-yourself (DIY) punk subculture. Also known as "fanzines" and "skinzines" (skinhead culture), zines were an essential method of ARA communication and networking.

NOTE

1   Devin Burghart, *Soundtracks to the White Revolution: White Supremacist Assaults on Youth Music Subcultures* (Chicago: Center for New Community, 1999).

A NOTE ON OUR SOURCES

In researching this book, we relied heavily on interviews with former members of ARA and others who had interacted with ARA. We are supremely grateful to each of these people for taking the time to share their stories. The interviewees include:

Asad Ismi (writer on international politics, Toronto), July 24, 2020
Bill Dunphy (journalist, Toronto area), March 5, 2018
Brandon (Baldies and Minneapolis ARA), November 24, 2020
Brandon Sledge (Las Vegas ARA), November 27, 2020
Charles (Detroit ARA), multiple interviews, 2020
Daryle Lamont Jenkins (One People's Project), multiple interviews, 2018 and 2020
David Miller (former Toronto city councilor), January 6, 2020
Davin Charney (Kitchener-Waterloo ARA), January 7, 2021
Devin Burghart (Institute for Research and Education on Human Rights), December 21, 2020
DJ (Baldies and Minneapolis ARA), October 6, 2018
Elizabeth Moore (former Heritage Front, Toronto), December 8, 2019
Emmy (Toronto ARA), November 22, 2019
Eric Johnson (SHARP, Cincinnati ARA, and Trotskyist League/US), September 23, 2020
Ernesto Todd Mireles (Lansing MEXA), November 20, 2020
Frank Meeink (ex–white power), January 13, 2021
George Matiasz (San Diego ARA), August 18, 2020
Gerry Bello (Columbus ARA), multiple interviews, 2019 and 2020
Giles (Toronto, Peterborough, and Vancouver ARA), October 11, 2020
Gremlin (Chicago ARA), January 30, 2021
Harry (Toronto ARA), December 13, 2019

Heather (Lansing and Chicago ARA), January 18, 2021

Howie (John Brown Anti-Klan Committee), July 15, 2020

Jane (Toronto ARA), January 29, 2020

Janusz Baraniecki (Toronto), December 12, 2019

John Bueno (Toronto ARA), January 18, 2018

Josh (Columbus ARA), multiple interviews, 2020

Judith (Toronto ARA), March 3, 2018

Julian Ichim (Kitchener-Waterloo ARA), August 31, 2021

Katrina (Minneapolis ARA), October 10, 2020

Kieran (Baldies; Minneapolis, Detroit, and Chicago ARA; Love and Rage Revolutionary Anarchist Federation), multiple interviews, 2019, 2020, and 2021

Lorraine (Baldies and Minneapolis ARA), September 3, 2020

Mac (Columbus ARA), multiple interviews, 2021

Malki C. Brown (SHOC-affiliated and Chicago ARA), October 15, 2020

Manny (Chicago ARA), multiple interviews, 2019 and 2020

Matt (SHARP, Cincinnati ARA, and Trotskyist League/US), October 2, 2020

Matthew Lyons (researcher, Three-Way Fight blog), July 1, 2021

Mic Crenshaw (Baldies and Minneapolis ARA), September 22, 2018

Michael Novick (Los Angeles ARA/People Against Racist Terror), multiple interviews, 2020

Michelle (SHOC- and Baldies-affiliated and Chicago and Minneapolis ARA), September 10, 2020

Nadia (Toronto ARA), January 26, 2020

Rath Skallion (Columbus and Nomadic ARA), February 1, 2021

Saba (Toronto ARA), January 26, 2020

Sheila (Bloomington, Chicago, and Louisville ARA), correspondence, February 14, 2021

Soheil (Toronto), July 27, 2020

Sprite (Chicago ARA), February 5, 2021

Steve (Lansing ARA/Active Transformation and Love and Rage Revolutionary Anarchist Federation), December 21, 2016 (interviewed by Dr. Ernesto Todd Mireles), and multiple interviews, 2019 and 2021 (by coauthor)

Thomas (Winnipeg ARA), September 28, 2020

Tito (Chicago ARA), September 22, 2020

Tom (SHARP and Portland ARA), February 22, 2019

Walter Tull (Edmonton Anti-Fascist League and Edmonton and Montréal ARA), multiple interviews, 2019

Xtn (Chicago ARA), multiple interviews, 2020 and 2021

Beyond interviews, our sources are generally referenced in the endnotes or the main body of this book. They fall into several categories: newspaper and magazine articles from the era we cover here; internal ARA documents that are largely not publicly accessible and are generally held in personal archives; public-facing ARA and anti-fascist material largely available on the internet; FBI files related to Anti-Racist Action obtained through the Freedom of Information Act; and some social media posts.

INDEX

Page numbers in *italic* refer to illustrations. "Passim" (literally "scattered") indicates intermittent discussion of a topic over a cluster of pages.

ABOUT THE AUTHORS

Shannon Clay is a historian and community activist from the Mountain West. Coming up after ARA had largely declined, he learned of its little-known history through anarchist networks and saw the need to document and publicize this history for a new generation of activists. He has been involved in student organizing and in prison solidarity and abolition work. Letters of love can be sent to ShannonClay@ protonmail.com. XVX.

Lady is from Columbus, Ohio, and is proud to be a working-class woman. She worked with ARA in the 1990s and 2000s, was a founding member of the Federation of Revolutionary Anarchist Collectives and a member of the Green Mountain Anarchist Collective from 2001 to 2007 and of the Northeastern Federation of Anarcho-Communists from 2001 until it ended in 2011. Lady founded Keystone ARA in 2016 and contributes to One People's Project/Idavox. She has dabbled in various anti-fascist how-to writings and community projects over the years. This is the first book she will take credit for. She lives with her family in Western Pennsylvania. Hate mail can be sent to lady@hushmail.com. FAFO.

Kristin Schwartz grew up with the Toronto chapter of ARA from 1992 to 2003 and is grateful to have had that opportunity to contribute to the long struggle against white supremacy. She went on to work in community radio and has produced several audio documentaries, including *Women: The Oppressed Majority* (2016), *The Latin American Revolution* (2014),  and *The Ravaging of Africa* (2007); some were syndicated across the Pacifica Network. Her writing has been published in *Our Times*, *Canadian Dimension*, the Canadian Centre for Policy Alternatives *Monitor*, and *Labour/Le Travail*.

Michael Staudenmaier is a veteran of many anti-fascist, anti-imperialist, and anarchist projects over the past quarter century, including work with ARA Chicago in the 1990s and 2000s. He is the author of *Truth and Revolution: A History of the Sojourner Truth Organization, 1969–1986* (AK Press, 2012), as well as many other shorter works of political analysis and historical scholarship. He works as assistant  professor of history at Manchester University in Indiana and lives in Chicago with his family.

Gord Hill, author of the foreword, is an Indigenous writer, artist, and activist of the Kwakwaka'wakw nation. He is the author and illustrator of *The 500 Years of Indigenous Resistance Comic Book*, *The Anti-Capitalist Resistance Comic Book*, and *The Antifa Comic Book* (all three published by Arsenal Pulp Press, in Vancouver, Canada), as well as the author of the book *500 Years of Indigenous Resistance*,  published by PM Press, in Oakland, California. His art and writing has also been published in numerous periodicals, including *Briarpatch*, *Canadian Dimension*, *Redwire*, *Red Rising Magazine*, *Dominion*, *Recherches Amerindiennes au Québec*, *Intotemak*, *Seattle Weekly*, and *Broken Pencil*.

ABOUT PM PRESS

PM Press is an independent, radical publisher of books and media to educate, entertain, and inspire. Founded in 2007 by a small group of people with decades of publishing, media, and organizing experience, PM Press amplifies the voices of radical authors, artists, and activists. Our aim is to deliver bold political ideas and vital stories to all walks of life and arm the dreamers to demand the impossible. We have sold millions of copies of our books, most often one at a time, face to face. We're old enough to know what we're doing and young enough to know what's at stake. Join us to create a better world.

PM Press
PO Box 23912
Oakland, CA 94623
www.pmpress.org

PM Press in Europe
europe@pmpress.org
www.pmpress.org.uk

FRIENDS OF PM PRESS

These are indisputably momentous times—the financial system is melting down globally and the Empire is stumbling. Now more than ever there is a vital need for radical ideas.

In the many years since its founding—and on a mere shoestring—PM Press has risen to the formidable challenge of publishing and distributing knowledge and entertainment for the struggles ahead. With hundreds of releases to date, we have published an impressive and stimulating array of literature, art, music, politics, and culture. Using every available medium, we've succeeded in connecting those hungry for ideas and information to those putting them into practice.

Friends of PM allows you to directly help impact, amplify, and revitalize the discourse and actions of radical writers, filmmakers, and artists. It provides us with a stable foundation from which we can build upon our early successes and provides a much-needed subsidy for the materials that can't necessarily pay their own way. You can help make that happen—and receive every new title automatically delivered to your door once a month—by joining as a Friend of PM Press. And, we'll throw in a free T-shirt when you sign up.

Here are your options:

- **$30 a month** Get all books and pamphlets plus 50% discount on all webstore purchases

- **$40 a month** Get all PM Press releases (including CDs and DVDs) plus 50% discount on all webstore purchases

- **$100 a month** Superstar—Everything plus PM merchandise, free downloads, and 50% discount on all webstore purchases

For those who can't afford $30 or more a month, we have **Sustainer Rates** at $15, $10, and $5. Sustainers get a free PM Press T-shirt and a 50% discount on all purchases from our website.

Your Visa or Mastercard will be billed once a month, until you tell us to stop. Or until our efforts succeed in bringing the revolution around. Or the financial meltdown of Capital makes plastic redundant. Whichever comes first.

ABOUT US

Working Class History is an international collective of worker-activists focused on the research and promotion of people's history through our podcast, books and social media channels.

We want to uncover stories of our collective history of fighting for better world and tell them in a straightforward and engaging way to help educate and inspire new generations of activists.

Through our social media outlets with over one million followers, we reach an audience of over 20 million per month. So if you're on social media, you can connect with us in the following ways:

- Instagram: @workingclasshistory
- Facebook: facebook.com/workingclasshistory
- Twitter: @wrkclasshistory
- YouTube: youtube.com/workingclasshistory
- Mastodon: mastodon.social/@workingclasshistory
- Tumblr: workingclasshistory.tumblr.com

We receive no funding from any political party, academic institution, corporation or government. All of our work is funded entirely by our readers and listeners on patreon. So if you appreciate what we do, consider joining us, supporting our work and getting access exclusive content and benefits at patreon.com/workingclasshistory.

500 Years of Indigenous Resistance

Gord Hill

ISBN: 978-1-60486-106-8
$12.00   96 pages

The history of the colonization of the Americas by
Europeans is often portrayed as a mutually beneficial
process, in which "civilization" was brought to the Natives,
who in return shared their land and cultures. A more
critical history might present it as a genocide in which
Indigenous peoples were helpless victims, overwhelmed and awed by European
military power. In reality, neither of these views is correct.

500 Years of Indigenous Resistance is more than a history of European colonization
of the Americas. In this slim volume, Gord Hill chronicles the resistance by
Indigenous peoples, which limited and shaped the forms and extent of colonialism.
This history encompasses North and South America, the development of nation-
states, and the resurgence of Indigenous resistance in the post-WW2 era.

Gord Hill is a member of the Kwakwaka'wakw nation on the Northwest Coast. Writer,
artist, and militant, he has been involved in Indigenous resistance, anti-colonial and
anti-capitalist movements for many years, often using the pseudonym Zig Zag.

Antifascism, Sports, Sobriety: Forging a Militant Working-Class Culture

Julius Deutsch
Edited and translated by Gabriel Kuhn

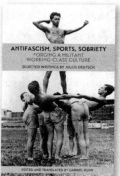

ISBN: 978-1-62963-154-7
$14.95   128 pages

The Austromarxist era of the 1920s was a unique chapter in socialist history. Trying to carve out a road between reformism and Bolshevism, the Austromarxists embarked on an ambitious journey towards a socialist oasis in the midst of capitalism. Their showpiece, the legendary "Red Vienna," has worked as a model for socialist urban planning ever since.

At the heart of the Austromarxist experiment was the conviction that a socialist revolution had to entail a cultural one. Numerous workers' institutions and organizations were founded, from education centers to theaters to hiking associations. With the Fascist threat increasing, the physical aspects of the cultural revolution became ever more central as they were considered mandatory for effective defense. At no other time in socialist history did armed struggle, sports, and sobriety become as intertwined in a proletarian attempt to protect socialist achievements as they did in Austria in the early 1930s. Despite the final defeat of the workers' militias in the Austrian Civil War of 1934 and subsequent Fascist rule, the Austromarxist struggle holds important lessons for socialist theory and practice.

Antifascism, Sports, Sobriety contains an introductory essay by Gabriel Kuhn and selected writings by Julius Deutsch, leader of the workers' militias, president of the Socialist Workers' Sport International, and a prominent spokesperson for the Austrian workers' temperance movement. Deutsch represented the physical defense of the working class against its enemies like few others. His texts in this book are being made available in English for the first time.

"An almost completely forgotten episode in labor history."
—Murray Bookchin, author of *Anarchism, Marxism and the Future of the Left*

"A foretaste of the socialist utopia of the future in the present."
—Helmut Gruber, author of *Red Vienna: Experiment in Working-Class Culture, 1919–1934*

Sober Living for the Revolution: Hardcore Punk, Straight Edge, and Radical Politics

Edited by Gabriel Kuhn

ISBN: 978-1-60486-051-1
$22.95   304 pages

Straight edge has persisted as a drug-free, hardcore punk subculture for 25 years. Its political legacy, however, remains ambiguous – often associated with self-righteous macho posturing and conservative puritanism. While certain elements of straight edge culture feed into such perceptions, the movement's political history is far more complex.

Since straight edge's origins in Washington, D.C., in the early 1980s, it has been linked to radical thought and action by countless individuals, bands, and entire scenes worldwide. *Sober Living for the Revolution* traces this history.

It includes contributions – in the form of in-depth interviews, essays, and manifestos – by numerous artists and activists connected to straight edge, from Ian MacKaye (Minor Threat/Fugazi) and Mark Andersen (*Dance of Days*/Positive Force DC) to Dennis Lyxzén (Refused/The (International) Noise Conspiracy) and Andy Hurley (Racetraitor/Fall Out Boy), from bands such as ManLiftingBanner and Point of No Return to feminist and queer initiatives, from radical collectives like CrimethInc. and Alpine Anarchist Productions to the Emancypunx project and many others dedicated as much to sober living as to the fight for a better world.

"Perhaps the greatest reason I am still committed to sXe is an unfailing belief that sXe is more than music, that it can be a force of change. I believe in the power of sXe as a bridge to social change, as an opportunity to create a more just and sustainable world."
—Ross Haenfler, professor of sociology at the University of Mississippi, author of *Straight Edge: Clean-Living Youth, Hardcore Punk, and Social Change*

"An 'ecstatic sobriety' which combats the dreariness of one and the bleariness of the other—false pleasure and false discretion alike—is analogous to the anarchism that confronts both the false freedom offered by capitalism and the false community offered by communism."
—CrimethInc. Ex-Workers' Collective

Working Class History: Everyday Acts of Resistance & Rebellion

Edited by Working Class History with a Foreword by Noam Chomsky

ISBN: 978-1-62963-823-2 (paperback)
      978-1-62963-887-4 (hardcover)
$20.00   352 pages

History is not made by kings, politicians, or a few rich individuals—it is made by all of us. From the temples of ancient Egypt to spacecraft orbiting Earth, workers and ordinary people everywhere have walked out, sat down, risen up, and fought back against exploitation, discrimination, colonization, and oppression.

Working Class History presents a distinct selection of people's history through hundreds of "on this day in history" anniversaries that are as diverse and international as the working class itself. Women, young people, people of color, workers, migrants, Indigenous people, LGBT+ people, disabled people, older people, the unemployed, home workers, and every other part of the working class have organized and taken action that has shaped our world, and improvements in living and working conditions have been won only by years of violent conflict and sacrifice. These everyday acts of resistance and rebellion highlight just some of those who have struggled for a better world and provide lessons and inspiration for those of us fighting in the present. Going day by day, this book paints a picture of how and why the world came to be as it is, how some have tried to change it, and the lengths to which the rich and powerful have gone to maintain and increase their wealth and influence.

This handbook of grassroots movements, curated by the popular Working Class History project, features many hidden histories and untold stories, reinforced with inspiring images, further reading, and a foreword from legendary author and dissident Noam Chomsky.

"This ingenious archive of working class history, organized as an extended calendar, is filled with little and better known events. Reading through the text, the power, fury, and persistence of the working-class struggles shine. 'Working class' is broader than unions and job struggles, and rather includes all emancipatory acts of working-class people, be they Indigenous peoples fighting for land rights, African Americans massively protesting police killings, anticolonial liberation movements, women rising up angry, or mass mobilizations worldwide against imperialist wars. It is international in scope as is the working class. This is a book the reader will open every day to recall and be inspired by what occurred on that date. I love the book and will look forward to the daily readings."
—Roxanne Dunbar-Ortiz, author of *An Indigenous Peoples' History of the United States*

The Future Is Unwritten:
A Working Class History
Blank Journal

Edited by Working Class History

ISBN: 978-1-62963-912-3
$21.95   224 pages

A classically elegant hardcover, sewn bound with
55lb paper. An enduring repository for your thoughts,
dreams, and battle plans for collective action. Includes
inspirational words of wisdom from the likes of: Audre Lorde, Emma Goldman,
Ambalavaner Sivanandan, George Lamming, Lucy Gonzalez Parsons, Marsha P
Johnson, He Zhen, Frantz Fanon, Albert Spies, CLR James, Ricardo Flores Magón,
Bhagat Singh, Walter Rodney, Ursula Le Guin, Pablo Neruda, Crawford Morgan,
Jayaben Desai and more.

*"In case you needed a reminder that ordinary people have the power to change history,
and have many times over, check out Working Class History."*
—Tom Morello, co-founder of Rage Against the Machine

*"Working Class History is broader than unions and job struggles; rather, it includes all
emancipatory acts of working-class people, be they Indigenous peoples fighting for
land rights, African Americans massively protesting against police killings, anticolonial
liberation movements, women rising up angry, or mass mobilizations worldwide
against imperialist wars. It is international in scope, as is the working class."*
—Roxanne Dunbar-Ortiz, author of *An Indigenous Peoples' History of the United
States*

*"Working Class History has hit upon a novel way to communicate our shared history to
a new generation of budding radicals and working-class revolutionaries. They make it
clear that today's victories build upon yesterday's struggles, and that, in order to push
forward into the liberated, equitable future we want, we must remember how far we've
come—and reckon with how much further there is to go."*
—Kim Kelly, journalist and labour columnist at *Teen Vogue*

*"Working Class History is essential reading for those seeking awareness of people who
made history in efforts and events to create a better world."*
—John O'Brien, Stonewall rebellion participant, Gay Liberation Front co-founder

*"Working Class History is global, diverse, and clear; bringing to our attention OUR
history which has so often been ignored, neglected or misrepresented."*
—Mike Jackson, co-founder Lesbians and Gays Support the Miners

Pacifism as Pathology: Reflections on the Role of Armed Struggle in North America Third Edition

Ward Churchill and Michael Ryan with a Preface by Ed Mead and Foreword by Dylan Rodríguez

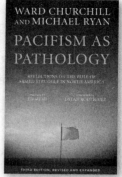

ISBN: 978-1-62963-224-7
$15.95   192 pages

Pacifism as Pathology has long since emerged as a dissident classic. Originally written during the mid-1980s, the seminal essay "Pacifism as Pathology" was prompted by veteran activist Ward Churchill's frustration with what he diagnosed as a growing—and deliberately self-neutralizing—"hegemony of nonviolence" on the North American left. The essay's publication unleashed a raging debate among activists in both the U.S. and Canada, a significant result of which was Michael Ryan's penning of a follow-up essay reinforcing Churchill's premise that nonviolence, at least as the term is popularly employed by white "progressives," is inherently counterrevolutionary, adding up to little more than a manifestation of its proponents' desire to maintain their relatively high degrees of socioeconomic privilege and thereby serving to stabilize rather than transform the prevailing relations of power.

This short book challenges the pacifist movement's heralded victories—Gandhi in India, 1960s antiwar activists, even Martin Luther King Jr.'s civil rights movement—suggesting that their success was in spite of, rather than because of, their nonviolent tactics. Churchill also examines the Jewish Holocaust, pointing out that the overwhelming response of Jews was nonviolent, but that when they did use violence they succeeded in inflicting significant damage to the nazi war machine and saving countless lives.

As relevant today as when they first appeared, Churchill's and Ryan's trailblazing efforts were first published together in book form in 1998. Now, along with the preface to that volume by former participant in armed struggle/political prisoner Ed Mead, new essays by both Churchill and Ryan, and a powerful new foreword by leading oppositionist intellectual Dylan Rodríguez, these vitally important essays are being released in a fresh edition.

"Although Churchill couches his psychological analysis in much more polite terms than I would, he believes that some white upper-middle-class activists are deeply conflicted about whether they really want to dismantle capitalism and give up their position of privilege."
—*Greanville Post*